2PH10

FLEET HISTORY

OF

GREENSLADES TOURS LTD, EXETER

PUBLISHED BY

THE PSV CIRCLE

JUNE 2013

FOREWORD

The draft for this publication was prepared by Kevin Pankhurst and the Publications team from the original PH10 publication and a large number of corrections and additional material. The assistance of Peter Bates, John Bennett, David Corke, Richard Gadsby, Dave Godley, Roger Grimley, Tony Holdsworth, Colin Martin, Peter Tulloch and Fred Ward is also gratefully acknowledged in the production of this edition.

This publication contains all material available in May 2013.

Photographs have been supplied by David Cornforth (via Peter Tulloch), Geoffrey Morant (courtesy Richard Morant), Kevin Pankhurst, Omnibus Society (photographs by A Broughall, Peter Henson, RHG Simpson, DHD Spray and from the Norris-Cull & XLTM collections).

Notes:

This is one of a range of publications produced by The PSV Circle primarily as a service to its members. The information contained herein has been taken from the range of sources indicated above; either from observation or other research, as well as the content of PSV Circle monthly news sheets and also includes information provided from other reputable sources. Considerable time and effort has been taken to ensure that the content of this publication is as complete and accurate as possible but no responsibility can be accepted for any errors or omissions.

Contents:

Foreword	page	2
Introduction	page	3
Fleet Details	page	8
Subsidary Operators	page	69
H & EA Belcher (Teignmouth) Ltd	page	69
Miller & Son (Exmouth) Ltd	page	71
Milton's Services (Crediton) Ltd	page	72
Regent Coaches (Teignmouth) Ltd	page	73
Vehicles of Acquired Operators	page	75
Ancillary Vehicles	page	96
Cross Reference of Registrations	page	97
County Codes	page	101

Any general comments on this publication may be sent to the Publications Manager, Unit GK, 436 Essex Road, London N1 3QP or via email to publications.manager@psv-circle.org.uk.

Details of how to join The PSV Circle and a list of all our publications can be obtained from The PSV Circle website - www.psv-circle.org.uk.

ISBN: 978-1-908953-14-8

Published by the PSV Circle
© The PSV Circle June 2013

W GREENSLADE, BRADNINCH (until 1918)
W & P GREENSLADE, EXETER (1918-1933)
GREENSLADES TOURS LTD, EXETER (From 5/33)

Samuel James Greenslade came from Shobrooke near Crediton and worked as a railway signalman at nearby Hele and Bradninch Station. He and his wife had five children, three boys and two girls. The eldest son, William, was born in 1894 and after leaving school he trained as a cycle mechanic with Davey's in Cowick Street, Exeter. His youngest brother, Percy, followed him and by 1912 they were able to set up their own bicycle rental and repair business in Bradninch. Bradninch needed a transport link to the nearest railway station at Hele so the Greenslades brothers purchased a Ford Model T taxi for £97. Three further taxis were soon acquired and a regular service was introduced between Bradninch and Hele railway station, in addition to providing normal taxi and private hire services. The first office was in Fore Street, Bradninch. Meanwhile, their brother, Gilbert, obtained a job with local auctioneer Percy Hexter and after three years became a qualified auctioneer's clerk.

With the outbreak of the First World War, all three joined the forces, with two brothers enlisting in the Royal Flying Corps as pilots, whilst the taxi business was run by their sister, Mrs Evelyn Dyer.

The brothers returned in 1918 and purchased a second-hand Mass touring car, which was rebodied as a 14-seat brake, using a body from a horse-drawn vehicle. The modification was carried out by William Greenslade, aided by an employee. It is reported that another similar vehicle was acquired also at the same time.

In 1919, the former stables of Collins Horse Repository, at 84A Paris Street, Exeter, was purchased and modified for use as a motor garage to house the current fleet of one Ford Model T, one landaulette, and the Maas brakes. One of the latter was replaced by a similar vehicle, based on a second-hand Maudslay chassis, in 1919. The site is today occupied by the Devon & Cornwall Housing Group and Exeter City Council offices.

During the next few years, the taxi side of the business was expanded, and a Dennis lorry was purchased to run a carrier's service between Exeter and Tiverton. Four Ford Model T vans were also purchased for use on Royal Mail contracts.

In 1924, an office was opened at 10 Queen Street, Exeter and by 1927 the coach and charabanc fleet comprised seven vehicles.

Vehicles of many different makes were purchased in the period before World War Two including examples of Dennis, GMC, Graham Dodge, Leyland, Reo and Thornycroft manufacture.

In December 1931 the first acquisition of another fleet took place, when Milton's of Crediton was taken over. Following the death of the company's founder, this operation was owned at the time by William Milton's executors AR Garnish and FM Milton, together with whom Greenslades formed a new company, Milton's Services (Crediton) Ltd, which was operated as a subsidiary company, retaining Milton's two-tone blue livery. The licences were transferred to this new company to obviate any problems from Devon General objecting to the take over. In 1933 the goods fleet acquired by Greenslade's from the Witheridge Transport Company Ltd was also licensed to Milton's Services (Crediton) Ltd. Milton's stage services passed to Devon General in 1936.

The next fleet to be acquired was that of H Belcher, of Teignmouth in January 1932. A new company, using the title H & EA Belcher Ltd, was formed in April 1932 and also remained as a subsidiary company. The original livery used by Belcher is not known, but from 1932 Greenslade's livery was used, with Belcher fleet names. In December 1939 the company's title became H & EA Belcher (Teignmouth) Ltd. The company owned no vehicles from October 1939 until December 1947, when the fleet was revived, and it then continued until January 1955.

In 1933, the Witheridge Motor Transport Company Ltd was acquired with the company name being changed to Greenslades Tours Ltd. The seven coaches passed to Greenslades with their goods fleet continuing to operate as a subsidiary company retaining the Witheridge Transport name, although licensed in the name of Milton's Services (Crediton) Ltd. This part of the operation was eventually sold to the haulage company Whitton's of Cullompton in 1946. The Witheridge Motor Transport stage services were retained and operated by Greenslades until they were acquired by Devon General in 1948.

In June 1936, the third fleet to be acquired and operated as a subsidiary was WH Broadbeer & Sons, trading as Regent Coaches, of Teignmouth. A limited company, Regent Coaches (Teignmouth) Ltd, was immediately formed and the registered office of the new company was moved to the Belcher office at 14, Wellington Street. The fleet was finally absorbed in January 1955.

Also in 1936, Greenslades head office was moved to 84 Queen Street, Exeter. This address is nowadays the location of the Boston Tea Party coffee house.

March 1938 saw the purchase of Sellers & Company {Arcadia Coaches} of Exmouth, which was owned by TW & RT Weller, with three vehicles and in November 1938 the business of HL Gunn of Rackenford, Tiverton, with four vehicles and stage services was purchased.

Also in 1938, six AEC Regal buses were purchased from Devon General and five AEC Regents were acquired from Exeter Corporation. However, the double-deckers were not used as such, three being rebuilt as single deckers by Tiverton Coachbuilders, one was not used and the other was dismatled for spares. All of these vehicles were purchased for contract work, with four of the Regals being sold the following year.

November 1939 saw the purchase of WJ Abbott (Exmouth) Ltd trading as Abbott's Blue Bus Service together with a solitary vehicle. This purchase included local stage services in Exmouth, which were transferred to Devon General on 24th April 1940.

By 1940 Greenslades had thirty coaches and a well-established taxi fleet based at Exeter. They also had control of three subsidiary coach fleets together with a road haulage department at Witheridge.

The war years saw an expansion of contract services to the various local War Department establishments, but the remainder of the coach side of the business was virtually dormant. Some thirteen Bedford OWBs were allocated to the Company for the contract services between 1942 and 1945, and these vehicles were to be the backbone of the immediate post-war coach fleet until replaced by Bedford OBs. Although delivered with wooden slatted seats, most were soon made more comfortable by the fitment of coach seats transferred from older vehicles. In 1943, the head office was moved to 14 Queen Street, Exeter.

Excursions and tours had been confined to day trips until 1948, when the first extended tour licence was granted. As a result heavyweight chassis began to be purchased, starting with a new AEC Regal III that had been displayed at the 1948 Commercial Motor Show at Earls Court. It was registered as HHP 755 and was badged as a Maudslay for its appearance at the Motor Show. Also in that year, the stage services which had been taken over with the various fleet acquisitions were transferred to Devon General Omnibus & Touring Co Ltd, including a Cheriton Fitzpayne to Exeter service which had been acquired from Mrs EJ Heywood & JE Greenslade together with two vehicles in November 1945.

The early post-war period saw attention concentrated on modernising the fleet and replacing existing vehicles. Some forty new vehicles were added to the fleets between 1946 and 1950, replacing all the pre-war vehicles by 1950. In the late 1940s Greenslades also acquired Cox Brothers (Exeter) Ltd, a car sales agency.

The taxi side of the company's activities had been formed into a separate business as Luxitax and this became Luxitax Ltd in 1948. A funeral service department had been set up in 1946 as Funeral Furnishers Ltd, but these two subsidiaries did not pass to BET. In 1949 Witheridge School contracts, together with two vehicles, were sold to DC Venner of Minehead.

In 1951 the Tiverton Tours licence which originated with J Thorne, acquired by HL Gunn and thence to Greenslades, was sold to SA Kingdom of Tiverton.

In April 1953 the Belcher company acquired the business of Miller & Sons (Exmouth) Ltd with eight vehicles being taken into the Belcher fleet. Miller's stage services at Exmouth had previously been acquired by Devon General in 1938.

The next few years were to be a period of great expansion for the company. On 31st October 1953, Greenslades Tours Ltd, together with subsidiary companies H & EA Belcher Ltd and Regent Coaches (Teignmouth) Ltd were acquired by the British Electric Traction Company. Percy Greenslade now retired from the business, but his brothers continued to serve on the board for another three years.

Under BET control, six fleets were acquired in the next four years. In 1954 the associated fleets of WJ Taylor (Central Garages) Ltd, of Exeter and Teign Cars Ltd, Teignmouth were purchased from HJ & FM Beal (an Exeter motor dealer), which had taken an interest in both fleets in 1948. This was the largest acquisition to date, involving fifteen Teign Cars and sixteen Taylor's vehicles. Only six Teign Cars and four Taylor's vehicles were used by Greenslades, as both fleets had been operating in competition with Greenslades and held similar excursions and tour licences which Greenslades were largely able to cover with their existing fleet.

In July 1954, Knight's Tours, of Exeter, was purchased and in October 1955 the extended tours licensed to Western Engineering & Motor Services Ltd {WEMS}, of Clevedon, Somerset were taken over. No vehicles were included with this acquisition. This gave Greenslades a large catchment area in north Somerset, including picking up points in Bath, Nailsea, Burnham and Bristol. The tours included a number to continental destinations.

During 1956, two Sidmouth fleets were absorbed. The first of these, the Sidmouth Motor Company and Dagworthy Ltd, was a long-established concern. This company was formed in November 1927 to take over the business previously run by Mr William Dagworthy who had been operating since before the 1914-1918 war. In late 1921 he had acquired the goodwill of the Sidmouth Motor Company Ltd, thereafter the Dagworthy and Sidmouth Motor Co names were used seemingly indiscriminately. There was intense rivalry on stage services from Sidmouth to Exeter and Sidbury until they were sold to the competitor, Devon General in April 1934. In the early 1930's two routes serving Peak Hill and Salcombe Hill were started. These two vantage points were situated on the heights overlooking the town and from where there were splendid views. Initially these two routes were operated by a Napier, later by a number of adapted Austin chassis, all fitted with toastrack bodies. The second operator acquired at Sidmouth was that of CG Burgoyne. Although sixteen vehicles were acquired with these two fleets, only one was used by Greenslades.

October 1957 saw the takeover of RC & CC Hopkins trading as Hopkins & Sons {Blue Moorland Coaches} of Dawlish, followed by the extended tours licences of Bowerman's Tours of Taunton in July 1958. Mr J Greenslade, son of Gilbert Greenslade, purchased the vehicles with the remainder of the tours licences and he continued to operate the business as Bowerman's Tours Ltd.

Twelve eight year old AEC Regal IIIs were transferred to Greenslades from the similarly BET owned, Devon General Grey Cars fleet in 1958. This was the start of the regular transfer of older vehicles that lasted until the Grey Cars fleet itself was placed under Greenslades control.

In 1959, the excursions and tours licences of Mrs WA Hart and her daughter Mrs KAM Bentham, trading as Hart's Tours, of Budleigh Salterton, were taken over.

During the next ten years, the company developed and consolidated its operations and opened a new garage at Willey's Avenue in Exeter, replacing the Paris Street premises, which had served the company for forty two years. The head office was relocated to 29, Paris Street, Exeter in 1963.

Vehicle policy from 1950 had been to purchase Bedfords for local tours, with Leylands, Maudslays and AECs for longer distance work. In 1955 two Commers were purchased and the first of many AEC Reliances arrived. More Bedfords came in 1956-1957 but from then until 1970, with the exception of four Fords in 1961, the only vehicles purchased new were AEC Reliances.

The Bowerman's Tours Ltd coach business was taken over by Berry's Transport Ltd, of Bradford-on-Tone in January 1965, but Mr Greenslade retained the company offices in Taunton and in Wellington for use as a travel agency. The Bathpool Garage was subsequently used by Taunton Meat Haulage Ltd.

William Greenslade purchased the business of E Clatworthy, of Fore Street Tiverton, in 1964. A limited company, E Clatworthy Ltd, was formed in April 1964, with an office at 15, Angel Hill, Tiverton and traded as "WJ Greenslade's Tiverton Coaches". This business was later sold, together with two vehicles, to Cox Bros (Exeter) Ltd, Tiverton in 6/71 and then sold on to Kingdom's Tours Ltd, of Tiverton, in 9/71.

The next changes occurred in 1969, when an exchange of licences was made with Wallace Arnold Tours, of Leeds. Greenslades' continental tours licences were transferred to Wallace Arnold in exchange for certain of Wallace Arnold's British extended tour licences based on Torquay.

Greenslades, as part of the BET group, passed to the Transport Holding Company on 1st January 1969, and subsequently to the National Bus Company on 1st January 1970. As a result, the company's registered office was moved to National House, Exeter on that date.

The livery had been buff (known as "chamois") since the early 1920s, with brown wings and green trim. Later two shades of green were used for trim and the brown was eliminated. This livery continued until October 1969, when the Western white and Ivy green livery, with large white fleet names, as dictated by THC policy, was introduced.

In 1971, day tours licensed to Western National Omnibus Company Ltd at Totnes, were acquired and on 2nd May 1971, the largest change in the company's history took place, when the Grey Cars fleet of Devon General was transferred to Greenslades. This added thirty five vehicles to the fleet, as well as licences for excursions and tours based on Torquay, Paignton, Newton Abbot and Broadclyst.

Fleet numbers were introduced in June 1971 and in May 1972 the company became part of the National Bus Company's Central Activities Group (South West). The registered office was moved back to 29 Paris Street, Exeter in October 1972. On 11th February 1974 Black & White Motorways Ltd was renamed National Travel (South West) Ltd and, for administrative purposes, Greenslades Tours Ltd, together with Shamrock and Rambler (Bournemouth) Ltd were placed under the control of this company. Wessex National became part of the same group in August 1974.

From 1971, Bristol RELH vehicles were favoured, but another AEC Reliance arrived in 1973. For 1974 another approach to new vehicle purchase was started with Bedfords and a Leyland being ordered; although the Leyland was diverted to Black and White before delivery.

The Western white and Ivy green livery was superseded by the standard National white coach livery from October 1972.

Apart from the vehicles transferred from Devon General, acquired fleets and from National Travel (South West) Ltd, very few second-hand vehicles have been purchased. From 1946 until 1967, only five such vehicles were acquired, and since then twenty three vehicles were transferred from other NBC fleets, with one Bristol LHL being purchased in 1974.

Prior to 1935, no one bodybuilder was particularly favoured, but from then until 1949 Tiverton Coachworks and Duple received all contracts. The early post-war period dictated that bodywork, like chassis, be obtained as available, with Burlingham, Gurney Nutting and Yeates products purchased as well; until 1953. From 1953 Duple came back into favour and from 1957, Harrington bodies were also obtained. Duple and Harrington were patronised until 1969; although from 1965 Duple (Northern) products were purchased rather than Duple. Three Plaxton bodies were delivered in 1967 and from 1970 until 1973 all vehicles ordered by Greenslades had Plaxton bodies. 1974 saw a return to Duple products.

With the advent of extended and continental tours, seating capacities were generally less than the maximum capacity for all front-line coaches, although many were re-seated to maximum capacities later in their lives, for use on local tours.

For the 1974 season, continental tours were recommenced using the Roscoff to Plymouth and Southampton to Le Havre ferry services. Later in 1974, Greenslades assumed responsibility, on behalf of National Travel (South West) Ltd, for the excursions and tours, based on Plymouth, of Western National Omnibus Company Ltd; with six vehicles allocated to Plymouth for this work.

Gilbert Greenslade retired from the board of Greenslades early in 1974. At the age of 76, he had been Mayor and Sheriff of Exeter and had served the Council from 1937 as a councillor and from 1952 as an alderman, as had William Greenslade, who was a councillor from 1941 until the late 1950s. Gilbert was also a director of Hammett's, the Exeter dairy company.

Fleet numbers, as such, were not used by Greenslades until June 1971, but after the BET take-over in 1953, each vehicle was allocated a running number "on paper" each season. For the period from 1960 until 1971, registration numbers were booked in blocks where possible; so as to run in sequence from the previous batch. For example 567-573 EFJ, 974 FFJ, 175-176 GFJ, AFJ 77-86B, avoiding numbers already in use. In June 1971 a numbering scheme was introduced intended to integrate with that of Western National. Subsequent events dictated that a renumbering took place in January 1975, to instead fit in with the other National Travel (South West) constituents, Black and White, Wessex National and Shamrock and Rambler.

Fleet numbers were displayed on black metal plates, with polished metal numbers, fitted front and rear, although some vehicles had still not received plates by 1974. From July 1974 subsequent new vehicles received standard NBC grey number transfers.

In January 1975, the head office was relocated to Musgrave House, Musgrave Road, Exeter. 1975 also saw the arrival of a batch of twelve Bristol LH6Ls with 7ft 6in wide Plaxton bodies to replace the Dartmoor and Exmoor tour fleet, together with further second-hand vehicles of AEC and Leyland manufacture. Bedford YMTs with Plaxton bodies were purchased in 1976, together with more second-hand vehicles of AEC, Bedford and Leyland manufacture. The final batch of Greenslades Tour vehicles was purchased in 1977 and, during that year, the first vehicles were transferred to the National Travel (South West) fleet.

During the 1970s, the garages at Budleigh Salterton, Dawlish, Exmouth, Sidmouth and Teignmouth, which had been purchased with the acquired companies, were closed and, by the beginning of 1978, the company was left with garages only in Plymouth, Torquay and Willeys Avenue, Exeter.

In April 1978 the Torquay and Plymouth operations were transferred to Western National Omnibus Company Ltd. Torwood Street garage in Torquay was closed in April 1978 and was later sold. The remaining Greenslades vehicles were gradually relicensed to National Travel (South West) Ltd during 1978, after which Greenslades Tours Ltd ceased to operate coaches. A proportion of the National Travel (South West) fleet was allocated to Exeter and those vehicles retained the Greenslades fleet name.

Musgrave House had closed in January 1978, when the head office returned again to 29, Paris Street, which remained the Exeter office of National Travel (South West) and, later, the coaching offices of Western National Omnibus Company Ltd until 1983, when the offices were transferred to Exeter Coach Station and Willeys Avenue garage. 29 Paris Street was then sold to an estate agency. It is currently the premises of estate agents Haart. In May 1981 the Exeter-based operations were transferred to Western National, together with the garage at Willeys Avenue. Western National retained the Greenslades fleet name on these vehicles. At the same time the Bournemouth and Swansea operations of National Travel (South West) were transferred to Hants and Dorset Motor Services Ltd and South Wales Transport Company Ltd respectively.

On 1st January 1983 a new company, Devon General Ltd, was formed to take over the Exeter, Torquay and East Devon areas of Western National Omnibus Company Ltd. This area being basically that associated with the original Devon General Omnibus & Touring Co Ltd and included the Willeys Avenue garage, together with the vehicles based there. These retained the Greenslades fleet name on the white National livery. Later a new Greenslades livery was introduced for the local tour coaches, of white with light and dark green stripes on a broad dark green waistband. Vehicles on National Express and National Holidays duties retained the National liveries.

In October 1984 Willeys Avenue garage was closed and the coaches were then based at the Belgrave Road, Exeter garage.

Devon General Ltd was privatised on 19th August 1986, when it was purchased by a group of its own managers. The Greenslades operations continued as before.

In 1987 Devon General Ltd decided to re-organize its coaching operations. In March the Torquay tours were sold to a resurrected Grey Cars company, which had been set up by a group of former drivers. In December the Greenslades private hire and tours operations at Exeter were sold to Paul Nightingale, the son of George Nightingale, who had operated from Budleigh Salterton, and latterly Exmouth, for many years. The sale included thirteen coaches and the dormant Greenslades Tours Ltd company. The National Express and Rapide vehicles were retained by Devon General, these vehicles receiving Devon General fleet names, together with the booking offices at Exeter and Exmouth.

In January 1988 the Greenslades operations were transferred to new premises at Peek House, Venny Bridges, Pinhoe, Exeter. At the same time a new livery was introduced, this was basically an updated version of the previous livery, retaining the white base and light and dark green.

The fleet was expanded with the purchase of three new Leyland Tigers, as well as seven second-hand vehicles.

In July 1988, the garage at Willeys Avenue, by now derelict, was sold for redevelopment, having remained with the National Bus Company when Devon General was privatised. The site is now the location of the appropriately named Greenslades Nursing Home.

On 1st August 1988, the dormant Greenslades Tours Ltd was resurrected by Paul Nightingale with vehicles licensed to that company.

So began another era which is beyond the scope of this publication.

VEHICLE DETAILS

1917

Vehicles acquired from Radford, Beer (DN) 7/17 (or 1918)

T 528	Mass 20hp	B7.230 ?			-/09	3/23
T 1246	Mass 20hp	? ?		14	5/10	1/20

Previous History:
  T 528: The registration was a re-issue. It is not confirmed that this vehicle was acquired.
  T 1246: This was originally a touring car, to which a brake body, originally fitted to a horse-drawn vehicle, was modified and fitted by Mr W Greenslade and Mr B Knight. It has been quoted as being new in 1908.

Disposal:
  T 528: No further operator.
  T 1246: W Cole, Ashton (DN) 1/20; J Moir & W Davie, Bovey Tracey use unknown 5/20.

1919

Vehicle acquired from Colonel Hill, Bickleigh (DN) -/19

T 6744	Maudslay 35hp	1/2892/3 (see below)	-14-	-/11	-/21

Previous History:
  This vehicle was acquired as a chassis, having been fitted with a touring car body when new. The chassis was probably from the War Department (Army) and was re-registered T 6744 in 4/19; previous registration(s) not known. The body was originally fitted to a horse-drawn vehicle and modified for fitment to T 6744 by Mr W Greenslade and Mr B Knight.

Disposal:
  T 6744: A Turner, Chulmleigh (DN) 8/21; VT Truman, Topsham (DN) (3/27?); last licensed 2/28; scrapped 5/29.

1921

New Vehicle

FJ 1679	Dennis Chara	25001 Tiverton	Ch20	5/21	11/27

Notes:
  FJ 1679: Named "Queen of the Exe".

Disposal:
  FJ 1679: Witheridge Motor Transport Co, Witheridge (DN) 11/27; becoming Witheridge Motor Transport Company Ltd 3/30; withdrawn 9/32; returned to Greenslades 6/33 (qv).

1922

New Vehicle

FJ 2074	Leyland C1 Special	19162 Westcott Bros	Ch20	5/22	-/28

Notes:
  FJ 2074: Westcott Bros was an Exeter coachbuilder; named "Pride of Devon".

Disposal:
  FJ 2074: Rebodied as C20- by an unknown manufacturer and transferred to Milton's Services (Crediton) Ltd, Crediton (DN) 12/31; BJ Elston, Honiton (GDN) as a lorry 1934; last licensed 12/38.

1924

New Vehicles

FJ 2852	Reo Speed Wagon Type F	98136 ?	Ch14	2/24	-/28
FJ 2932	Dennis 2½ ton	30632 ?	Ch20	5/24	-/31

Disposals:
FJ 2852: Discombe and Way, Crediton (DN) 1928; withdrawn 3/32.
FJ 2932: Witheridge Motor Transport Co Ltd, Witheridge (DN) 1931; returned to Greenslades 6/33 (qv).

1926

New Vehicle

FJ 4163	Thornycroft A2 Long	12444	Torquay Carriage	Ch20	4/26	by-/40

Notes:
FJ 4163: Modified to C18F configuration, probably by Westcott Bros of Exeter, by 1931.

Disposal:
FJ 4163: Not traced, but probably requisitioned by the War Department (GOV). Tax records show last licensed to Greenslades 11/45.

1927

New Vehicles

FJ 4986	Reo Sprinter	G5699	Westcott Bros	C19F	5/27	-/32
FJ 4987	Reo Sprinter	G6787	Westcott Bros	C17F	5/27	-/32

Disposals:
FJ 4986: CE Heard, Burlescombe (DN) 1932; WH Tazwell, Hatch Beauchamp (GSO) as a farm tractor (unlicensed) 12/43; scrapped by HG Hooper, Bathealton, Somerset 11/46 (or 1/46).
FJ 4987: A Temby, Okehampton (DN) 1932; withdrawn 9/35; Ware (dealer), Plymouth for scrap 11/35.

Vehicle acquired from Trelawny Cars, Penzance (CO) -/27

AF 2589	Dennis Subsidy 4 ton	12904	Dennis?	Ch28	3/20	-/28

Previous History:
AF 2589: New to Smiths Motors (Engineers) Ltd {Silver Cars}, Falmouth (CO); from whom it was acquired at an unknown date.

Disposal:
AF 2589: Scrapped 1928.

1928

New Vehicles

FJ 5623	Dennis E	17352	Westcott Bros	C32F	4/28	-/39
FJ 5688	Graham Dodge	A586037	Westcott Bros	C20F	5/28	5/30
FJ 5689	Dennis 30 cwt	52746	(Dennis?)	C14F	5/28	-/30
FJ 5731	Graham Bros	GB4678	Westcott Bros	C20-	6/28	-/39

Notes:
FJ 5623: Re-seated to C26F 5/36; reverting to C32F 5/38.

Disposals:
FJ 5623: Witheridge Motor Transport Co, Witheridge (GDN) as a lorry 1/39; withdrawn 12/41.
FJ 5688: WWA Mason {White Hart Service}, Morchard Bishop (DN) 5/30; Witheridge Motor Transport Co Ltd, Witheridge (GDN) as a cattle lorry 1933; withdrawn 9/35; WG Mudge, Exeter (GDN) as a cattle lorry 10/35; withdrawn 10/36.
FJ 5689: A Turner, Chulmleigh (DN) 7/30 withdrawn 9/35; Worthmore (builder), London SW1 (XLN) 1/36; Escott & Co Ltd (dealer), London SW2 for scrap 1/36.
FJ 5731: Fulford, Bideford (GDN) as a lorry 7/40; Twose, Westward Ho! (GDN) by 7/47; EH May, Langtree (GDN) 7/47; last licensed 12/50.

1929

New Vehicles

FJ 6172	Graham Bros	D200128	Westcott Bros		C18F	3/29	-/31
FJ 6308	GMC T30C	301356	Duple	1572	C20F	5/29	-/33

FJ 6320	Graham Bros		D201038	Duple	1571	C20F	5/29	-/32

Disposals:
  FJ 6172: FW Dowell {Orange and Black Coaches}, Branscombe (DN) 1/31; Male, Henford (DN) 4/32; Hanson, London N7 (GLN) as a van 7/32; last licensed 9/35; JG Auto Spares (dealer), London W6 for scrap 1/36.
  FJ 6308: Witheridge Motor Transport Co Ltd, Witheridge (DN) 1933; returned to Greenslades 6/33 (qv).
  FJ 6320: A Temby, Okehampton (DN) 4/32; NC Born, Northlew (DN) 9/37; LE Adams, Northlew (GDN) as a cattle lorry by 8/44; last licensed 12/46.

1930

New Vehicles

FJ 7010	GMC T19	19152B	?		C18-	6/30	-/35
FJ 7011	Reo Pullman	GE144	Abbott (Farnham)		C25F	6/30	-/36
FJ 7012	Reo Pullman	GE129	Abbott (Farnham)		C25F	6/30	-/33
FJ 7042	Reo Speed Wagon	FB1420	?		C20-	6/30	-/31

Notes:
  FJ 7010: Re-seated to C14- at an unknown date; the chassis number is also quoted as 15192B.

Disposals:
  FJ 7010: WA Woof {Premier Motor Services}, Calshot (HA) for spares 3/35; engine transferred to GMC T19C TR 9679.
  FJ 7011: CA Gayton {Gayton's Coaches}, Ashburton (DN) 11/36 withdrawn 9/49; scrapped 4/51.
  FJ 7012: A & SJ Stevens {W Stevens & Sons / The Harrier}, Modbury (DN) 4 3/33 withdrawn 9/49.
  FJ 7042: Discombe and Way, Crediton (DN) 8/31; C Way & Son, Crediton (DN) 10/39; withdrawn 12/51.

1931

New Vehicle

FJ 7716	Morris Viceroy	161Y	Westcott Bros		C20F	6/31	-/40

Disposal:
  FJ 7716: WRJ & JE Herring {Herring Brothers}, Burnham-on-Sea (SO) 10/40; withdrawn 12/44.

Vehicle acquired from Milton's Services (Crediton) Ltd, Crediton (DN) 12/31

FJ 5607	Graham Dodge	A587848	?		B14F	4/28	-/33

Previous History:
  FJ 5607: New to Milton's Services.

Disposal:
  FJ 5607: WH Luxton {Luxton Brothers}, Exeter as a lorry 11/33 withdrawn 3/34.

Vehicle acquired from E Burrows & Sons, Cullompton (DN)

UO 8211	Chevrolet LP	46159	?		C14F	8/28	9/34

Previous History:
  UO 8211: New to Burrows.

Disposal:
  UO 8211: Scrapped.

1932

New Vehicles

FJ 8278	Morris Director	007RP	Duple	2860	C14F	4/32	12/36
FJ 8351	Morris Director	075RP	Duple	2861	C14F	7/32	6/36

Notes:
  FJ 8351: Re-seated to C20F at an unknown date.

Disposals:
    FJ 8278: Scrapped.
    FJ 8351: H & EA Belcher (Teignmouth) Ltd {Empress Coaches}, Teignmouth (DN) 6/36; withdrawn 10/39; WGL Waterman, Spaxton (SO) 3/40; JA Edwards (showman), Winchester as goods 12/46.

Vehicle acquired from Hellier, Honiton (DN) 12/32

UO 1895	Reo Major	G5922	?		C14F	4/27	12/32

Previous History:
    UO 1895: New to Hellier.

Notes:
    UO 1895: Used as a towing vehicle for a short time.

Disposal:
    UO 1895: CE Heard, Burlescombe (DN) 12/32; last licensed 11/36; sold for scrap.

1933

New Vehicles

FJ 9060	Dennis Lancet	170318	Duple	3381	C32R	5/33	6/33
FJ 9061	Dennis Lancet	170387	Duple	3382	C32R	5/33	9/39
FJ 9066	Commer Centaur	46189	?		C20F	6/33	4/37

Notes:
    FJ 9060-9061: Had canvas roofs which folded back from the front bulkhead to the waistrail at the rear, with no rear dome.

Disposals:
    FJ 9060: War Department (GOV) 9/39; WC Jones {Hanworth Coaches}, Hanworth (MX) 12/45 (7/46 also quoted); becoming Acorn Coaches Ltd, Hanworth (MX) 8/46.
    FJ 9061: War Department (GOV) 9/39; WC Jones {Hanworth Coaches}, Hanworth (MX) 7/46; becoming Acorn Coaches Ltd, Hanworth (MX) 49 8/46; loaned to London Transport (LN) during 1948 and 1949; withdrawn 4/49; a fixed roof was added to the body by/for Jones / Acorn at an unknown date.
    FJ 9066: A Temby, Okehampton (DN) 4/37; NC Born, Northlew (DN) 9/37; L Roberts, Dolton (GDN) as a lorry 6/44; last licensed 12/44.

Vehicles acquired from Witheridge Motor Transport Co Ltd, Tiverton (DN) 6/33

DV 1370	Chevrolet LQ	51951	?		C18-	6/29	by -/40
DV 5712	Reo Speed Wagon	FB1421	?		C20-	6/30	by -/39
FJ 1679	Dennis Chara	25001	Tiverton		Ch20	5/21	n/a
FJ 2932	Dennis 2½ ton	30632	?		Ch20	5/24	-/35
FJ 6308	GMC T30C	301356	Duple	1572	C20F	5/29	-/38
TT 9819	Chevrolet X	10637	?		C14F	10/26	by -/36
UO 7110	Reo Sprinter	FAX5798	?		C20-	6/28	-/33

Previous History:
    These vehicles were new to Witheridge Motor Transport, except for:-

    FJ 1679: New to Greenslades; from whom it was acquired 11/27.
    FJ 2932: New to Greenslades; from whom it was acquired 1931.
    FJ 6308: New to Greenslades; from whom it was acquired 1933.

Notes:
    FJ 1679: Had been unlicensed since 9/32 and was not relicensed when reacquired by Greenslades.

Disposals:
    DV 1370: AFC & WH Greenslade {F Greenslade & Sons}, Dulverton (SO) as C14- by 1940; EC Jones, London SE6 (GLN) as a lorry by 6/49; Shepherd (dealer?), London SE6; last licensed 6/49.
    DV 5712: WG Friend & Son, Ivybridge (DN) at an unknown date; JA Watson, Gunnislake (CO) 3/39; CG Yeo & Turner {Woolacombe and Mortehoe Motor Co}, Mortehoe (DN) 5/46; unidentified owner as a caravan 2/53.

FJ 1679: Not traced.
FJ 2932: Loveridge, Hawkchuch use unknown 1935; last licensed 9/35.
FJ 6308: E Saunders, Winkleigh (DN) as C19F 4/38; withdrawn 12/50; scrapped 3/54.
TT 9819: Felgate, Stonehouse as goods vehicle 9/36; last licensed as a showman's caravan at an unknown date.
UO 7110: Discombe and Way, Crediton (DN) 6/33; withdrawn 9/36.

1934

Vehicles acquired from Western National Omnibus Co Ltd, Exeter (DN) 11/34

DR 3421	Maudslay ML3	?	Hall Lewis	B32-	4/28	-/40
RL 3361	Thornycroft A1	12428	Vickers	B20F	4/26	-/38
UU 3022	Maudslay ML3B	4615	Vickers	B32R	7/29	n/a
YH 3796	Maudslay ML3A	4100	Buckingham	C32D	5/27	n/a
YV 1103	Maudslay ML3B	4267	Strachan & Brown	C31D	3/28	8/40
YV 1104	Maudslay ML3B	4272	Strachan & Brown	C31D	4/28	9/37
YV 1105	Maudslay ML3B	4274	Strachan & Brown	C31D	4/28	by 4/39

Previous History:
DR 3421: New to Mrs MM Williams {Embankment Motor Company}, Plymouth (DN); from whom it was acquired as fleet number 3426 in 4/33.
RL 3361: New to Devon Motor Transport Co Ltd, Okehampton (DN) 150; from whom it was acquired as fleet number 2715 in 11/27.
UU 3022: Ordered by the Great Western Railway (Road Motor Division), but delivered direct to Western National as fleet number 1582.
YH 3796: New to the Great Western Railway (Road Motor Division) 1224; from whom it was acquired as fleet number 1224 in 1929.
YV 1103: New to the Great Western Railway (Road Motor Division) 1503; from whom it was acquired as fleet number 1503 in 1929.
YV 1104: New to the Great Western Railway (Road Motor Division) 1504; from whom it was acquired as fleet number 1504 in 1929.
YV 1105: New to the Great Western Railway (Road Motor Division) 1505; from whom it was acquired as fleet number 1505 in 1929.

Notes:
UU 3022: Not operated by Greenslades.
YH 3796: Not operated by Greenslades.
YV 1103-1105: Not licensed by Greenslades withdrawn 5/35.

Disposals:
DR 3421: Not traced.
RL 3361: Not traced.
UU 3022: Unidentified operator at an unknown date; converted to an ambulance by 1/41; last noted with an unidentified contractor, Devonport (XDN) 5/55.
YH 3796: Chassis used for spares; body taken to Dawlish Warren for use as a caravan.
YV 1103: War Department (GOV) 8/40.
YV 1104: War Department (GOV) 9/39.
YV 1105: Scrapped 4/39.

1935

New Vehicles

AFJ 738	Bedford WLB	109994	Duple	4903	B20F	5/35	-/35
AFJ 782	Bedford WTL	875342	Duple	5081	C25R	6/35	-/35

Disposals:
AFJ 738: WH Kestel, Bodmin (CO) 7/35; SA Blake {Blake's Bus Services}, Delabole (CO) 8/42; becoming Blake's Bus Services Ltd, Delabole (CO) 1949; Southern National Omnibus Co Ltd, Exeter (DN) 3810 4/52; S Jewell (dealer), Wadebridge 5/52.
AFJ 782: H & EA Belcher Ltd {Empress Coaches}, Teignmouth (DN) 6/35; Lamboll and Ingham {Ruby Cars}, Paignton (DN) 5/39; AA Woodbury, Wellington (SO) 10/39; WJ Redwood, Hemyock (DN) 7/50; Batten and Thorne Ltd, Tiverton (DN) 7/50; withdrawn 12/52; SA Kingdom {Tivvy Coaches}, Tiverton (DN) 5/53; withdrawn 5/55; D Leach, Great Yarmouth (GNK) as a van at an unknown date; last licensed 6/59.

Vehicles acquired from Western National Omnibus Co Ltd, Exeter (DN) 1935

GU 9528	Thornycroft A2	15906	Duple	1533	B20F	5/29	12/40
TR 2129	Maudslay ML4	3934	Buckingham		C32-	5/26	-/38
UU 973	Thornycroft A2	15908	Duple	1540	B20F	6/29	12/38
YV 1102	Maudslay ML3B	4264	Strachan & Brown		C32D	3/28	n/a
YV 8565	Maudslay ML3B	4279	Strachan & Brown		C26D	5/28 by	10/38
YV 8567	Maudslay ML3B	4288	Strachan & Brown		C26D	5/28	9/38
YV 8568	Maudslay ML3B	4290	Strachan & Brown		C26D	6/28	6/40

Previous History:
  GU 9528: Ordered by the Great Western Railway, but delivered direct to Western National as fleet number 1484.
  TR 2129: New to J Jackson {Jackson's Low Level Tours}, Southampton (HA); Tourist Motor Coaches (Southampton) Ltd, Southampton (HA) 14 9/34; Western National 3530 5/35.
  UU 973: Ordered by the Great Western Railway (Road Motor Division), but delivered direct to Western National as fleet number 1491.
  YV 1102: New to the Great Western Railway (Road Motor Division) 1505; from whom it was acquired as fleet number 1502 in 1929.
  YV 8565: New to the Great Western Railway (Road Motor Division) 1507; from whom it was acquired as fleet number 1507 in 1929.
  YV 8567: New to the Great Western Railway (Road Motor Division) 1505; from whom it was acquired as fleet number 1509 in 1929.
  YV 8568: New to the Great Western Railway (Road Motor Division) 1505; from whom it was acquired as fleet number 1510 in 1929.

Notes:
  TR 2129: Not licensed by Greenslades withdrawn 5/36.
  YV 1102: Not operated by Greenslades.
  YV 8565: Not licensed by Greenslades withdrawn 5/36.
  YV 8567-8568: Not licensed by Greenslades withdrawn 5/36.

Disposals:
  GU 9528: Not traced; last licensed to Greenslades 12/40.
  TR 2129: No further operator.
  UU 973: Not traced; last licensed to Greenslades 12/38.
  YV 1102: Chassis used for spares; body taken to Dawlish Warren for use as a caravan.
  YV 8565: Scrapped 10/38.
  YV 8567: Not traced; last licensed to Greenslades 9/38.
  YV 8568: Not traced; last licensed to Greenslades 6/40.

Vehicle acquired from J Geddes {Burton Cars}, Brixham (DN) 3/35

DV 3371	Thornycroft A2	15410	Mumford	C20F	12/29	-/36

Previous History:
  DV 3371: New to Geddes.

Disposal:
  DV 3371: CA Gayton {Gayton's Coaches}, Ashburton (DN) 1936; withdrawn 12/39.

Vehicle acquired from Milton's Services (Crediton) Ltd, Crediton (DN) by 11/35

FH 4762	Dennis F	80010	GRCW	C26-	5/27	---

Previous History:
  FH 4762: New to Davis & Sons {Westgate}, Gloucester (GL); from whom it was acquired c1934.

Notes:
  FH 4762: Not operated by Greenslades.

Disposal:
  FH 4762: AE Thomas, Chagford (DN) 11/35; withdrawn 12/42.

1936

Vehicles acquired from Milton's Services (Crediton) Ltd, Crediton (DN) 4/36

FJ 8005	Dennis Lancet	170012	Duple	2715	B32R	2/32	-/39

Previous History:
FJ 8005: New to Milton's Services.

Disposals:
FJ 8005: J Geddes {Burton Cars}, Brixham (DN) as B30R 3/39; War Department (GOV) M1261543 7/43; scrapped 11/43.

Vehicle acquired from WH Broadbeer & Sons {Regent Coaches}, Teignmouth (DN) 6/36

OD 6288	Commer Corinthian	56002	?		C20F	7/33	-/39

Previous History:
OD 6288: New to Broadbeer.

Disposal:
OD 6288: AH Young, Moorlinch (SO) by 1940; BC Leather, Maiden Bradley (WI) 1941; withdrawn 1/49; Iles, Bristol (GGL) as a lorry at an unknown date; last licensed 8/52.

Vehicle acquired from H & EA Belcher Ltd {Empress Coaches}, Teignmouth (DN) 6/36

DV 9548	Bedford WLG	113380	Mumford		C14F	6/31	n/a

Previous History:
DV 9548: New to Belcher.

Notes:
DV 9548: Not operated by Greenslades.

Disposal:
DV 9548: H Hayes, Wellington (SO) 6/36; AA Woodbury, Wellington (SO) by 12/38; Veal, Cullompton (GDN) as a lorry by 12/42.

Vehicles acquired from Western National Omnibus Co Ltd, Exeter (DN) 1936

GU 2928	Maudslay ML3B	4595	Vickers	B32R	6/29	n/a
GU 2929	Maudslay ML3B	4596	Vickers	B32R	4/29	n/a
GU 2931	Maudslay ML3B	4598	Vickers	B32R	6/29	n/a
RL 7545	Lancia Pentaiota	2374	?	C25-	4/28	n/a
RL 8061	Lancia Pentaiota	2676	?	C26-	6/28	n/a
UU 3012	Maudslay ML3B	4602	Vickers	B32R	6/29	n/a
UU 3015	Maudslay ML3B	4606	Vickers	B32R	6/29	n/a
UU 4811	Maudslay ML3B	4617	Vickers	B32R	4/29	n/a
UU 4813	Maudslay ML3B	4671	Vickers	B32R	4/29	n/a
YV 1111	Maudslay ML3B	4234	Short	B32R	3/28	n/a
YV 1112	Maudslay ML3B	4269	Short	B32R	5/28	n/a

Previous History:
GU 2928: Ordered by the Great Western Railway (Road Motor Division) but delivered direct to Western National as fleet number 1567 in GWR livery.
GU 2929: Ordered by the Great Western Railway (Road Motor Division) but delivered direct to Western National as fleet number 1568 in GWR livery.
GU 2931: Ordered by the Great Western Railway (Road Motor Division) but delivered direct to Western National as fleet number 1570 in GWR livery.
RL 7545: New to GR Hocking {Silver Tours}, Newquay (CO); National Omnibus & Transport Co Ltd, London SW3 (LN) 2770 7/28; from whom it was acquired as fleet number 2770 1929.
RL 8061: Ordered by GR Hocking {Silver Tours}, Newquay (CO) but delivered new to National Omnibus and Transport Company Ltd, London SW3 (LN) 2763; from whom it was acquired as fleet number 2763 1929.
UU 3012: Ordered by the Great Western Railway (Road Motor Division) but delivered direct to Western National as fleet number 1572 in GWR livery.

UU 3015: Ordered by the Great Western Railway (Road Motor Division) but delivered direct to Western National as fleet number 1575 in GWR livery.
UU 4811: Ordered by the Great Western Railway (Road Motor Division) but delivered direct to Western National as fleet number 1584 in GWR livery.
UU 4813: Ordered by the Great Western Railway (Road Motor Division) but delivered direct to Western National as fleet number 1586 in GWR livery.
YV 1111: New to the Great Western Railway (Road Motor Division) 1517; from whom it was acquired as fleet number 1517 1929.
YV 1112: New to the Great Western Railway (Road Motor Division) 1518, from whom it was acquired as fleet number 1517 1929.

Notes:
None of these vehicles were operated by Greenslades.

Disposals:
GU 2928: Not traced, but believed chassis scrapped and body taken to Dawlish Warren, for use as a caravan.
GU 2929: Slade (dealer), Penzance for scrap.
GU 2931: Slade (dealer), Penzance, for scrap.
RL 7545: GG Warren, St Ives (CO) at an unknown date; withdrawn 9/38.
RL 8061: Not traced, but believed chassis scrapped and body taken to Dawlish Warren, for use as a caravan.
UU 3012: Not traced, but believed chassis scrapped and body taken to Dawlish Warren, for use as a caravan.
UU 3015: Not traced, but believed chassis scrapped and body taken to Dawlish Warren, for use as a caravan.
UU 4811: Not traced, but believed chassis scrapped and body taken to Dawlish Warren, for use as a caravan.
UU 4813: Not traced, but believed chassis scrapped and body taken to Dawlish Warren, for use as a caravan.
YV 1111: Not traced, but believed chassis scrapped and body taken to Dawlish Warren, for use as a caravan.
YV 1112: Not traced, but believed chassis scrapped and body taken to Dawlish Warren, for use as a caravan.

1937

New Vehicles

CFJ 942	Dodge RB	RB1551	Tiverton		C14F	5/37	-/46
CFJ 943	Bedford WTB	111064	Tiverton		C20F	5/37	-/47
CFJ 995	Bedford WTB	110906	Duple	8487	C25F	5/37	-/49

Disposals:
CFJ 942: AA Woodbury, Wellington (SO) 5/46; withdrawn 3/48; Parsons Motors, Wells (SO) at an unknown date; last licensed 1/50.
CFJ 943: F Trott and VC Winter, Ilminster (SO) as C25F 11/47; FW Parker {Empress Coaches}, Ilminster (SO) 6/50; withdrawn 11/56.
CFJ 995: NH Ashton {Ashtonville Coaches}, Halwill Junction (DN) 10/49; withdrawn 9/54; last licensed 12/55; noted derelict on a farm 8/58.

Vehicle acquired from A Temby, Okehampton (DN) 4/37

BX 7340	Leyland A13	36412	?		C26-	7/26	n/a

Previous History:
BX 7340: New to EJ Dunn, Carmarthen (CR); transferred to EJ Dunn, Taunton (SO) at an unknown date; from whom it was acquired 10/35.

Notes:
BX 7340: Not operated by Greenslades.

Disposal:
BX 7340: Not traced.

1938

New Vehicles

EFJ 76	Bedford WTB	112075	Tiverton	C25F	5/38	-/48
EFJ 77	Bedford WTB	112062	Tiverton	C25F	5/38	-/48
EFJ 78	Bedford WTB	112328	Tiverton	C25F	5/38	-/48
EFJ 79	Bedford WTB	112324	Tiverton	C25F	5/38	-/48
EFJ 548	Bedford WTB	7890	Tiverton	B20F	11/38	-/48

Notes:
EFJ 79: Body stored from 10/39 until 4/45, during which time its chassis was ftted with a cattle lorry body for use by Witheridge Motor Transport Co (GDN).
EFJ 548: Re-seated to B25F at an unknown date.

Disposals:
EFJ 76: A & SJ Stevens {W Stevens & Sons / The Harrier}, Modbury (DN) 1 4/48; C Daniels, Ivybridge (XDN) 10/54; DC Slade, Plymouth (XDN) 3/56; last licensed 9/56.
EFJ 77: NH Ashton {Ashtonville Coaches}, Halwill Junction (DN) 1/48; last licensed 3/55; noted derelict on a farm 5/58.
EFJ 78: FG & EG Trathen {FG Trathen & Son}, Yelverton (DN) 6/48; Ritchie, Crays Pond (OX) 3/53; Sydney Green & Sons (contractors), Henley on Thames at an unknown date; withdrawn 12/58.
EFJ 79: FG & EG Trathen {FG Trathen & Son}, Yelverton (DN) 1/48; Wasilewski, London E4 (GLN) as a mobile shop 6/54; Loy, Leicester (GLN) as a mobile shop 6/57.
EFJ 548: Devon General Omnibus & Touring Co Ltd, Torquay (DN) M610 1/48; withdrawn 12/50; Mitchley (dealer), Birmingham 12/51.

Vehicles acquired from TW & RT Weller {Sellers & Co/Arcadia Coaches} Exmouth (DN) 3/38

DV 833	Thornycroft A6	18277	Mumford		C20F	5/29	9/40
DV 9046	Thornycroft A12	20916	?		C20-	5/31	12/38?
OD 9843	Dodge KB	KB171	Thurgood	522	C20R	6/34	-/38

Previous History:
These vehicles were all new to Sellers.

Disposals:
DV 833: Scrapped by Greenslades.
DV 9046: Possibly to War Department (GOV) and returned at unknown dates; last licensed to Greenslades 12/44; scrapped at an unknown date.
OD 9843: JH Maineard, Dulverton (SO) 12/38; Batten and Thorne Ltd, Tiverton (DN) 10/45; withdrawn 6/50.

Vehicles acquired from Exeter Corporation (DN) 9/38

FJ 7411	AEC Regent	6611092	RSJ	H28/20R	1/31	-/41
FJ 7412	AEC Regent	6611094	RSJ	H28/20R	1/31	-/40
FJ 7414	AEC Regent	6611091	RSJ	H28/20R	1/31	-/41
FJ 7820	AEC Regent	6611574	NCME	H28/20R	7/31	n/a
FJ 7825	AEC Regent	6611579	NCME	H28/20R	7/31	n/a

Previous History:
FJ 7411-7412: New as Exeter Corporation 17-18.
FJ 7414: New as Exeter Corporation 20.
FJ 7820: New as Exeter Corporation 22.
FJ 7825: New as Exeter Corporation 27.

Notes:
FJ 7411-7412: Rebuilt to single-deck as B31R by Tiverton Coachworks before entering service.
FJ 7414: Rebuilt to single-deck as B32R by Tiverton Coachworks before entering service.
FJ 7820: Not operated by Greenslades.
FJ 7825: Not operated by Greenslades.

Disposals:
FJ 7411: HJ, JH & GH Yeomans {Yeomans Motors}, Canon Pyon (HR) 31 8/41; rebodied Strachan B32F and fitted with an AEC 7.7 litre oil engine 2/46; JH & GH Yeomans {Yeomans Motors}, Canon Pyon (HR) 31 11/47; withdrawn 11/55; AMCC (dealer), London E15 11/55.

FJ 7412: War Department (GOV) 7/40; A Timpson & Sons Ltd, London SE6 (LN) assuming the identity of GN 7283 (ch.662575) 1942; C Houchin {Charing Cross Motors}, Ilford and London WC2 (LN) by 4/48; licensed 8/48; reverted to original identity (FJ 7412) late 1948; withdrawn 8/52.

FJ 7414: HJ, JH & GH Yeomans {Yeomans Motors}, Canon Pyon (HR) 32 8/41; rebodied Duple B32F (33761) 11/44; fitted with an AEC 7.7 litre oil engine 6/46; JH & GH Yeomans {Yeomans Motors}, Canon Pyon (HR) 32 11/47; withdrawn 12/54; scrapped by Yeomans.

FJ 7820: EH & PH Ludlow {Ludlow Brothers}, Birmingham (WK) 30 12/42; rebodied Duple H30/26R (33760) 12/42; withdrawn 5/50; Remnant (dealer), Birmingham at an unknown date.

FJ 7825: Last licensed 12/38; dismantled for spares; scrapped 7/40.

Vehicles acquired from Devon General Omnibus & Touring Co Ltd (DN) 10/38

DV 9216	AEC Regal	662681	Park Royal	B3090	B32F	5/31	-/39
DV 9218	AEC Regal	662680	Park Royal	B3092	B32F	5/31	-/40
DV 9220	AEC Regal	662676	Park Royal	B3094	B32F	5/31	-/40
DV 9335	AEC Regal	662806	Park Royal	B3097	B32F	6/31	-/39
DV 9336	AEC Regal	662805	Park Royal	B3098	B32F	6/31	-/39
DV 9337	AEC Regal	662677	Park Royal	B3099	B32F	6/31	-/39

Previous History:
DV 9216: New as Devon General 180 as DP26F; re-seated to B32F 1935.
DV 9218: New as Devon General 182 as DP26F; re-seated to B32F 1935.
DV 9220: New as Devon General 184 as DP26F; re-seated to B32F 1935.
DV 9335-9337: New as Devon General 187-189 as DP26F; re-seated to B32F 1935.

Disposals:
DV 9216: Gough's Garages Ltd {Queen of the Road}, Bristol (GL) 1939; War Department (GOV) 1940.
DV 9218: War Department (GOV) M1260485 7/40; GJ Miller {GJ Miller & Son}, Cirencester (GL) 1943; AH Kearsey Ltd, Cheltenham (GL) 41 8/47; rebodied Burlingham C33F (2971) 1947; withdrawn 1/55; GB Green & TH Griffin {G & G Coaches}, Leamington Spa (WK) 3/54; FS Dunn, Bestwood Village (NG) by 9/57.
DV 9220: War Department (GOV) M1260486 7/40; GJ Miller {GJ Miller & Son}, Cirencester (GL) 1945; AH Kearsey Ltd, Cheltenham (GL) 39 5/46; withdrawn 10/51; scrapped by Kearsey.
DV 9335: Gough's Garages Ltd {Queen of the Road}, Bristol (GL) 21 1939; withdrawn 1/57.
DV 9336: Gough's Garages Ltd {Queen of the Road}, Bristol (GL) 1939; not operated; War Department (GOV) 1940; returned to Gough's Garages Ltd {Queen of the Road}, Bristol (GL) at an unknown date; Bristol Co-operative Society Ltd {Queen of the Road}, Bristol (GL) 8/47.
DV 9337: Gough's Garages Ltd {Queen of the Road}, Bristol (GL) 22 1939; rebuilt by Longwell Green as C33F at an unknown date (post-war); withdrawn 9/52.

Vehicles acquired from HL Gunn {Gunn's Tours}, Rackenford, Tiverton (DN) 11/38

AG 5348	Reo Pullman	GE177	Taylor (Eaton)	C20F	3/30	-/47
DV 4280	GMC T30	303230	Gunn	C20F	3/30	n/a
OD 2686	Reo	ML241	Gunn	C20F	6/32	n/a
RX 7787	Reo Speed Wagon	FD4335	?	C26-	12/30	9/39
VF 6229	Reo Pullman	GE84	Taylor (Eaton)	C26F	6/29	-/45

Previous History:
AG 5348: New to D. Blane {Blane's Pullman Service}, Kilmarnock (AR) as B26F; Scottish General Transport Co Ltd, Kilmarnock (AR) 48 9/31; Western SMT Co Ltd, Kilmarnock (AR) 9/31; Gilford Motor Co Ltd (as dealer), London N7 1932; FH Nugas, Herongate (EX) 1932; City Coaches Ltd, Brentwood (EX) 5/36; not operated; from whom it was acquired 5/36.
DV 4280: New to Gunn.
OD 2686: New to Gunn.
RX 7787: New to Elliotts of Newbury Ltd, Newbury (GBE) as a van; JW Barnard {B & B Services}, Potten End (HT) rebodied C26- by an unknown manufacturer 7/37; from whom it was acquired 1/38.
VF 6229: New to WJ Crisp, Northwold (NK); from whom it was acquired 6/35.

Notes:
DV 4280: Not operated by Greenslades.
OD 2686: Not operated by Greenslades.

Disposal:
> AG 5348: F Baker and F Bowden {Bradninch Tours}, Bradninch (DN) 3/48; withdrawn 10/49; last licensed 12/49; scrapped 10/50.
> DV 4280: Chassis to E Saunders, Winkleigh (DN) and fitted with an unidentified body from an unknown source (possibly from a different Greenslades vehicle) 12/38; last licensed 9/44.
> OD 2686: Scrapped by Greenslades 9/41.
> RX 7787: Transferred to the Ancillary Fleet (qv).
> VF 6229: F Baker {Bradninch Tours}, Bradninch (DN) 4/45; withdrawn 12/45; scrapped 1946.

1939

New Vehicle

FFJ 116	Bedford WTB	7517	Tiverton		C25F	5/39	-/49

Disposal:
> FFJ 116: DC Venner, Witheridge (DN) 1/50 to 9/53; AJ Reed, Chulmleigh (DN) 10/53; withdrawn 3/54; PA Newton, Chulmleigh (DN) 9/54; withdrawn 6/55; sold for scrap.

Vehicles acquired from H & EA Belcher Ltd {Empress Coaches}, Teignmouth (DN) 10/39

DV 1082	Lancia Torino	2743	Duple	1586	C26F	5/29	n/a
OD 2488	Morris Viceroy	240Y	?		C20F	5/32	-/40
AUO 454	Dodge PLB	PLB1028	Thurgood	557	C20R	6/35	-/39
DFJ 46	Bedford WTB	111152	Tiverton		C20F	5/37	-/48
DFJ 47	Bedford WTB	111307	Tiverton		C20F	5/37	-/48
DFJ 114	Bedford WTB	111501	Duple	8893	C25F	6/37	12/42

Previous History:
> These vehicles were new to Belcher except for:
>
> AUO 454: New to WH Broadbeer & Sons {Regent Coaches}, Teignmouth (DN); from whom it was acquired 5/37.

Notes:
> DV 1082: Not operated by Greenslades.

Disposal:
> DV 1082: Last licensed by Belcher 8/38; scrapped.
> OD 2488: WEJ & JE Herring {Herring Brothers}, Burnham-on-Sea (SO) 10/40; Springett (farmer), Oakford Fitzpayne as a lorry at an unknown date; last licensed 12/47.
> AUO 454: JH Maineard, Dulverton (SO) 10/39; Batten and Thorne Ltd, Tiverton (DN) 10/45; withdrawn 10/49; scrapped 9/50.
> DFJ 46: ST Wills, Atherington (DN) 2/48; WSJ Farley, Ashreigney (DN) 9/53; withdrawn 9/54.
> DFJ 47: A Millman {FJ Millman & Sons}, Buckfastleigh (DN) 2/48; withdrawn 2/52; GE Nightingale, Budleigh Salterton (DN) fitted with the 1939 Duple C25F body (5945) transferred from Western National Omnibus Co Ltd, Exeter (DN) Bedford WTB DDV 22 10/53; it has been suggested this may have been a change of identity, rather than a body change; last licensed 6/59; withdrawn 5/60; still owned 3/61; no further owner.
> DFJ 114: Last licensed by Greenslades 12/42; not traced.

Vehicle acquired from WJ Abbott (Exmouth) Ltd {Abbott's Blue Bus Service}, Exmouth (DN) 11/39

JX 501	Albion PH49	15004H	ECOC	2908	B20F	3/33	n/a

Previous History:
> JX 501: New to Hebble Motor Services Ltd, Halifax (WR) 94; from whom it was acquired by 9/38.

Notes:
> JX 501: Not operated by Greenslades.

Disposal:
> JX 501: Last licensed 3/40.

Vehicle acquired from Regent Coaches (Teignmouth) Ltd (DN) 11/39

JY 454	Morris Director	077RP	Mumford		C18-	7/32	-/39

Previous History:
JY 454: New to WH Broadbeer & Sons {Regent Coaches}, Teignmouth (DN); becoming Regent Coaches (Teignmouth) Ltd 6/36.

Disposal:
JY 454: JH Clark {Tally Ho! Coaches}, East Allington (DN) 6 as C20- 1940; withdrawn 9/50.

1940

Vehicle acquired from E Clatworthy, Tiverton (DN) -/40

VV 10	Reo Pullman	GE155	Duple	1887	C20F	-/30	12/44

Previous History:
VV 10: New to Allchin {Cream Cars}, Torquay (DN); from whom it was acquired c1936 (by 5/37).

Disposal:
VV 10: F Baker {Bradninch Tours}, Bradninch (DN) 12/44; last licensed 6/46.

1942

New Vehicles

FFJ 909	Bedford OWB	8615	Duple	31672	B32F	7/42	-/48
FFJ 916	Bedford OWB	9048	Duple	31707	B32F	8/42	-/50
FFJ 917	Bedford OWB	9116	Duple	31708	B32F	8/42	-/50
FFJ 918	Bedford OWB	8988	Duple	31709	B32F	8/42	-/49
FFJ 948	Bedford OWB	11180	Mulliner		B32F	11/42	-/48
FFJ 953	Bedford OWB	11303	Duple	31886	B32F	12/42	-/48
FFJ 954	Bedford OWB	11309	Duple	31885	B32F	12/42	-/53

Notes:
FFJ 916: Fitted with coach seats as DP30F 1942.
FFJ 917: Fitted with coach seats as DP30F 1942.
FFJ 918: Fitted with coach seats as DP28F 1942.
FFJ 953: Fitted with coach seats as DP31F 1943.

Disposals:
FFJ 909: RC Williams {Godolphin Motors}, Breague (CO) 5/48; Grenville Motors Ltd, Camborne (CO) 9/48; withdrawn 8/55; Daniels, Pool (GCO) as a mobile shop; last licensed 12/60.
FFJ 916: WL Heard {Hartland Coaches}, Hartland (DN) 12/50; fitted with a Perkins oil engine and licensed 5/51; this vehicle either assumed the identity of Bedford OWB FFJ 969 (ch.13033) or was fitted with the Duple B24F body (32046) from that vehicle 10/56; withdrawn 12/63; scrapped.
FFJ 917: EM Richards (Kingsbridge Motor Works), Kingsbridge (DN) as B32F 9/50; EM Wray {Primrose Coaches}, Kingsbridge (DN) 12/54; CJ Prowse {Primrose Coaches}, Kingsbridge (DN) 5/57; FET Baker (showman), Millbay, Plymouth 1958; last licensed 9/60.
FFJ 918: PW Steer (Bow Belle), Bow (DN) 9/49; withdrawn 9/55; Jest and Ruskin (contractor), Waltham Cross (XHT) by 1/56; disused at Hainault by 5/61; JE Pipkin, Barkingside use and date unknown; last licensed 4/64.
FFJ 948: A & SJ Stevens {W Stevens & Sons / The Harrier}, Modbury (DN) 9 1/48; withdrawn 3/56; WF Glynn (showman), Efford, Plymouth 1956; last licensed 8/61.
FFJ 953: WF Berriman, Troon (CO) 3/48; Grenville Motors Ltd, Camborne (CO) 8/48; withdrawn 10/57; unknown owner, Perranporth as a mobile snack bar 11/57.
FFJ 954: J, EM & AB Geddes {JM Geddes & Son / Burton Cars}, Brixham (DN) 9/53; Berry Head Lime & Stone Co, Brixham, (XDN) 10/54; English China Clay Quarries Ltd, Exeter (XDN) 12/58; transferred to English China Clay Quarries Ltd, St Austell (XCO) 12/59; scrapped 12/61.

1943

New Vehicle

FFJ 996	Bedford OWB	16768	Duple	34019	B32F	10/43	-/50

Disposal:
   FFJ 996: HC Kingcombe, Newton Ferrers (DN) 1/50; withdrawn 9/58; no further operator.

1944

New Vehicles

| GFJ 40 | Bedford OWB | 22898 | Duple | 39087 | B32F | 10/44 | -/50 |
| GFJ 41 | Bedford OWB | 22919 | Duple | 38966 | B32F | 10/44 | -/50 |

Notes:
   GFJ 40: Fitted with coach seats as DP28F soon after entry into service. The front dome of the body was replaced with a more rounded design, possibly also the rear dome.
   GFJ 41: Fitted with coach seats as DP29F soon after entry into service; rebuilt by Tiverton c1948.

Disposals:
   GFJ 40: E Saunders, Winkleigh (DN) as B30F 11/50; withdrawn 12/62; sold for use as a farm storeshed.
   GFJ 41: DC Venner, Witheridge (DN) 4/50; PA Newton, Chulmleigh (DN) 4/54; withdrawn 3/56; HGJ Bruce & RRH Parker, Lewdown (DN) 9/56; JEB Gregory, Launceston (CO) 10/58 withdrawn 7/60; WR Bridge, Clitheroe (XLA) at an unknown date; last licensed 2/61.

1945

New Vehicles

| GFJ 101 | Bedford OWB | 29791 | Duple | 41358 | B32F | 8/45 | -/50 |
| GFJ 102 | Bedford OWB | 29471 | Duple | 41356 | B32F | 8/45 | -/50 |

Notes:
   GFJ 101: Fitted with coach seats as DP28F before entry into service.
   GFJ 102: Fitted with coach seats as DP28F before entry into service.

Disposals:
   GFJ 101: Last licensed by Bowaters Services & Transport Ltd, London SW1 (XLN) 12/61.
   GFJ 102: Last licensed by W Pilkington, Liverpool (GLA) as a mobile shop 9/60.

Vehicles acquired from Mrs EJ Heywood & JE Greenslade, Cheriton Fitzpayne (DN) 11/45

| FH 5515 | Dennis G | 70150 | ? | | C20F | 5/28 | n/a |
| BFJ 938 | Bedford WTB | 110644 | Tiverton | | C26F | 6/36 | -/47 |

Previous History:
   FH 5515: New to Davis & Sons {Westgate}, Gloucester (GL); PA Grindle {Forest Greyhound}, Cinderford (GL) c1930; from whom it was acquired.
   BFJ 938: New to Heywood & Greenslade.

Notes:
   FH 5515: Not operated by Greenslades.

Disposals:
   FH 5515: Scrapped by Kelly, Crediton at an unknown date.
   BFJ 938: AA Woodbury, Wellington (SO) 4/47; F Petherick, Chawleigh (DN) 9/50; withdrawn 4/51.

Vehicle acquired from Henry Turner & Co Ltd, Exeter (GDN?)

| FJ 5123 | Thornycroft A2 | 14545 | ? | | C14- | 7/27 | -/47 |

Previous History:
   FJ 5123: New to Henry Turner & Co Ltd, Exeter probably as a goods vehicle; from whom it was probably acquired c1945 and fitted with the (second-hand?) C14- body by an unknown manufacturer.

Disposal:
   FJ 5123: Batten and Thorne Ltd, Tiverton (DN) 4/47; withdrawn 7/48; C Buckland, Burnham-on-Sea (GSO) as a van 1948; last licensed 12/48.

1946

New Vehicle

GFJ 632	Bedford OB	29712 Duple	43125	C29F	9/46	-/53

Disposal:
GFJ 632: A & SJ Stevens {W Stevens & Sons / The Harrier}, Modbury (DN) 2 1/53; becoming C Nuttall {Stevens Garage/The Harrier}, Modbury (DN) 2 5/62; withdrawn 8/69.

Vehicles acquired from Exeter Corporation (DN) 5/46

FFJ 967	Bedford OWB	12797 Duple	32021	B32F	2/43	n/a
FFJ 968	Bedford OWB	13030 Duple	32068	B32F	3/43	n/a
FFJ 969	Bedford OWB	13033 Duple	32046	B32F	3/43	-/49
FFJ 970	Bedford OWB	13087 Duple	32049	B32F	3/43	n/a
FFJ 971	Bedford OWB	13475 Duple	32102	B32F	4/43	n/a
FFJ 972	Bedford OWB	13465 Duple	32083	B32F	4/43	1/50

Previous History:
FFJ 967: New as Exeter Corporation 71; from whom it was acquired via Tiverton Motor Co Ltd (dealer), Tiverton 5/46.
FFJ 968: New as Exeter Corporation 72; from whom it was acquired via Tiverton Motor Co Ltd (dealer), Tiverton 5/46.
FFJ 969: New as Exeter Corporation 73; from whom it was acquired via Tiverton Motor Co Ltd (dealer), Tiverton 5/46; fitted with coach seats as DP28F before entering service with the front and possibly the rear dome of the body being replaced by a more rounded design.
FFJ 970: New as Exeter Corporation 74; from whom it was acquired via Tiverton Motor Co Ltd (dealer), Tiverton 5/46.
FFJ 971: New as Exeter Corporation 75; from whom it was acquired via Tiverton Motor Co Ltd (dealer), Tiverton 5/46.
FFJ 972: New as Exeter Corporation 76; from whom it was acquired via Tiverton Motor Co Ltd (dealer), Tiverton 5/46; fitted with coach seats as DP28F before entering service with the front dome of the body being replaced by a more rounded design.

Notes:
FFJ 967-968: Not operated by Greenslades.
FFJ 970-971: Not operated by Greenslades.

Disposals:
FFJ 967: SJ Wakley {Rambler Coaches}, Axminster (DN) 6 as B28F 5/46; becoming SJ Wakley Ltd {Rambler Coaches}, Axminster 5/54; withdrawn 12/58; Wessex Motorways (Bristol) Ltd, Chard (SO) 1/60; used as a towing vehicle; last licensed 12/60; scrapped at Chard 8/62.
FFJ 968: Sidmouth Motor Co and Dagworthy Ltd, Sidmouth (DN) 7/46; re-seated to B30F; returned to Greenslades 6/56 (qv).
FFJ 969: PA Norman {Kingston Coaches}, Combe Martin (DN) as B24F 9/49; JE Lee, Meddon, Hartland (DN) 5/54; withdrawn 9/56; WL Heard {Hartland Coaches}, Hartland (DN) 10/56. Either the body of this vehicle was transferred onto Bedford OWB FFJ 916 or the identity of this vehicle was then assumed by FFJ 916 (qv).
FFJ 970: SJ Wakley {Rambler Coaches}, Axminster (DN) 5 5/46; becoming SJ Wakley Ltd {Rambler Coaches}, Axminster 5/54; withdrawn 12/58; Wessex Motorways (Bristol) Ltd, Chard (SO) 1/60; used as a non-psv; scrapped at Chard at an unknown date.
FFJ 971: Sidmouth Motor Co and Dagworthy Ltd, Sidmouth (DN) as B31F 7/46; returned to Greenslades 6/56 (qv).
FFJ 972: NH Ashton {Ashtonville Coaches}, Halwill Junction (DN) 1/50; last licensed 12/60; withdrawn 10/61; scrapped at Halwill Junction at an unknown date.

Vehicle acquired from Western National Omnibus Co Ltd, Exeter (DN) 1946

TW 9856	Leyland PLSC3	45754 Mumford		C29R	6/27	-/47

Previous History:
TW 9856: New to National Omnibus & Transport Co Ltd, London SW3 (LN) 2367 with a Beadle C26D body; Western National Omnibus Co Ltd, Exeter (DN) 2367 6/30; rebodied by Mumford, originally as C25R 2/35.

Disposal:

TW 9856: F Baker {Bradninch Tours}, Bradninch (DN) 11/47; WJO Jennings Ltd, Morwenstow (CO) 1/48; withdrawn 1/50. Although tax records quote this vehice as being last licensed 12/39 by Jennings, it is confirmed as operating for Jennings between 1/48 and 1/50.

1947

New Vehicles

HFJ 147	Bedford OB	44583	Duple	43360	C29F	3/47	-/52
HFJ 148	Bedford OB	36003	Duple	43128	C29F	3/47	-/50
HFJ 149	Bedford OB	36215	Duple	43189	C29F	3/47	-/55
HFJ 152	Bedford OB	35324	Duple	43127	C29F	3/47	-/51
HFJ 153	Bedford OB	34991	Duple	43126	C29F	3/47	-/52
HFJ 507	Bedford OB	55565	Duple	43361	C29F	5/47	-/54
HFJ 836	Bedford OB	63155	Duple	43363	C29F	12/47	9/57

Disposals:

HFJ 147: SJ Wakley {Rambler Coaches}, Axminster (DN) 11 5/52; becoming SJ Wakley Ltd {Rambler Coaches}, Axminster (DN) 5/54; withdrawn 10/59; Wessex Motorways (Bristol) Ltd, Chard 1/60; not operated; Luxury Coaches (Stow) Ltd, Stow-on-the-Wold (GL) 3/60; Sussex and Dorking Brick Co Ltd, Dorking (XSR) 7/63; Redland Transport Ltd, Reigate (XSR) 1963; last licensed 11/63; scrapped at an unknown date.

HFJ 148: A & SJ Stevens {W Stevens & Sons / The Harrier}, Modbury (DN) 4 11/50; becoming C Nuttall {Stevens Garage/The Harrier}, Modbury (DN) 5/62; withdrawn 1/64; unidentified owner, Bourton-on-the-Water (GGL) as a mobile fish and chip shop 4/65; registration void 12/71.

HFJ 149: F Cowley (dealer), Salford 10/55; Miller, Port St Mary, Isle of Man (IM) re-registered UMN 137 10/55; Kirkby (dealer), South Anston 6/64.

HFJ 152: J Fry, Tintagel (CO) 7/51; TJ Hutchinson {Woodside Coaches}, London SE18 (LN) 5/58; licensed 7/58; withdrawn 1/60; BD Cook {Karefree Travel}, West Croydon (LN) 9/60; withdrawn 4/61; TT French {French Car Service}, London SW18 (LN) 7/62; withdrawn 7/65; Bexleyheath Transport Co Ltd, Bexleyheath (LN) for spares 1966; scrapped 1968.

HFJ 153: JS Jenkins {Duchy Tours}, Penzance (CO) 3/52; becoming Jenkins {Duchy Tours} Ltd, Penzance (CO) 6/53; S Hillier, Shangri-la Caravan Camp, St Osyth (XEX) 3/59; last licensed 12/60; Lamb (dealer), Tendring for scrap 5/62.

HFJ 507: J Parkinson, Adlington (LA) 6/54; licensed 12/55; WR & MA Martin, Weaverham (CH) 4/61; withdrawn 8/61; M Hassan, Liverpool use and date unknown; last licensed 3/65.

HFJ 836: AMCC (dealer), London E15 by 2/58; Ellinas (dealer), Nicosia (O-CY) 2/58; Kaimakli Bus Co, Kaimakli (O-CY) re-registered TAP 139 4/58; Papapetrou, Evrykhou (O-CY) 5/59; rebodied Trimbakiri FB35F 11/68; Evrykhou Transport Co, Evrykhou, Cyprus (O-CY) 1/86; withdrawn 12/89.

1948

New Vehicles

JFJ 14	Bedford OB	66020	Duple	43365	C29F	3/48	9/57
JFJ 15	Bedford OB	73541	Duple	46958	C29F	3/48	-/58
JFJ 16	Austin K4/CXB	109735	Tiverton		C29F	3/48	-/51
JFJ 178	Bedford OB	67196	Duple	46959	C29F	5/48	-/58
JFJ 179	Bedford OB	55508	Tiverton		C29F	5/48	-/53
JFJ 180	Bedford OB	69970	Tiverton		C29F	6/48	-/53
JFJ 181	Bedford OB	63312	Tiverton		C25F	6/48	-/51
JFJ 260	Bedford OB	60870	Tiverton		C29F	6/48	-/53
JFJ 261	Bedford OB	68687	Tiverton		C25F	6/48	-/53

Notes:

JFJ 181: Re-seated to C29F at an unknown date.
JFJ 261: Re-seated to C29F at an unknown date.

Disposals:

JFJ 14: AMCC (dealer), London E15 1957; Ellinas, Nicosia (O-CY) 1/58; re-registered TAM 159; Papa Georghiou, Exometokhi (O-CY) 7/58; Tembria Car Co, Korakou (O-CY) 5/59; Petrou, Aglandjia (O-CY) 1/60; Tricomitis (dealer), Famagusta 9/68.

JFJ 15: J Heathcoat and Co Ltd, Tiverton (XDN) 6/58; RCL Tomlinson {Dawlish Coaches}, Dawlish (DN) 6/61; Dawlish Coaches Ltd, Dawlish (DN) 7/62; WWS & SEJ Ridler {WS Ridler & Son}, Dulverton 3/63; withdrawn 11/65.

JFJ 16: SA Kingdom {Tivvy Coaches}, Tiverton (DN) 1/51; withdrawn 3/56; Kinnear, Moodie and Co, London SE13 use unknown 12/59; withdrawn 2/63.

JFJ 178: Exeter Laundries Ltd, Exeter (XDN) 9/58; Paladin Paint Contractors, Tiverton (XDN) by 5/64; CW Raven Products Ltd, Filkins (XOX) 6/65; last noted 8/65.

JFJ 179: Mrs WA Hart and KAM Bentham {Hart's Services and Tours}, Budleigh Salterton (DN) 6/53; SA Kingdom {Tivvy Coaches}, Tiverton 6/59; withdrawn 4/64; Alf Moseley & Son Ltd (dealer), Loughborough 1/65.

JFJ 180: JH Wellington {W Wellington & Son / Kingsbridge Belle}, Kingsbridge (DN) 2 10/53; Tally Ho! Coaches Ltd, East Allington (DN) 10/64; last licensed 12/65; scrapped 1/66.

JFJ 181: WJ Nicholas {Riviera Tours}, Penzance (CO) 4/51; WK & MM Roberts {Cornish Riviera Tours}, Penzance (CO) 5/56; Notre Dame School, Plymouth (XDN) 2/57; withdrawn 5/61; Rev J Jones, Efford, Plymouth (XDN) at an unknown date; last licensed 12/64; Rundle (dealer), Plymouth for scrap by 3/65.

JFJ 260: EC & WC Mansell {Mansell's Garage / Blue Motors}, Lynmouth (DN) 3/53; SA Kingdom {Tivvy Coaches}, Tiverton (DN) 1/55; scrapped 2/60.

JFJ 261: EC & WC Mansell {Mansell's Garage / Blue Motors}, Lynmouth (DN) 3/53; withdrawn 1/55; CE Christian Ltd, Newquay (XCO) by 4/62; scrapped 8/62.

Vehicle acquired from Maudslay Motor Co Ltd, Coventry -/48

HHP 755	AEC Regal III	9621E612	Duple	51484	FC33F	9/48	-/61

Previous History:
HHP 755: Exhibited at the 1948 Earls Court Commercial Motor Show, carrying Maudslay badges. AEC badges were fitted before it entered service with Greenslades in 12/48.

Disposal:
HHP 755: AMCC (dealer), London E15 10/61; Collins Fruit Farm, Weeley Heath (XEX) 10/64; East London Transport Society for preservation 6/78; West of England Transport Collection, Winkleigh for preservation by 10/82; Tony Blackman, Halifax for preservation c6/89; Ashley Blackman, Halifax for preservation by 5/07; returned to Winkleigh 8/07; Quantock Motor Services, Wiveliscombe (SO) for preservation by 1/08; moved to Bishops Lydeard by 5/11; D Shears, Winkleigh for preservation 2/12.

1949

New Vehicles

JFJ 822	Maudslay Marathon III	70350	Duple	51690	FC33F	3/49	-/60
JFJ 938	Maudslay Marathon III	70439	Duple	51691	C33F	5/49	-/59
JFJ 939	Bedford OB	105898	Duple	46962	C29F	5/49	1/59
JFJ 949	Maudslay Marathon III	70432	Whitson		C33F	5/49	-/52
KFJ 55	Maudslay Marathon III	70430	Burlingham	3675	C33F	6/49	-/60
KFJ 172	AEC Regal III	9621E800	Gurney Nutting	1002	FC33F	8/49	-/60
KFJ 173	Albion FT3AB	70755D	Tiverton		C31F	7/49	-/49
KFJ 222	Albion FT3AB	70756A	Tiverton		C33F	8/49	-/52

Notes:
Four further Albion FT3AB were ordered by Greenslades (ch.70816A-D) but subsequently cancelled and delivered to W Alexander & Sons Ltd, Falkirk (SN) with Strachan bodies registered CWG 228, 230, 226-227 respectively.

Disposals:
JFJ 822: AMCC (dealer), London E15 12/60; Lansdowne Luxury Coaches Ltd, London E11 (LN) by 6/61; AMCC (dealer), London E15 by 2/62; last licensed 11/63.

JFJ 938: W & J Glossop Ltd, Exeter (XDN) by 3/61.

JFJ 939: AMCC (dealer), London E15 1/59; Sheerlines Ltd, Southend-on-Sea (EX) 6/59; RJ Copeman {C & R Coaches}, Little Tey (EX) 2/63; withdrawn 8/70; unknown owner, Eight Ash Green as a mobile caravan at an uknown date; Dale, Little Tay as a mobile caravan by 7/98; S Golynia, Long Melford for preservation by 9/10.

JFJ 949: HC Kingcome, Newton Ferrers (DN) 9/52; JGF Galpin, Newton Ferrers (DN) 10/62; withdrawn 11/62.

KFJ 55: AMCC (dealer), London E15 12/60; Lansdowne Luxury Coaches Ltd, London E11 (LN) 1/61.
KFJ 172: AMCC (dealer), London E15 12/60; Limmer & Trinidad Lake Asphalt Co Ltd, London EC1 (GLN) 814 as a tar boiler lorry by 7/71.
KFJ 173: Mrs WA Hart & KAM Bentham {Hart's Services and Tours}, Budleigh Salterton (DN) as C33F 11/49; withdrawn 3/59; GS Carnall, Aylesbeare (DN) 1/60; W Bennetto {Majestic}, Fraddon (CO) 9/60, licensed 1/61; W & B Bennetto {W Bennetto & Son / Majestic}, Fraddon (CO) 8/62; withdrawn 10/62.
KFJ 222: SA Kingdom {Tivvy Coaches}, Tiverton (DN) 5/52; DS & RV Kingdom {Tivvy Coaches}, Tiverton (DN) 2/61; Kingdom's Tours Ltd {Tivvy Coaches}, Tiverton (DN) 10/61; withdrawn 1/63; scrapped.

1950

New Vehicles

KFJ 607	Leyland PS2/3	494736	Gurney Nutting		C33F	3/50	-/60
KFJ 609	AEC Regal III	9621E1067	Gurney Nutting		C33F	3/50	-/61
KFJ 610	AEC Regal III	9621E1066	Gurney Nutting		C33F	3/50	-/61
KFJ 611	AEC Regal III	9621E1069	Gurney Nutting	1036	C33F	3/50	-/61
KFJ 612	AEC Regal III	9621E1068	Gurney Nutting	1037	FC33F	3/50	-/61
KFJ 613	AEC Regal III	9621E1070	Gurney Nutting	1038	C33F	7/50	-/63
KFJ 614	AEC Regal III	9621E1071	Gurney Nutting	1039	C33F	7/50	-/62
KFJ 684	Bedford OB	130606	Duple	46964	C29F	5/50	-/59

Notes:
KFJ 612: Re-seated as FC35F 5/60.

Disposals:
KFJ 607: AMCC (dealer), London E15 10/60.
KFJ 609: AMCC (dealer), London E15 10/61.
KFJ 610: AMCC (dealer), London E15 10/61.
KFJ 611: AMCC (dealer), London E15 10/61; Martin-Baker Aircraft Co Ltd, Higher Denham (XBK) 1/62; replaced by 12/91, probably for scrap.
KFJ 612: AMCC (dealer), London E15 10/61; Martin-Baker Aircraft Co Ltd, Higher Denham (XBK) 1/62; transferred to Langford Lodge, Co Antrim by 8/65; withdrawn 6/70; unidentified dealer for scrap by 1/73.
KFJ 613: AMCC (dealer), London E15 10/63; Vines Luxury Coaches Ltd, Great Bromley (EX) 6/64; AC Peck {Cedric Coaches}, Wivenhoe (XEX) 19 1/65; Cedric Contracts Ltd, Wivenhoe (XEX) 8/67; Blackwell (dealer), Earls Colne 11/68; chassis derelict on premises 1/70.
KFJ 614: Junior Leaders Regiment, Royal Signals, Denbury (XDN) 11/62; sold for scrap by 1967.
KFJ 684: AMCC (dealer), London E15 1959; AC Peck (Cedric Coaches), Wivenhoe (EX) 12 5/59; transferred to Peck's non-psv fleet (XEX) 5/66; Cedric Contracts Ltd, Wivenhoe (XEX) 8/67; scrapped 12/67.

1951

New Vehicles

LFJ 737	Bedford SB	1144	Duple	56665	C35F	5/51	-/52
LFJ 801	Maudslay Marathon III	38/79535	Gurney Nutting	1253	FC33C	5/51	-/61
LFJ 804	Maudslay Marathon III	38/79536	Gurney Nutting	1254	FC35C	5/51	-/61
LFJ 876	Leyland PS2/3	496172	Yeates	239	C37F	7/51	-/63
LFJ 877	Leyland PS2/3	500449	Yeates	240	C37F	7/51	-/63

Notes:
LFJ 801: Re-seated as FC26C; reverted to FC35C at unknown dates.
LFJ 804: Re-seated as FC26C; reverted to FC35C at unknown dates.
LFJ 876: Chassis extended by Yeates prior to bodying.
LFJ 877: Chassis extended by Yeates prior to bodying.

Disposals:
LFJ 737: SA Kingdom {Tivvy Coaches}, Tiverton (DN) 5/52; RG Rowland & WS Pocklington {Rambler Coaches}, St Leonards (ES) 3 5/57; withdrawn 4/62; HR Richmond Ltd {Epsom Coaches}, Epsom (SR) 6/62; withdrawn 9/64; Kenson Construction Co Ltd (contractor), Purbrook (XSR) 10/64.
LFJ 801: AMCC (dealer), London E15 11/61; Lansdowne Luxury Coaches Ltd, London E11 (LN) 5/62; Chalkes Hill Motor Sales (dealer), Leigh-on-Sea 12/64; GC Bickers, Coddenham (EK) 12/65;

withdrawn 1/69; Cedric Contracts Ltd, Wivenhoe (XEX) 8/69; Blackwell (dealer), Earls Colne 7/70.
LFJ 804: AMCC (dealer), London E15 11/61; Mrs ME Lewington {Clintona Coaches}, Harold Hill (LN) 3/63; R Staines {Clintona Coaches}, Brentwood (EX) 10/63; P Rice {Southgate Coaches}, London N11 (LN) 2/64; withdrawn 6/64; Luton Commercial Motors Ltd (dealer), Dunstable at an unknown date.
LFJ 876: Bowerman's Tours Ltd, Taunton (SO) 10/63; licensed 11/63; withdrawn 12/64; CS Williams (Taunton) Ltd (contractor), Taunton (XSO) by 4/66; still owned 7/67.
LFJ 877: Bowerman's Tours Ltd, Taunton (SO) 10/63; licensed 11/63; withdrawn 8/64; Staverton Contractors Ltd (contractor), Totnes (XDN) 194 at an unknown date; West of England Transport Collection, Winkleigh for preservation 9/71; G Ledger, Northampton as spares for preserved vehicle 6/74; body to Midlands Omnibus Preservation Society.

1952

New Vehicles

MFJ 551	Bedford SB	4394	Duple	1006/340	C33F	5/52	-/59
MFJ 552	Bedford SB	5495	Duple	1006/448	C33F	3/52	2/53
MFJ 553	Bedford SB	5564	Duple	1006/481	C33F	3/52	-/61
MFJ 608	Leyland PSU1/15	520441	Burlingham	4925	C28C	4/52	-/63

Disposals:
MFJ 551: GE Wright {Bow Belle}, Bow (LN) 4/60; Ongar Motors and Transport Co Ltd, Ongar (EX) 2/62.
MFJ 552: Regent Coaches (Teignmouth) Ltd, Teignmouth (DN) 2/53; returned to Greenslades 1/55 (qv).
MFJ 553: A Millman {Millman & Sons}, Buckfastleigh (DN) 3/62; withdrawn 3/68.
MFJ 608: M & P Philipson {P Philipson & Son / Dearneways}, Goldthorpe 46 (SY) as C41C 10/63; Grayline Luxury Coaches Ltd, Bicester (OX) 3/66; Garnham's Garage Ltd, Woodbridge (EK) 9/66; withdrawn 9/69; Mills (dealer), Hollesley Bay for scrap.

1953

Vehicles acquired from H & EA Belcher (Teignmouth) Ltd {Empress Coaches}, Teignmouth (DN) 2/53

MFJ 609	Leyland PSU1/15	520442	Burlingham	4926	C41C	4/52	-/63
MFJ 900	Bedford SB	9121	Gurney Nutting	1307	C36F	6/52	-/60
MFJ 901	Bedford SB	8359	Gurney Nutting	1308	C35F	6/52	-/59

Previous History:
These vehicles were all new to Belcher.

Notes:
MFJ 609: Re-seated to C28C at an unknown date.
MFJ 901: Re-seated to C36F at an unknown date.

Disposal:
MFJ 609: M & P Philipson {P Philipson & Son / Dearneways}, Goldthorpe 45 (WR) as C41C 10/63; WS Yeates Ltd (dealer), Loughborough 5/66.
MFJ 900: J Heathcoat and Co Ltd, Tiverton (XDN) by 1961; last noted 4/68.
MFJ 901: J Heathcoat and Co Ltd, Tiverton (XDN) by 4/60.

1954

New Vehicles

OFJ 790	Bedford SBG	27337	Duple	1051/79	C34F	4/54	-/61
OFJ 791	Bedford SBG	27516	Duple	1051/98	C34F	4/54	-/61
OFJ 792	Bedford SBG	27391	Duple	1051/99	C34F	4/54	-/62
OFJ 793	Bedford SBG	27776	Duple	1051/115	C36F	4/54	-/61
OFJ 794	Bedford SBG	27551	Duple	1051/129	C36F	4/54	-/62
OFJ 795	Bedford SBG	28192	Duple	1051/159	C36F	6/54	-/61

Disposals:
OFJ 790: AMCC (dealer), London E15 10/61; Wiffen's Coaches Ltd, Finchingfield (EX) as C36F 5/62; HG Chapman, Sawtry (CM) 11/62; withdrawn 6/67; Marriott (contractor), Rushden (XNO) by 8/68; Errington (dealer), Oadby by 8/68.

OFJ 791: AMCC (dealer), London E15 10/61; F Thompson & Sons (Dereham) Ltd {Eniway Coaches}, East Dereham (NK) 5/62; withdrawn 6/67; EE Smith & Sons Ltd, Attleborough (NK) 1/69; withdrawn 1/73.
OFJ 792: HF & FM Beal (dealer), Exeter 10/62; RW Toop, WJ Ironside and PW Davies {Bere Regis and District Motor Services}, Dorchester (DT) 12/62; licensed 3/63; withdrawn 12/64; scrapped at Dorchester 1965.
OFJ 793: HF & FM Beal (dealer), Exeter 12/61; J, EM & AB Geddes {JM Geddes & Son / Burton Cars}, Brixham (DN) 5/62; AM & K Sargeant {Sargeant Brothers}, Kington (HR) 12/66; withdrawn 5/69.
OFJ 794: HF & FM Beal (dealer), Exeter 10/62; RW Toop, WJ Ironside & PW Davies {Bere Regis and District Motor Services}, Dorchester (DT) 12/62; licensed 3/63; withdrawn 3/69.
OFJ 795: HF & FM Beal (dealer), Exeter 12/61; J Heathcoat and Co Ltd, Tiverton (XDN) by 5/62; last noted 4/68.

Vehicles acquired from Taylor's Central Garages (Exeter) Ltd, Exeter (DN) 1/54

FW 7106	AEC Regal	6621788	Willowbrook	2852	C32F	2/36	n/a
DVH 531	Bedford OB	76861	Duple	50419	C29F	6/48	n/a
DVH 837	Bedford OB	83793	Duple	50420	C29F	8/48	n/a
EBU 13	Bedford OB	34093	Pearson		C26F	7/47	n/a
EBU 223	Bedford OB	65698	Pearson		C25F	1/48	n/a
ECX 566	Bedford OB	108291	Duple	54362	C29F	6/49	n/a
GTD 460	AEC Regal	O6624695	Santus		C32F	8/46	-n/a
HFJ 117	Daimler CVD6	13337	Heaver		C33F	3/47	9/56
HFJ 300	Daimler CVD6	13336	Heaver		C35F	5/47	9/56
HFJ 390	Daimler CVD6	13866	Heaver		C35F	6/47	9/56
JFJ 198	Bedford OB	67396	Heaver		C25F	6/48	n/a
JFJ 346	Bedford OB	70107	Heaver		C25F	8/48	n/a
LDH 712	Daimler CVD6	15943	Plaxton	149	C33F	10/48	n/a
LFJ 931	Daimler CVD6	17661	Duple	50209	C37F	7/51	-/61
LPC 187	Foden PVSC5	23004	Whitson		C35F	3/47	n/a
MMT 880	Bedford OB	37258	Duple	43162	C27F	11/46	n/a

Previous History:
These vehicles were new to Taylor's except for the following:-

FW 7106: New to Enterprise and Silver Dawn Motors Ltd, Scunthorpe (LI) 12; becoming Enterprise (Scunthorpe) Passenger Services Ltd, Scunthorpe (LI) 12 5/47; from whom it was acquired 8/48.
DVH 531: New to Hansons Buses Ltd, Huddersfield (WR) 263; from whom it was acquired 1/52.
DVH 837: New to Hansons Buses Ltd, Huddersfield (WR) 264; from whom it was acquired 1/52.
EBU 13: New to Shearings Tours Ltd, Oldham (LA); from whom it was acquired 5/49.
EBU 223: New to H Harrison, Chadderton (LA); from whom it was acquired 3/49.
ECX 566: New to Hansons Buses Ltd, Huddersfield (WR) 272; from whom it was acquired 1/52.
GTD 460: New to Mittons Motors Ltd, Colne (LA); from whom it was acquired 7/49.
LDH 712: New to J Boult & Sons, Walsall (WM) 42; from whom it was acquired 5/51.
LPC 187: New to WS Hunt, Ottershaw (SR) F1; from whom it was acquired 7/49.
MMT 880: New to WJ Ray {Ray Coaches}, Edgware (MX); from whom it was acquired 7/51.

Notes:
FW 7106: Licence had expired when acquired; not operated by Greenslades.
DVH 531: Not operated by Greenslades.
DVH 837: Not operated by Greenslades.
EBU 13: Not operated by Greenslades.
EBU 223: Not operated by Greenslades.
ECX 566: Not operated by Greenslades.
GTD 460: Not operated by Greenslades.
JFJ 198: Not operated by Greenslades.
JFJ 346: Not operated by Greenslades.
LDH 712: Not operated by Greenslades.
LPC 187: Not operated by Greenslades.
MMT 880: Not operated by Greenslades.

Disposals:

FW 7106: No further operator.

DVH 531: Burrett and Wells Ltd, Melksham (WI) 37 6/54; Chiltonian Motors Ltd, Chilton Foliat (WI) 4/57; SR Gough {Gough's Coaches), Bracknell (BE) 3/58; becoming Gough's Garages Ltd, Bracknell (BE) by 3/61; withdrawn 3/63; L Wilson, Reading (GBE) by 5/65; last licensed 3/66.

DVH 837: J & FR Parsons & AJH Codd, Holsworthy (DN) 6/54; J, FR & EM Parsons and AJH Codd, Holsworthy (DN) c1955; withdrawn 1/70.

EBU 13: C Lindsay & ET Latham {L and L Coaches}, Worthing (WS) 8/54; withdrawn 12/54; J Davis & Son Ltd, Hawkhurst (KT) 4/55; withdrawn 5/56; RM Holtby, Guildford (GSR) at an unknown date; GR Holtby, Guildford (GSR) probably as a mobile shop at an unknown date; last licensed 2/58.

EBU 223: E Vernon, Northleigh (DN) 7/54; withdrawn 10/64; last owner J Jones (dealer?), (Chersey?) 1/65.

ECX 566: Burrett & Wells Ltd, Melksham (WI) 38 6/54; withdrawn 4/57; H & J Homer & D Jones, Quarry Bank (WM) 4/57; withdrawn 7/59; RB Talbott {Barry's Coaches}, Moreton-in-Marsh (GL) 10/59; EHJ, DL, EO & D Kear {Duchess}, Bristol (GL) 4/60; withdrawn 6/67.

GTD 460: A Turner, Chulmleigh (DN) 7/54; withdrawn 5/59; Higgs & Hill (contractor), London SW8 (XLN) 5/59.

HFJ 117: AMCC (dealer), London E15 by 10/56; Autobuses Interurbanos Canarios, SA {AICASA}, Gran Canaria (O-IC) 137 as B30F re-registered GC12312 9/58; sold by auction for scrap 10/74.

HFJ 300: AMCC (dealer), London E15 by 10/56; Autobuses Interurbanos Canarios, SA {AICASA}, Gran Canaria (O-IC) 119 as B30F re-registered GC10730 5/57; sold by auction for scrap 10/74.

HFJ 390: AMCC (dealer), London E15 by 10/56; Autobuses Interurbanos Canarios, SA {AICASA}, Gran Canaria (O-IC) 121 as B33C re-registered GC10839 5/57; sold by auction for scrap 10/74.

JFJ 198: LFJ Ley {Treley Motors}, St Buryan (CO) 8/54; withdrawn 5/60; Barnard and Barnard (dealer), London SE26.

JFJ 346: J Heathcoat and Co Ltd, Tiverton (XDN) 6/54; last noted 7/59.

LDH 712: AMCC (dealer), London E15 7/54; Autobuses Interurbanos Canarios, SA {AICASA}, Gran Canaria (O-IC) 133 re-registered GC11938 4/58; sold by auction for scrap 10/74.

LFJ 931: DP Gourd, Bishopsteignton (DN) 1/61; Dawlish Coaches Ltd, Dawlish (DN) 1/66; JGF Galpin {Sunshine Coaches}, Plymouth (DN) 2/68; Plymouth Rowing Club, Plymouth (XDN) 7/68; N Pomeroy, Croydon for preservation 2/73; D Brewer, Pilton for preservation by 6/83; vandalised 11/84; unidentified dealer, Frome at an unknown date; West of England Transport Collection, Winkleigh for preservation 6/91; D Slater, Newcastle for preservation c12/91; North East Bus Breakers (dealer), Annfield Plain as spares for preserved vehicles; R Duffley, C Hatton & A Mould, Chase Terrace as spares for preserved vehicle by 11/97; dismantled for spares 2007.

LPC 187: Don Everall (Commercial Vehicles) Ltd (dealer), Wolverhampton 6/54; Joseph Dean & Sons Ltd, Wolverhampton (ST) 6/54; sold by 12/60; possibly returned to Don Everall (Commercial Vehicles) Ltd (dealer), Wolverhampton.

MMT 880: CW & WHM Terraneau, South Molton (DN) 5/54; LA Arscott (Chagford) Ltd, Chagford (DN) 5/58; RW Jefferies {Moorland Heather Coaches}, Chagford (DN) 2/61 and withdrawn 10/62.

Vehicles acquired from Teign Cars Ltd, Teignmouth (DN) 1/54

FW 7107	AEC Regal	6621789	Willowbrook	2853	C32F	2/36	n/a	
ACN 682	Daimler CVD6	15557	ACB		C33F	1/48	-/56	
DVH 434	Bedford OB	74943	Duple	50407	C29F	5/48	n/a	
EBU 771	Bedford OB	72999	Pearson		C26F	7/48	n/a	
ECX 412	Bedford OB	103155	Duple	50412	C29F	4/49	n/a	
ECX 413	Bedford OB	104100	Duple	50413	C29F	4/49	n/a	
EUO 122	Bedford WTB	112206	Heaver		C20F	5/38	n/a	
EUO 123	Bedford WTB	112202	Heaver		C20F	5/38	n/a	
GDV 885	Daimler CVD6	13867	Heaver		C33F	7/47	-/56	
HDV 357	Daimler CVD6	14339	Heaver		C33F	8/47	-/56	
JNC 214	Daimler CVD6	13888	KW Bodies		FC33F	4/48	n/a	
JOD 354	Bedford OB	68371	Heaver		C29F	5/48	n/a	
MMT 879	Bedford OB	37115	Duple	43163	C29F	11/46	n/a	
MOD 533	Daimler CVD6	17637	Duple	50210	C37F	7/51	-/60	

Previous History:

These vehicles were new to Teign Cars except for:-

FW 7107: New to Enterprise and Silver Dawn Motors Ltd, Scunthorpe (LI) 14; becoming Enterprise (Scunthorpe) Passenger Services Ltd, Scunthorpe (LI) 14 5/47; from whom it was acquired 9/48.

ACN 682: First registered by Walton (dealer), Gateshead and used as a demonstrator for Associated Coachbuilders, Sunderland; from whom it was acquired.
DVH 434: New to Hansons Buses Ltd, Huddersfield (WR) 262; Taylor's Central Garages Ltd, Exeter (DN) 1/52; from whom it was acquired.
EBU 771: New to Hilditch Tours Ltd, Oldham (GM); from whom it was acquired.
ECX 412: New to Hansons Buses Ltd, Huddersfield (WR) 270; from whom it was acquired.
ECX 413: New to Hansons Buses Ltd, Huddersfield (WR) 271; from whom it was acquired.
JNC 214: New to Sharp's Motor Services (Manchester) Ltd, Manchester (LA); TW Mundy {Silver Queen}, Camborne (CO) 6/49; from whom it was acquired; believed to have been rebuilt with full-front by Heaver 5/51.
MMT 879: New to WJ Ray {Ray Coaches}, Edgware (MX); from whom it was acquired.

Notes:
FW 7107: Not operated by Greenslades.
DVH 434: Not operated by Greenslades.
EBU 771: Not operated by Greenslades.
ECX 412-413: Not operated by Greenslades.
EUO 122-123: Not operated by Greenslades.
JNC 214: Not operated by Greenslades.
JOD 354: Not operated by Greenslades.
MMT 879: Not operated by Greenslades.

Disposals:
FW 7107: Greenslades Tours Ltd, Exeter (DN) 1/54; withdrawn 2/54; Marston Coaches Ltd, Oxford (OX) 2/54; SG Taylor {Enterprise Coaches}, Newbury (BK) 12/55; last licensed 3/56.
ACN 682: AMCC (dealer), London E15 by 10/56; Autobuses Interurbanos Canarios SA {AICASA}, Gran Canaria (O-IC) 117 re-registered GC10689 as B33F 4/57; sold for scrap 10/74.
DVH 434: Excelsior Coaches (Torquay) Ltd, Torquay (DN) 3/54; withdrawn 8/56; Wallace Arnold Tours Ltd, Leeds (WR) 3/57; not operated; Florence Excursions (Morecambe) Ltd, Morecambe (LA) 6/57; withdrawn 10/57; S Hughes (dealer), Gomersal 11/57; D Thomas, Llangynwyd (GG) 3/58; withdrawn 5/61.
EBU 771: L Slater {Dorothy Coaches}, Weston-super-Mare (SO) 4/54; withdrawn 6/59.
ECX 412: J, FR & EM Parsons and AJH Codd, Holsworthy (DN) c1955; withdrawn 10/71.
ECX 413: EJH & AJ Lovering {Lovering Brothers}, Combe Martin (DN) 3/54; AJ Lovering Ltd, Combe Martin 6/57; withdrawn 1/65.
GDV 885: AMCC (dealer), London E15 by 10/56; Autobuses Interurbanos Canarios SA {AICASA}, Gran Canaria (O-IC) 123 as B33F re-registered GC10953 6/57; sold for scrap 10/74.
HDV 357: AMCC (dealer), London E15 by 10/56; Autobuses Interurbanos Canarios SA {AICASA}, Gran Canaria (O-IC) 116 as B33F re-registered GC10671 4/57; sold for scrap 10/74.
JNC 214: AMCC (dealer), London E15 1954; Autobuses Interurbanos Canarios, SA {AICASA}, Gran Canaria (O-IC) 132 as B33F (probably rebuilt back to half-cab configuration) re-registered GC11937 4/58.
JOD 354: GE Nightingale, Budleigh Salterton (DN) 6/54; withdrawn 12/57; scrapped.
MMT 879: HE Butler, Milborne St Andrew (DT) 6/54; withdrawn 8/56; Craeg, Newchurch (XIW).
MOD 533: Staverton Contractors Ltd (contractor), Totnes (XDN) 10/60; Small (dealer), Newton Abbot for scrap 6/69.

Vehicles acquired from Devon General Omnibus & Touring Co Ltd, Torquay (DN) 3/54

JUO 605	Bedford OB	71454	Duple	47695	C29F	3/48	-/58
JUO 606	Bedford OB	73118	Duple	47696	C29F	3/48	-/58
JUO 608	Bedford OB	76097	Duple	47697	C29F	6/48	-/58

Previous History:
JUO 605-606: New as Devon General TCB605-606.
JUO 608: New as Devon General TCB 608.

Disposals:
JUO 605: AMCC (dealer), London E15 1958; Kyriakou, Limassol (O-CY) re-registered TAV 704 7/59; withdrawn 12/71.
JUO 606: AMCC (dealer), London E15 1958; Kyriakou, Limassol re-registered TAY 31 (O-CY) 10/59; Hamboullas, Limassol (O-CY) 2/60; Shiakli, Evdhimou (O-CY) 5/60; Osman, Kato Polemidhia (O-CY) 7/66; Djemal, Limassol (O-CY) 3/69; rebodied unknown FB32F 10/69; Christodoulou,

Vatili (O-CY) 9/71; re-seated FB34F 12/71; Atil, Elea (O-CY) 4/72; Pavlides (dealer), Nicosia (O-CY) 6/72.

JUO 608: AMCC (dealer), London E15 1958; TK Roberts & JAC Davies {Brechfa Express}, Felingwm (CR) 11/58; DV Bonnell {Bonnell's Blue Line Coaches}, Pwll (CR) 7/59; withdrawn 7/63; Gwyn Williams & Sons Ltd, Lower Tumble (CR) 6 9/66; D Jones {Ffoshelig Coaches}, Newchurch (CR) 2/68; used as a store shed from 10/69; West of England Transport Collection, Winkleigh for preservation 5/71; N Robertson, Sible Hedingham for preservation 5/71; Piper, Great Yeldham for preservation c1975; sold for scrap late 1975 or early 1976.

Vehicles acquired from Knight's Tours (Exeter) Ltd, Exeter (DN) 7/54

EFR 226	Bedford OB	134738	Duple	56105	C29F	4/50	-/57
EVJ 439	Bedford OB	56990	Duple	46453	C29F	8/47	10/56
GFJ 867	Bedford OB	34543	Duple	43087	C29F	11/46	-/55

Previous History:
EFR 226: New to A Whiteside Ltd, Blackpool (LA); from whom it was acquired 3/53.
EVJ 439: New to WE Morgan {Wye Valley Motors}, Hereford (HR); from whom it was acquired 7/50.
GFJ 867: New to Knight.

Disposals:
EFR 226: GH High, Tilney St. Lawrence (NK) 3/57; R Payne, Tilney St. Lawrence (NK) 5/57; W Carter, Marham (NK) 1/64; withdrawn 4/64.
EVJ 439: J Heathcoat and Co Ltd, Tiverton (XDN) 10/56; last licensed 12/61.
GFJ 867: JH Clark {Tally Ho! Coaches}, East Allington (DN) 15 1/55; renumbered 10 at an unknown date; HMS Adamant, Devonport (XDN) by 4/64; last licensed with Lt Dando, HMS Adamant, Devonport (XDN) 2/66.

1955

New Vehicles

RFJ 12	Commer Avenger III	T84A0001	Devon Coachbuilders		C31F	2/55	-/61
RFJ 380	AEC Reliance	MU3RV545	Duple	212/7	C41F	4/55	-/68
RFJ 381	AEC Reliance	MU3RV546	Duple	212/8	C41F	4/55	-/68
RFJ 395	Commer Avenger III	T84A0018	Devon Coachbuilders		C31F	4/55	-/62

Notes:
RFJ 12: Fitted with the 1950 Devon Coachbuilders body transferred from Belcher, Teignmouth Commer Avenger LOD 266.
RFJ 395: Fitted with the 1950 Devon Coachbuilders body transferred from Belcher, Teignmouth Commer Avenger MTA 173.

Disposals:
RFJ 12: AG & KM Spiers, Henley-on-Thames (OX) 6/61; licensed 11/61; withdrawn 8/63.
RFJ 380: AMCC (dealer), London E15 2/68.
RFJ 381: AMCC (dealer), London E15 2/68.
RFJ 395: Western Motor Works (Ashford) Ltd {Belmont Coaches}, Woodchurch (KT) 4/62; licensed 10/62; withdrawn 9/66.

Vehicles acquired from Regent Coaches (Teignmouth) Ltd, Teignmouth (DN) 1/55

HFJ 834	Bedford OB	58801	Duple	43362	C29F	12/47	-/58
HFJ 835	Bedford OB	63622	Duple	43364	C29F	12/47	-/58
JFJ 259	Bedford OB	76613	Duple	46960	C29F	6/48	-/58
JFJ 867	Bedford OB	92701	Duple	46961	C29F	3/49	-/58
KFJ 606	Leyland PS2/3	494660	Gurney Nutting		C33F	3/50	-/60
KFJ 608	Leyland PS2/3	494737	Gurney Nutting		C33F	3/50	-/60
KFJ 683	Bedford OB	121961	Duple	46963	C29F	5/50	-/59
MFJ 552	Bedford SB	5495	Duple	1006/448	C33F	3/52	-/61

Previous History:
HFJ 834: New to H & EA Belcher {Empress Coaches}, Teignmouth (DN); from whom it was acquired 4/53.
HFJ 835: New to H & EA Belcher {Empress Coaches}, Teignmouth (DN), from whom it was acquired 4/53.
JFJ 259: New to Regent.
JFJ 867: New to Regent.

KFJ 606: New to H & EA Belcher {Empress Coaches}, Teignmouth (DN), from whom it was acquired 2/53.
KFJ 608: New to Regent.
KFJ 683: New to Regent.
MFJ 552: New to Greenslades; from whom it was acquired 2/53.

Disposals:
HFJ 834: AMCC (dealer), London E15 6/58; J Heathcoat and Co Ltd, Tiverton (XDN) at an unknown date; last licensed 10/60; scrapped 12/60.
HFJ 835: AMCC (dealer), London E15 6/58; DJ Mainwaring, Gilfach Goch (GG) 1/59; withdrawn 10/61; scrapped 1962.
JFJ 259: Exeter Laundries Ltd, Exeter (XDN) 2 1958; withdrawn 1/64; Fulham St Andrews Scout Group, London SW6 (XLN) by 10/65; last licensed with R Swerdloft, Brentwood, Essex 3/66.
JFJ 867: AMCC (dealer), London E15 1958; R Taylor, London SE1 (LN) 5/58; withdrawn 7/58; Arlington Motors (dealer), Potters Bar 1959; Versil, Cardiff (GGG) as a mobile shop 4/60.
KFJ 606: AMCC (dealer), London E15 10/60; Precelly Motors Ltd, Clynderwen (CR) 11/60; licensed 1/61; withdrawn 12/64; noted at Haverfordwest partially scrapped 4/69.
KFJ 608: AMCC (dealer), London E15 10/60; Precelly Motors Ltd, Clynderwen (CR) 11/60; licensed 1/61; withdrawn 12/64.
KFJ 683: AMCC (dealer), London E15 1959; HR Figg {Henridor Coaches}, Thorpe Bay (EX) 5/59; AH George {Pelere Motors}, Penryn (CO) 2/60; Willis (Central Garage) Ltd, Bodmin (CO) 4/64; withdrawn 11/66; scrapped by 8/70.
MFJ 552: AMCC (dealer), London E15 10/61; E, VC, VM & ELR Barnes {CF Barnes & Son}, Clacton-on Sea (EX) 10/61; withdrawn 1/68; AC Peck {Cedric Coaches}, Wivenhoe (EX) 1/68; Cedric Contracts Ltd, Wivenhoe (XEX) 9/68; scrapped 9/70.

Vehicles acquired from H & EA Belcher (Teignmouth) Ltd {Empress Coaches}, Teignmouth (DN) 1/55

LOD 266	Commer Avenger	23A0313	Devon Coachbuilders		C31F	5/50	n/a
LTA 185	Guy Vixen	LLV41247P	Devon Coachbuilders		FC24F	7/49	n/a
MTA 173	Commer Avenger	23A0534	Devon Coachbuilders		C31F	7/50	n/a
NDV 263	Bedford SB	9009	Duple	1020/19	C33F	5/52	-/63

Previous History:
These vehicles were all new to Miller & Son (Exmouth) Ltd (DN); from whom they were acquired 4/53.

Notes:
LOD 266: Not operated by Greenslades.
LTA 185: Not operated by Greenslades.
MTA 173: Not operated by Greenslades.

Disposals:
LOD 266: Body transferred to new Commer Avenger III RFJ 12; chassis to Hammetts Dairies (Exeter) Ltd (GDN) as a lorry 1/55.
LTA 185: Hammetts Dairies (Exeter) Ltd (GDN) 1/55; converted to a lorry.
MTA 173: Body transferred to new Commer Avenger III RFJ 395; chassis to Hammetts Dairies (Exeter) Ltd (GDN) as a lorry 1/55.
NDV 263: AMCC (dealer), London E15 10/63; E, VC, VM & ELR Barnes {CF Barnes & Son}, Clacton-on-Sea (EX) 11/63; withdrawn 5/67; scrapped.

1956

New Vehicles

SFJ 902	Bedford SBG	44470	Duple	1060/293	C41F	5/56	-/66
SFJ 903	Bedford SBG	44559	Duple	1060/294	C41F	5/56	-/66
SFJ 904	Bedford SBG	44731	Duple	1060/295	C41F	5/56	-/66
SFJ 905	Bedford SBG	44755	Duple	1060/296	C41F	5/56	-/66
SFJ 906	Bedford SBG	44307	Duple	1060/291	C41F	5/56	-/68
SFJ 907	Bedford SBG	44303	Duple	1060/292	C41F	5/56	-/66
SFJ 908	Bedford SBG	45360	Duple	1060/297	C41F	5/56	-/66
SFJ 909	Bedford SBG	43359	Duple	1060/285	C28F	5/56	-/67
SFJ 910	Bedford SBG	43873	Duple	1060/286	C28F	5/56	-/67
TFJ 436	Bedford SBG	45929	Duple	1060/443	C41F	6/56	-/67
TFJ 437	Bedford SBG	45953	Duple	1060/444	C41F	6/56	-/68
TFJ 438	Bedford SBG	46061	Duple	1060/445	C36F	6/56	-/67

| TFJ 439 | Bedford SBG | 46178 | Duple | 1060/446 | C36F | 6/56 | -/67 |
| TFJ 440 | Bedford SBG | 46198 | Duple | 1060/447 | C36F | 6/56 | -/67 |

Notes:
SFJ 909: Re-seated to C33F 1959; to C41F 1963.
SFJ 910: Re-seated to C33F 1959; to C41F 1963.

Disposals:
SFJ 902: Kingdom's Tours Ltd {Tivvy Coaches}, Tiverton (DN) 10/66; CJ Down, Mary Tavy (DN) 3/69; HEC Ball, Plymouth (DN) 8/72; withdrawn 10/74.
SFJ 903: Kingdom's Tours Ltd {Tivvy Coaches}, Tiverton (DN) 10/66; Westosdeal (dealer), Hayle 11/71.
SFJ 904: Gorey Coaches, St Helier, Jersey (CI) re-registered J 9040 3/67; Tantivy Motors, St Helier, Jersey (CI) 26 3/70; Smith, Meir for preservation re-registered GRE 63T 7/79; withdrawn 6/81; RA & CM Ayton {Ayton's Coaches}, Shavington (CH) by 10/84, not operated; AJ, JA & S Boulton, Cardington (SH) 2/86; to service re-registered UJT 384 by 10/87; BH Botley, Swanmore (HA) 1/91; Rogers, Gosport for preservation 1/92; A Saunders, Ipswich for preservation 12/92; reverted to original registration SFJ 904 4/93; V Foster, Droitwich for preservation 11/98; Rixon & Williams, Porthcawl (MG) for preservation with operator by 8/01; Lewis Coaches (Stalbridge) Ltd, Henstridge (SO) for preservation with operator 3/03.
SFJ 905: Gorey Coaches, St Helier, Jersey (CI) re-registered J 9050 3/67; Tantivy Motors, St Helier, Jersey (CI) 25 3/70.
SFJ 906: Lansdowne (dealer), Frating 2/68; E, VC, VM & ELR Barnes {CF Barnes & Son}, Clacton-on-Sea (EX) 7/68; withdrawn 2/74.
SFJ 907: HF & FM Beal (dealer), Exeter by 10/66; LM & HW Pridham {Pridham Brothers}, Lamerton (DN) 6/67; PI & JL Ford {Watson's Coaches}, Gunnislake (CO) 5/68; FR Guscot, Halwill (DN) 9/74; withdrawn 6/79.
SFJ 908: HF & FM Beal (dealer), Exeter by 10/66; LM & HW Pridham {Pridham Brothers}, Lamerton (DN) 6/67; PI & JL Ford {Watson's Coaches}, Gunnislake (CO) 5/68; HGJ Bruce and RRH Parker {Born's Tours}, Okehampton (DN) 8/71; withdrawn 5/78.
SFJ 909: HF & FM Beal (dealer), Exeter by 10/66; DC Venner, Witheridge (DN) 1/67; Mascot Motors Ltd, St Helier, Jersey (CI) 7 re-registered J 6419 2/68; withdrawn by 1977.
SFJ 910: Lansdowne (dealer), Frating 1/67; AC Peck {Cedric Coaches}, Wivenhoe (EX) 2/67; Cedric Garages (Wivenhoe) Ltd, Wivenhoe (EX) 8/67; fitted with a Bedford 300 oil engine; Elim Church, Barking (XLN) 10/71; Cedric Contracts Ltd, Wivenhoe (XEX) 2/75; Essex University Students, Colchester (XEX) 2/77.
TFJ 436: Lansdowne (dealer), Frating 1/67; G Douglas {Douglas Greyhound}, St Helier, Jersey (CI) re-registered J 22898 2/67; not operated; WP Le Marquand {Holiday Coach Tours}, St Peter, Jersey (CI) 1 4/67; renumbered 4 1971; renumbered 7 1974.
TFJ 437: Lansdowne (dealer), Frating 2/68; P Le Cuirot {St Aubin's Tours}, St Peter, Jersey (CI) 2 re-registered J 2239 4/69.
TFJ 438: HF & FM Beal (dealer), Exeter by 12/66; AO Sherrin, Carhampton (SO) 1/67; GW Pitt {Doug Jones Coaches}, Littleton (SR) 3/74; Whites of Camberley Ltd, Camberley (SR) 12/74; withdrawn 4/75; TD & RH Barnes & JTL & EER Hewlett {TD Barnes & Sons}, Aldbourne (WI) 7/76; withdrawn 10/76.
TFJ 439: Lansdowne (dealer), Frating 1/67; Southend Municipal Airport Committee, Southend-on-Sea (XEX) 88 6/67; General Autos (dealer), London SW18 10/75.
TFJ 440: E Clatworthy Ltd {WJ Greenslade's Tiverton Coaches}, Tiverton (DN) 6/67; C Pugsley {Imperial Coaches}, Yeo Vale (DN) 11/67; JW Pugsley, Swimbridge (DN) 11/73; withdrawn 3/76.

Vehicles acquired from Sidmouth Motor Co & Dagworthy Ltd, Sidmouth (DN) 6/56

CDV 772	Austin 16	EIRZ53790			Car6	11/38	n/a
EDV 433	Bedford WTB	14309	Duple	6027	C20F	3/39	n/a
FFJ 968	Bedford OWB	13030	Duple	32068	B30F	2/43	n/a
FFJ 971	Bedford OWB	13475	Duple	32102	B31F	2/43	n/a
GDV 802	Guy Vixen	LV29603	Guy		FB18F	8/47	-/57
HOD 471	Guy Vixen	LV38778	?		FB24F	3/48	n/a
JUO 324	Bedford OB	43981	Duple	46524	C29F	3/47	n/a
KOD 276	Guy Vixen	LLV40907P	Devon Coachbuilders		FC27F	5/49	n/a
KOD 363	Guy Vixen	LLV40344P	Wadham		FC27F	6/49	n/a
KOD 364	Guy Vixen	LV38950	Devon Coachbuilders		FC23F	6/49	n/a
KOD 983	Guy Vixen	LV40440	Devon Coachbuilders		FC23F	7/49	n/a
NUO 651	Bedford SB	7694	Duple	1009/144	C33F	3/52	-/58

Previous History:

These vehicles were new to Sidmouth Motor Co & Dagworthy except for:-

CDV 772: New to Sidmouth Motor Co and Dagworthy, but not licensed by them as a psv until 1/51.
FFJ 968: New to Exeter Corporation (DN) 72 as B32F; Greenslades 5/46; from whom it was acquired 7/46.
FFJ 971: New to Exeter Corporation (DN) 75 as B32F; Greenslades 5/46; from whom it was acquired 7/46.
GDV 802: Body new 1930 transferred from Guy ONDL YC 9715, having been rebuilt with no side windows and fitted behind a lorry style cab with full front.
HOD 471: Had a pre-war coach body with folding canvas roof possibly transferred from Commer Centurion B50 ATA 507; rebuilt to full-front configuration with bus seats and without side windows by Tiverton, for fitting to the new chassis.

Notes:

With the exception of GDV 802 and NUO 651, none of these vehicles were operated when acquired (or re-acquired in the case of FFJ 968, 971) by Greenslades.

Disposals:

CDV 772: Not traced.
EDV 433: JH Powell, Charmouth (DT) 11/56; withdrawn 5/60; no further owner.
FFJ 968: AMCC (dealer), London E15 10/56; EE Fossett (circus showman), Northampton at an unknown date; noted at Kelvedon 9/62; last licensed 10/64.
FFJ 971: AMCC (dealer), London E15 10/56; Miller (contractor), London E7 (XLN) at unknown date; Ashwell Hall Fruit Farm, Finchingfield, Essex at an unknown date; last licensed 11/65.
GDV 802: Last licensed 7/56; returned to Sidmouth Motor Co Ltd, who continued to operate their car hire and repair business, used as a towing vehicle; Windmill Garage, near Honiton, as a towing vehicle at an unknown date: West of England Transport Collection, Winkleigh for preservation 10/75; Bevan Funnell {Reprodux}, Newhaven for preservation 12/84; rebodied as a van by 3/92; M Cornwall, Sheffield Park for preservation by 12/05; M & S Kemp, Kent/Sussex for preservation by 7/07.
HOD 471: Last licensed with Sidmouth Motor Co 6/55.
JUO 324: Okeridge Motor Services Ltd, Okehampton (DN) 5/56; withdrawn 1/63; no further owner.
KOD 276: Silverline Taxis Ltd, Newport (MH) 6/56; licensed 11/56; withdrawn 10/58; DW Tibbs, Newport (GMH) as a mobile shop; withdrawn 4/62; scrapped.
KOD 363: Mrs LF Lord {Astley Garage}, South Milton (DN) 6/56 withdrawn 4/57; RW & E Bloomfield, South Milton (DN) 8/61; AG Preston, Devonport (GDN) as a mobile shop 8/64; withdrawn 10/67; scrapped.
KOD 364: WE Taylor & Sons Ltd, Clyst Honiton (XDN) 6/56; last licensed with J Johnstone, Exeter 9/64.
KOD 983: Unidentified owner, Exeter (GDN) as a mobile shop by 2/60; last licensed with J Johnstone, Exeter 1/62.
NUO 651: AMCC (dealer), London E15 10/58; A Green (Coaches) Ltd, London E17 (LN) 6/59; licensed 7/59; withdrawn 9/59; AS Drury, Langley (HT) 9/59; withdrawn 4/62; Arlington Motor Co Ltd (dealer), Potters Bar 1962; "The Norland Service", Borehamwood (XLN) c6/62; EW Winterbourne (scrap dealer), London E3 at an unknown date; last licensed 6/67.

Vehicles acquired from CG Burgoyne, Sidmouth (DN) 7/56

DUJ 253	Bedford OB	49817	Duple	43231	C29F	5/47	n/a
DUX 586	Bedford OB	60927	Duple	43233	C29F	10/47	n/a
HSP 144	Commer Avenger	23A0181	Harrington		C32F	-/49	n/a
LUO 359	Commer Avenger	23A0152	Harrington	666	C31F	12/49	n/a

Previous History:

DUJ 253: New to JT, FW & GE Whittle {JT Whittle & Sons}, Highley (SH); from it was acquired 3/49.
DUX 586: New to JT, FW & GE Whittle {JT Whittle & Sons}, Highley (SH); from it was acquired 4/49.
HSP 144: New to T Brown, Kelty (SE); A Ferguson & GB Murray {Comfort Coaches}, Dunfermline (FE) at an unknown date; H Collinson, Dewsbury (WY) 3/52; E & S Talbott {E Talbott & Son}, Gawthorpe (WR) 5/54; withdrawn 11/54; from whom it was acquired 5/55.
LUO 359: New to Burgoyne.

Notes:

None of these vehicles were operated by Greenslades.

Disposals:
> DUJ 253: Kyriakou, Limassol (O-CY) re-registered TAA 748 9/56; Cyprus Palestine Plantation Co, Nicosia (O-CY) re-registered AA 748 3/64; Phassouri Plantations, Limassol (O-CY) by 3/68; rebodied by the operator for own use as B29F 9/68; withdrawn by 4/81
> DUX 586: E Saunders, Winkleigh (DN) 7/56; withdrawn 3/68; derelict at Winkleigh until at least 7/72.
> HSP 144: TW Humphries, Bridgend (GG) 10/56; ES & DG Evans {Evans Brothers}, Aberayron (CG) 6/58 withdrawn 7/65; T Jones, Llanrhystyd (CG) 9/65; withdrawn 6/66.
> LUO 359: ME & ET Carter {Carter Brothers Coaches}, Mount Hawke (CO) 12/56; B Hopley, Mount Hawke (CO) 8/64; withdrawn 5/65.

1957

New Vehicles

UFJ 300	AEC Reliance	MU3RA1622	Harrington	1919	C41F	5/57	-/70
UFJ 301	AEC Reliance	MU3RA1621	Harrington	1918	C41F	5/57	-/70
UFJ 303	Bedford SBG	50749	Duple	1074/308	C41F	4/57	-/67

Notes:
> UFJ 300: Re-seated to C28F 1958; to C35F 1959; to C36F 5/70.
> UFJ 301: Re-seated to C36F; then to C37F at unknown dates.
> UFJ 303: Originally intended for Falkland Garages Ltd, Torquay (DN).

Disposals:
> UFJ 300: Rhys {Fydust Coaches}. Port Talbot (GG) 3/71; G Collins, Barlby (ER) 9/71; Advance Roadways Ltd, Goole (WR) 9/73.
> UFJ 301: Rhys {Fydust Coaches}. Port Talbot (GG) 3/71; B Hackett {Sapphire Tours}, London W7 (LN) 8/71; RA Jefferiss {R & J Coaches}, London NW2 (LN) 1/73; JD De Leon {John Dean Coaches}, London NW10 (LN) 3/73; returned to RA Jefferiss {R & J Coaches}, London NW2 (LN) 4/74; named "Miss Gemini" licensed 8/74; withdrawn 11/74.
> UFJ 303: E Clatworthy Ltd {WJ Greenslade's Tiverton Coaches}, Tiverton (DN) 12/67; C Pugsley {Imperial Coaches}, Yeo Vale (DN) 10/68; JW Pugsley, Swimbridge (DN) 11/73; withdrawn 9/74.

Vehicles acquired from C Hopkins & Sons {Blue Moorland Coaches}, Dawlish (DN) 10/57

MOD 737	Bedford SB	1749	Duple	57025	C33F	7/51	-/59
NTT 578	Bedford SB	6686	Duple	1013/15	C33F	1/52	-/67
UTT 985	Bedford SBG	42981	Duple	1060/283	C41F	2/56	-/66
VOD 549	Bedford SBG	50779	Duple	1074/204	C41F	2/57	-/68

Previous History:
> These vehicles were all new to Hopkins.

Notes:
> MOD 737: Operated in Hopkins dark blue, light blue and brown livery, with Blue Moorland fleetnames, until withdrawal.
> NTT 578: Operated in Hopkins dark blue, light blue and brown livery, with Blue Moorland fleetnames, until 5/60.
> UTT 985: Operated in Hopkins dark blue, light blue and brown livery, with Blue Moorland fleetnames, until 5/60.
> VOD 549: Operated in Hopkins dark blue, light blue and brown livery, with Blue Moorland fleetnames, until an unknown date.

Disposals:
> MOD 737: AMCC (dealer), London E15 1959; HR Figg {Henridor Coaches}, Thorpe Bay (EX) 11/59; AA Ford, Althorne (EX) 1/60; withdrawn 5/64; RE Gale {Gale's Coaches}, Haslemere (SR) 7/64; withdrawn 8/65; Ellis, Etchingham (XES) by 8/68.
> NTT 578: HG Kinsman & Son Ltd, Bodmin (CO) 2/67; withdrawn after an accident 3/70; sold for scrap.
> UTT 985: AMCC (dealer), London E15 10/66; E, VC, VM & ELR Barnes {CF Barnes & Son}, Clacton-on-Sea (EX) 11/66; withdrawn 7/73.
> VOD 549: AMCC (dealer), London E15 1/68; E, VC, VM & ELR Barnes {CF Barnes & Son}, Clacton-on-Sea (EX) 1/68; withdrawn 10/71, sold for scrap.

1958

New Vehicles

VFJ 991	AEC Reliance	MU3RV1991	Duple	1094/7	C41C	5/58	-/70
VFJ 992	AEC Reliance	MU3RV1992	Duple	1094/8	C41C	5/58	-/70
VFJ 993	AEC Reliance	MU3RV1993	Duple	1094/9	C41C	5/58	-/70
VFJ 994	AEC Reliance	MU3RV1994	Duple	1094/10	C41C	6/58	-/70

Disposals:

VFJ 991: W Norths (PV) Ltd (dealer), Sherburn in Elmet 12/70; Walker's Garage (Tadcaster) Ltd, Tadcaster (WR) 4/71; ER Speak, Normanton (WR) 4/73; Hudson's Coaches, Hull (EY) 11/73; withdrawn 4/74; T Ward & Son Ltd, Middlestown (WR) 2/75.

VFJ 992: W Norths (PV) Ltd (dealer), Sherburn in Elmet 12/70; Rhys {Fydust Coaches}, Port Talbot (CC) 4/71; G Collins, Barlby (ER) 8/71; EW & KE Maule & E Catley {K & A Coaches}, Hull (ER) 9/73; E Catley, Hull (ER) 4/74; C & A Pearson, Aldbrough (NY) 5/74; unidentified tug-of-war team at an unknown date; RE Talbot, Anstey as a mobile caravan re-registered AJU 264A by 7/78; last noted in Leicester 5/82.

VFJ 993: W Norths (PV) Ltd (dealer), Sherburn in Elmet 12/70; D Little, Leeds (XWR) 2/71; returned to W Norths (PV) Ltd (dealer), Sherburn in Elmet by 10/76; Budge, Scunthorpe (XLI) by 6/77.

VFJ 994: W Norths (PV) Ltd (dealer), Sherburn in Elmet 12/70; W Davies {Marino Coaches}, Ferryhill (DM) 3/71; withdrawn 3/72; St Marks School, Warrenpoint (XDO) by 6/73.

Vehicles acquired from Devon General Omnibus & Touring Co Ltd, Torquay (DN) 4/58

LTA 623	AEC Regal III	9621A773	Duple	55181	C32F	5/50	-/61
LTA 624	AEC Regal III	9621A774	Duple	55177	C32F	5/50	-/60
LTA 625	AEC Regal III	9621A775	Duple	55178	C32F	5/50	-/60

Previous History:

LTA 623-625: New as Devon General TCR623-625.

Disposals:

LTA 623: AG Bowerman Ltd {Bowerman's Tours}, Taunton (SO) 1/61; withdrawn 10/64; unidentified showman 10/64.

LTA 624: AG Bowerman Ltd {Bowerman's Tours}, Taunton (SO) 9/60; withdrawn 1964; unidentified showman, noted at Wanstead Flats 3/64.

LTA 625: Philip & Son Ltd (shipbuilders and engineers), Dartmouth (XDN) 12/60; Riverside Building and Construction Co Ltd, Dartmouth (XDN) by 12/63.

Vehicles acquired from Devon General Omnibus & Touring Co Ltd, Torquay (DN) 5/58

LTA 626	AEC Regal III	9621A776	Duple	55179	C32F	5/50	-/63
LTA 627	AEC Regal III	9621A777	Duple	55180	C32F	5/50	-/60
LTA 628	AEC Regal III	9621A778	Duple	55183	C32F	5/50	-/60
LTA 629	AEC Regal III	9621A779	Duple	55182	C32F	5/50	-/66
LTA 630	AEC Regal III	9621A780	Duple	55184	C32F	5/50	-/66
LTA 631	AEC Regal III	9621A781	Duple	55185	C32F	5/50	-/60
LTA 632	AEC Regal III	9621A782	Duple	55186	C32F	5/50	-/60
LTA 633	AEC Regal III	9621A783	Duple	55188	C32F	5/50	-/63
LTA 634	AEC Regal III	9621A784	Duple	55187	C32F	5/50	-/61

Previous History:

LTA 626-628: New as Devon General TCR626-628.

LTA 629: New as Devon General TCR629; used as a towing vehicle for a period before withdrawal, whilst still in use as a psv.

LTA 630-634: New as Devon General TCR630-634.

Disposals:

LTA 626: AMCC (dealer), London E15 11/63; Lansdowne Luxury Coaches Ltd, London E11 (LN) 8/64; withdrawn 3/65; Homeworthy Furniture, London E9 (GLN) as a van by 11/65.

LTA 627: AG Bowerman Ltd {Bowerman's Tours}, Taunton (SO) 10/60; withdrawn 6/64; Dyer (contractor), Weston-Super-Mare (XSO) 7/64; Penfold (dealer), Hewish for scrap 3/66.

LTA 628: W & LR Hard {W Hard & Sons / The Avon}, South Brent (DN) as C33F 10/60; becoming LR Hard {The Avon}, South Brent (DN) 6/65; RW Jefferies {Moorland Heather Coaches}, Chagford (DN) 9/66; withdrawn 12/69; GW Glover, Crediton for preservation 1/70; G & M Brown, Newton

Abbot for preservation 12/72; West of England Transport Collection, Winkleigh for preservation 1973; R Greet, Ipplepen for preservation 1973; believed scrapped 1974.

LTA 629: GW Glover, Crediton for preservation 4/66; D Sayer, Halifax for preservation 1/73; G Bedford, Scarborough for preservation 11/79; Grey Cars Ltd, Torquay (DN) 1/88; GM Goodwin, Ilfracombe (DN) by 5/89; DN Dean {Classique Saloon Luxury Coaches}, Paisley (SC) 3/92; C Cowdery, East Markham for preservation 5/08.

LTA 630: AMCC (dealer), London E15 4/66; Homeworthy Furniture, London E9 (GLN) as a van by 10/66.

LTA 631: WJ Down {Otter Coaches}, Ottery St Mary (DN) 9/60; Rowe (dealer), Exeter for scrap 5/65.

LTA 632: AMCC (dealer), London E15 12/60; LF Everson {RE Everson}, Wix (EX) 6/61; FAE Mann {Everson's Coaches}, Dovercourt (EX) (1963?); AC Peck {Cedric Coaches}, Wivenhoe (EX) 20 2/65; Cedric Contracts Ltd, Wivenhoe (XEX) 20 9/65; used as a store by 6/68; scrapped at Wivenhoe 8/70.

LTA 633: AMCC (dealer), London E15 11/63; Homeworthy Furniture, London E9 (GLN) as a van by 2/64.

LTA 634: AMCC (dealer), London E15 5/61; J Navarro {Transportes Guanarteme}, Las Palmas, Gran Canaria (O-IC) 16 re-registered GC 18719 10/61; still in use having been rebuilt to B30C 6/71.

1959

New Vehicles

XFJ 590	AEC Reliance	2MU3RV2380	Duple	1109/26	C36F	5/59	-/71
XFJ 591	AEC Reliance	2MU3RV2381	Duple	1109/27	C36F	5/59	-/71
XFJ 592	AEC Reliance	2MU3RV2383	Duple	1109/30	C36F	5/59	-/71
XFJ 593	AEC Reliance	2MU3RV2382	Duple	1109/31	C36F	5/59	-/71
XFJ 875	AEC Reliance	2MU3RV2570	Duple	1109/37	C41F	6/59	-/71

Note:

XFJ 875: Ordered by AG Bowerman Ltd, Taunton (SO).

Disposals:

XFJ 590: Europa Commercial Vehicles (dealer), London SE19 7/71; Flights of Birmingham Ltd, Birmingham (WK) 7/71; JW Runnalls {Primrose Coaches}, Hayle (CO) 12/71; re-seated to C40F by 5/72; West of England Transport Collection, Winkleigh for preservation 7/79; Devon Bus Preservation Group, Exeter for preservation 10/79; unidentified dealer, Kingsteignton for scrap 7/84.

XFJ 591: W Norths (PV) Ltd (dealer), Sherburn in Elmet 3/71; ED & REG Morris {Morris Brothers / M Tours and Excursions}, Swansea (GG) 4/71; Morris Brothers of Swansea Ltd, Swansea (WG) by 1975; withdrawn by 3/76; unidentified dealer, Swansea for scrap 9/76.

XFJ 592: Europa Commercial Vehicles (dealer), London SE19 7/71; Flights of Birmingham Ltd, Birmingham (WK) 7/71; Fountain Luxury Coaches Ltd, Twickenham (MX) 1/72; withdrawn 1/75; RA Jefferies {R and J Coaches}, Southall (LN) 2/76; CD Plume, Staines as a caravan by 9/78; unidentified owner as a caravan in the South West at an unknown date; still in use as a caravan 6/88; parked on a gypsy site Sowton Trading Estate, Exeter Sowton 8/91; scrapped 2/96.

XFJ 593: W Norths (PV) Ltd (dealer), Sherburn in Elmet 3/71; ED & REG Morris {Morris Brothers / M Tours and Excursions}, Swansea (GG) 4/71; Morris Brothers of Swansea Ltd, Swansea (WG) by 1975; withdrawn by 3/76; unidentified dealer, Swansea for scrap 9/76.

XFJ 875: W Norths (PV) Ltd (dealer), Sherburn in Elmet 3/71; ED & REG Morris {Morris Brothers / M Tours and Excursions}, Swansea (GG) 4/71; Morris Brothers of Swansea Ltd, Swansea (WG) by 1975; withdrawn by 3/76; unidentified dealer, Swansea for scrap 9/76.

1960

New Vehicles

554 AFJ	AEC Reliance	2MU3RV2904	Harrington	2242	C36F	4/60	-/72
555 AFJ	AEC Reliance	2MU3RV2903	Harrington	2241	C36F	6/60	-/72
556 AFJ	AEC Reliance	2MU3RV2902	Harrington	2240	C36F	6/60	-/71
557 AFJ	AEC Reliance	2MU3RA2901	Harrington	2239	C41F	7/60	-/71
558 AFJ	AEC Reliance	2MU3RA2900	Harrington	2238	C41F	7/60	-/71
559 AFJ	AEC Reliance	2MU3RA2899	Harrington	2237	C41F	7/60	-/71

Notes:

554 AFJ: Re-seated to C40F in 3/71; numbered 396 6/71.
555 AFJ: Re-seated to C40F in 3/71; numbered 397 6/71.
556 AFJ: Re-seated to C40F in 3/71; allocated fleet number 398 in 6/71, but never carried.

557 AFJ: Repainted in the white and ivy green livery 3/71; allocated fleet number 399 6/71, but never carried.
558 AFJ: Repainted in the white and ivy green livery 3/71; allocated fleet number 400 6/71, but never carried.
559 AFJ: Allocated fleet number 401 6/71, but never carried.

Disposals:

554 AFJ (396): Europa Commercial Motors (dealer), London SE19 4/72; Flights of Birmingham Ltd, Birmingham (WK) 6/72; withdrawn 1/74; JE Morris & Son (Bearwood) Ltd, Bearwood (WK) 1/74; AE & CE Thomas {Bert Thomas & Son}, Usk (GT) 7/75; burnt out 3/76.

555 AFJ (397): Europa Commercial Motors (dealer), London SE19 4/72; Flights of Birmingham Ltd, Birmingham (WK) 4/72; withdrawn 12/73; H & J Homer, Quarry Bank (ST) 3/74; Prospect Coach Group Ltd, Lye (WM) 10/75; not operated; Jameson (dealer), Dunscroft 4/80.

556 AFJ: Europa Commercial Motors (dealer), London SE19 10/71; Flights of Birmingham Ltd, Birmingham (WK) as C36F 12/71; TEA Bowles Ltd, Ford (GL) 2 4/74; withdrawn 5/80.

557 AFJ: Europa Commercial Motors (dealer), London SE19 10/71; Flights of Birmingham Ltd, Birmingham (WK) 12/71; Brownhills Comprehensive School, Brownhills (XWM) 6/74; scrapped by 1/79.

558 AFJ: Europa Commercial Motors (dealer), London SE19 10/71; Flights of Birmingham Ltd, Birmingham (WK) 12/71; R Irving, Carlisle (CA) 4/74; MD Brown {Sheerline Services}, Wide Open (TW) 2/75; Law's Coaches, Aberdeen (GN) 8/75; withdrawn by 10/77.

559 AFJ: Europa Commercial Motors (dealer), London SE19 10/71; Flights of Birmingham Ltd, Birmingham (WK) 12/71; TEA Bowles Ltd, Ford (GL) 1 4/74; withdrawn 10/79; West of England Transport Collection, Winkleigh for preservation 6/80; used as a spares store; J Sykes (dealer), Carlton 3/86.

1961

New Vehicles

540 CFJ	AEC Reliance	2MU3RV3553	Harrington	2455	C36F	4/61	-/73
541 CFJ	AEC Reliance	2MU3RV3554	Harrington	2456	C36F	5/61	-/73
542 CFJ	AEC Reliance	2MU3RV3555	Harrington	2457	C36F	5/61	-/73
543 CFJ	Ford 570E	510E62766	Duple	1139/241	C41F	5/61	-/68
544 CFJ	Ford 570E	510E63348	Duple	1139/242	C41F	5/61	-/68
545 CFJ	Ford 570E	510E63362	Duple	1139/243	C41F	5/61	-/68
546 CFJ	Ford 570E	510E63902	Duple	1139/244	C41F	5/61	-/68

Notes:

540 CFJ: Re-seated as C40F 3/71; numbered 403 6/71; repainted in the white and ivy green livery in 1971; repainted with dark blue waistbands and given Royal Blue fleet names in 5/73, for loan to Western National Omnibus Co Ltd (DN) from 6/73 until 9/73.

541 CFJ: Re-seated as C40F in 3/71; numbered 404 6/71; repainted in the white and ivy green livery in 1972; repainted with dark blue waistbands and given Royal Blue fleet names in 5/73, for loan to Western National Omnibus Co Ltd (DN) from 6/73 until 9/73.

542 CFJ: Re-seated as C41F with seat coming from 1293 WE in 3/71; numbered 405 6/71; repainted in the white and ivy green livery in 1971.

Disposals:

540 CFJ (403): Blackbrooker (dealer), London SE20 12/73; W Cullinan, London E11 (LN) 4/74; AJ Risby {Falcon Travel}, Godalming (SR) 5/75.

541 CFJ (404): Blackbrooker (dealer), London SE20 12/73; Thamesmead Motor Services Ltd, London SE18 (LN) 34 1/74; Bishop Challoner School, Shortlands (XLN) 6/76; fitted with bus seats by 10/81; withdrawn 12/82; sold for scrap 1983.

542 CFJ (405): Blackbrooker (dealer), London SE20 12/73; R Staines {Crusader Coaches}, Clacton-on-Sea (EX) 4/74; GEW Dack {Rosemary Coaches}, Terrington St Clement (NK) 12/75; Ensign (Mobil), Grays (XEX) 4/78; D Walton, Gravesend for preservation 6/78; West of England Transport Collection, Winkleigh for spares by 12/80; T Wigley (dealer), Carlton for scrap 9/83.543 C

544 CFJ: Lansdowne (dealer), Frating 11/68; ER Sutton and NE Pawsey {Sutton's Crossley Coaches}, Clacton-on-Sea (EX) 1/69; withdrawn 1/76; BM Brandon {Osborne Coaches}, Blackmore End (EX) 4/76; Barrier, Isleworth as a caravan 1/82; entered in "Showbus 83" by Sheals and Barrett, Baldock 9/83.

545 CFJ: Lansdowne (dealer), Frating 11/68; WK Tait, Morpeth (ND) 10/69; NK Green and CA Field {Nu-Venture Coaches}, Maidstone (KT) 5/72; withdrawn 9/73.

546 CFJ: Lansdowne (dealer), Frating 11/68; ER Sutton and NE Pawsey {Sutton's Crossley Coaches}, Clacton-on-Sea (EX) 1/69; BJ & PM Whincop, Peasenhall (SK) 1/75 withdrawn 10/80; Gates (Irish Travellers Council), Yate as a mobile caravan at an unknown date; sold by 1/94.

Vehicles acquired from Devon General Omnibus & Touring Co Ltd, Torquay (DN) 3/61

NUO 680	AEC Regal IV	9822S1624	Willowbrook	53094	C41F	5/53	-/63
NUO 681	AEC Regal IV	9822S1625	Willowbrook	53096	C41F	5/53	-/64
NUO 682	AEC Regal IV	9822S1626	Willowbrook	53095	C41F	6/53	-/65

Previous History:
NUO 680-682: New as Devon General TCR680-682.

Disposals:
NUO 680: Lansdowne (dealer), Frating 1/64; HAC Claireaux {CJ Partridge & Son}, Hadleigh (WF) 1/64; Blackwell (dealer), Earls Colne 4/66; in use as a store-shed by 7/73; S Gilkes, Chislehurst for preservation 7/85; Gilkes & Rudkin, Chislehurst for preservation 8/85; unidentified group, Horsham for preservation 1/88; Rollinson (dealer), Carlton for scrap 2/88.
NUO 681: Lansdowne (dealer), Frating 11/64; Lefkaritis, Larnaca (O-CY) 12/64; re-registered TCM 598 2/65; withdrawn 6/71; derelict until destroyed by fire 7/84.
NUO 682: Lansdowne (dealer), Frating 11/65; Lefkaritis, Larnaca (O-CY) 12/65; re-registered TCU 654 2/66; withdrawn by 10/72; derelict until destroyed by fire 7/84.

Vehicle acquired from Devon General Omnibus & Touring Co Ltd, Torquay (DN) 4/61

| NUO 684 | AEC Regal IV | 9822S1628 | Willowbrook | 53098 | C41F | 6/53 | -/63 |

Previous History:
NUO 684: New as Devon General TCR684.

Disposals:
NUO 684: AG Bowerman Ltd {Bowerman's Tours}, Taunton (SO) 3/64; Kingdom's Tours Ltd {Tivvy Coaches}, Tiverton (DN) 1/65; DP Gourd, Bishopsteignton (DN) 4/67; A, J & K Millman, Buckfastleigh (DN) 4/68; withdrawn 3/69; Ninestones Riding School, Liskeard (XCO) by 3/75; D Sayer, Halifax for preservation 7/79; Wombwell Diesels Co Ltd (dealer), Wombwell for scrap 10/80.

Vehicles acquired from Devon General Omnibus & Touring Co Ltd, Torquay (DN) 6/61

NUO 683	AEC Regal IV	9822S1627	Willowbrook	53097	C41F	5/53	-/64
NUO 685	AEC Regal IV	9822S1629	Willowbrook	53099	C41F	6/53	-/64
NUO 688	AEC Regal IV	9822S1632	Willowbrook	53102	C41F	6/53	-/63

Previous History:
NUO 683: New as Devon General TCR683.
NUO 685: New as Devon General TCR685.
NUO 688: New as Devon General TCR688.

Disposals:
NUO 683: Lansdowne (dealer), Frating 11/64; Vines Luxury Coaches Ltd, Great Bromley (EX) 11/64; Shaw and Kilburn (dealer), London W3 10/67; RW Denyer {Denyer Brothers}, Brentwood (EX) 5/68, not operated; derelict on premises 5/73; still there 3/01.
NUO 685: Lansdowne (dealer), Frating 11/64; AC Peck {Cedric Coaches}, Wivenhoe (EX) 11/64; EJ Deeble & Son, Upton Cross (CO) 6/66; RK & RE Webber {Webber Brothers}, Blisland (CO) 5/71; withdrawn 9/71; returned to EJ Deeble, Upton Cross (CO) 8/72.
NUO 688: SG Parnell {Seatax Coaches}, Paignton (DN) 10/63; Dawlish Coaches Ltd, Dawlish (DN) 3/65; withdrawn 9/65; Ascough (dealer), Dublin 2/66; Cronin's Coaches Ltd, Cork (EI) by 8/67; re-registered MPI 624; withdrawn by 1973.

Vehicles acquired from Devon General Omnibus & Touring Co Ltd, Torquay (DN) 7/61

| NUO 686 | AEC Regal IV | 9822S1630 | Willowbrook | 53100 | C41F | 5/53 | -/63 |
| NUO 687 | AEC Regal IV | 9822S1631 | Willowbrook | 53101 | C41F | 6/53 | -/65 |

Previous History:
NUO 686-687: New as Devon General TCR686-687.

Disposals:
NUO 686: AG Bowerman Ltd {Bowerman's Tours}, Taunton (SO) 3/64; Kingdom's Tours Ltd {Tivvy Coaches}, Tiverton (DN) 1/65; Ascough (dealer), Dublin 2/66; Richardson's Fertilizers, Belfast (XAM) 5/66.
NUO 687: Lansdowne (dealer), Frating 11/65; Lefkaritis, Larnaca (O-CY) 12/65; re-registered TCU 656 2/66; withdrawn by 10/72; derelict until destroyed by fire 7/84.

1962

New Vehicles

567 EFJ	AEC Reliance	2MU4RA4274	Harrington	2631	C36F	5/62	-/73
568 EFJ	AEC Reliance	2MU4RA4275	Harrington	2632	C36F	5/62	-/73
569 EFJ	AEC Reliance	2MU4RA4276	Harrington	2633	C36F	5/62	-/73
570 EFJ	AEC Reliance	2MU4RA4277	Harrington	2634	C36F	5/62	-/73
571 EFJ	AEC Reliance	2U3RA4271	Harrington	2635	C49F	6/62	-/73
572 EFJ	AEC Reliance	2U3RA4272	Harrington	2636	C49F	6/62	-/73
573 EFJ	AEC Reliance	2U3RA4273	Harrington	2637	C49F	6/62	-/73

Notes:
567 EFJ: Re-seated as C40F 5/65; numbered 415 6/71; repainted in the white and ivy green livery 1972.
568 EFJ: Re-seated as C40F 5/65; numbered 416 6/71; repainted in the white and ivy green livery 1972.
569 EFJ: Re-seated as C40F 5/65; numbered 417 6/71; repainted in the white and ivy green livery 1972.
570 EFJ: Re-seated as C40F 5/65; numbered 418 6/71; repainted in the white and ivy green livery 1971.

571-573 EFJ: Were the first batch of 36ft long vehicles for Greenslades.

571 EFJ: Allocated fleet number 419 6/71, but never carried; repainted in the white and ivy green livery in 1972.
572 EFJ: Numbered 420 6/71; repainted in the white and ivy green livery 1971.
573 EFJ: Allocated fleet number 421 6/71, but never carried. It was the last vehicle to carry Greenslades "The Silent Guide" triangle motif on the rear panels and was repainted in the white and ivy green livery in 1972.

Disposals:
567 EFJ (415): Blackbrooker (dealer), London SE20 12/73; Thamesmead Motor Services Ltd, London SE18 (LN) 36 1/74; BH Maybury, Cranborne (DT) 4/77; withdrawn 7/77; A Ward {Websters}, Hognaston (DE) 12/77; not operated.
568 EFJ (416): Blackbrooker (dealer), London SE20 12/73; Goldline Coaches Ltd, London E14 (LN) 4/74; licensed 1/75; withdrawn 12/75.
569 EFJ (417): RK Webber {Webber Brothers}, Blisland (CO) 9/73; LJ Hubber {Streamline Coaches}, Newquay (CO) 3/74; DF Piper {Silverline Coaches}, Paignton (DN) 5/79; West of England Transport Collection, Winkleigh for preservation 10/79; R Paye, South Newton for preservation 6/82; J Sykes (dealer), Carlton 2/86; West of England Transport Collection, Winkleigh for preservation 3/86; Morris, Wiveliscombe for preservation by 9/92; transferred to Rexquote, Bishops Lydeard (SO) for preservation by 9/97; moved to Norton Fitzwarren by 6/02; R Evans, Swansea as spares for preservation project 11/02; still at Winkleigh 9/03; dismantled for spares by 12/06.
570 EFJ (418): F, TJ & GM Stoneman {Currian Road Tours}, Nanpean (CO) 10/73; Nadder Valley Coaches Ltd, Tisbury (WI) 3/75; withdrawn 4/78; JC Retallick and RC Kernutt {Sureline Coaches}, Goldalming (SR) 7/78; moved to Guildford (SR) 12/79; withdrawn 8/80; White {White's Travel}, Woodbury Salterton (location possibly Axminster originally) (DN) 9/80; withdrawn 9/81; 299 Squadron, Air Training Corps, Exmouth (XDN) 2/82; West of England Transport Collection, Winkleigh for spares 1986; R Neal, East Dean for preservation 5/87; R Neal, East Dean (ES) licensed as a psv 2/89; Crowther, High Wycombe for preservation 12/92; Crowther, Booker (BK) 4/93; F Tresham, Leighton Buzzard for preservation 5/00.
571 EFJ: Sadler (dealer), North Waltham 11/73; R Smith, Branton (SY) 5/74; P Sheffield, Cleethorpes (LI) 6/75; withdrawn after an accident 6/78.
572 EFJ (420): F & TG Stoneman and MG Brown {Currian Road Tours}, Nanpean (CO) 4/74; Mitchell's (Perranporth) Ltd, Perranport (CO) 6/75; WC Richardson {Flora Motors}, Helston (CO) 2/76; withdrawn 2/80.
573 EFJ: FJ & JA Fry {Fry's Tours}, Tintagel (CO) 1/74; withdrawn 8/80; still owned 6/82.

Vehicles acquired from Devon General Omnibus & Touring Co Ltd, Torquay (DN) 3/62

NUO 689	AEC Regal IV	9822S1633	Willowbrook	53103	C41F	7/53	-/64
NUO 690	AEC Regal IV	9822S1634	Willowbrook	53104	C41F	7/53	n/a
NUO 691	AEC Regal IV	9822S1635	Willowbrook	53105	C41F	7/53	-/66
PDV 692	AEC Regal IV	9822S1786	Park Royal	B37246	C41F	7/54	-/65
PDV 693	AEC Regal IV	9822S1787	Park Royal	B37247	C41F	7/54	-/65
PDV 694	AEC Regal IV	9822S1788	Park Royal	B37248	C41F	7/54	-/65
PDV 695	AEC Regal IV	9822S1789	Park Royal	B37249	C41F	7/54	-/65
PDV 696	AEC Regal IV	9822S1790	Park Royal	B37250	C41F	7/54	-/66
PDV 697	AEC Regal IV	9822S17891	Park Royal	B37251	C41F	7/54	-/65

Previous History:
NUO 689-691: New as Devon General TCR689-691.
PDV 692-697: New as Devon General TCR692-697.

Notes:
NUO 690: Not operated by Greenslades.

Disposals:
NUO 689: Lansdowne (dealer), Frating 12/64; Vines Luxury Coaches Ltd, Great Bromley (EX) 12/64; Shaw & Kilburn Ltd (dealer), London W3 9/67; loaned to County Coaches (Brentwood) Ltd, Brentwood (EX) 10/67; RW Denyer {Denyer Brothers}, Stondon (EX) 5/68; withdrawn 5/70; still derelict on premises 3/01.
NUO 690: AG Bowerman Ltd {Bowerman's Tours}, Taunton (SO) 5/62; Kingdom's Tours Ltd {Tivvy Coaches}, Tiverton (DN) 1/65; Dawlish Coaches Ltd {Tomlinson's}, Dawlish (DN) 1/66; DC Venner, Witheridge (DN) 3/66; LJ Hubber {Streamline Coaches}, Newquay (CO) 5/66; HG Brown & G Davies {Truronian Coaches}, Truro (CO) 5/68; withdrawn 6/70; Cornish Gliding and Flying Club, Perranporth as a clubhouse by 8/72; Orchard (dealer), St Day for scrap by 4/79.
NUO 691: Lansdowne (dealer), Frating 4/66; Lefkaritis, Larnaca (O-CY) 1966; not operated; derelict until destroyed by fire 7/84.
PDV 692: Lansdowne (dealer), Frating 11/65; Lefkaritis, Larnaca (O-CY) 12/65; re-registered TCU 655 2/66; withdrawn by 10/72; derelict until destroyed by fire 7/84.
PDV 693: Lansdowne (dealer), Frating 12/65; Lefkaritis, Larnaca (O-CY) 12/65; not operated; derelict until destroyed by fire 7/84.
PDV 694: Lansdowne (dealer), Frating 11/65; Lefkaritis, Larnaca (O-CY) 12/65; re-registered TCU 658 2/66; withdrawn by 10/72; derelict until destroyed by fire 7/84.
PDV 695: Lansdowne (dealer), Frating 11/65; Lefkaritis, Larnaca (O-CY) 12/65; re-registered TCU 657 2/66; withdrawn by 10/72; derelict until destroyed by fire 7/84.
PDV 696: Lansdowne (dealer), Frating 4/66; Lefkaritis, Larnaca (O-CY) 1966; not operated; derelict until destroyed by fire 7/84.
PDV 697: Lansdowne (dealer), Frating 11/65; Lefkaritis, Larnaca (O-CY) 12/65, re-registered TCU 659 2/66; withdrawn by 10/72; derelict until destroyed by fire 7/84.

1963

New Vehicles

974 FFJ	AEC Reliance	2MU3RA3467	Harrington	2701	C41F	6/63	-/73
175 GFJ	AEC Reliance	2MU4RA4706	Harrington	2786	C36F	4/63	-/73
176 GFJ	AEC Reliance	2MU4RA4707	Harrington	2787	C36F	4/63	-/73

Notes:
974 FFJ: Originally intended for an unidentified operator; numbered 441 6/71; repainted in the white and ivy green livery 1971.
175 GFJ: Re-seated to C40F 4/65; numbered 439 6/71; repainted in the white and ivy green livery 1971.
176 GFJ: Re-seated as C40F in 4/65; numbered 440 6/71; repainted in the white and ivy green livery 1971.

Disposals:
974 FFJ (441): Blackbrooker (dealer), London SE20 12/73; R Staines {Crusader Coaches}, Clacton-on-Sea (EX) 5/74; GEW Dack {Rosemary Coaches}, Terrington St Clement (NK) at an unknown date; Ensign Bus Co Ltd (dealer), Grays 4/78; E Beckett (dealer), Carlton for scrap 4/78.
175 GFJ (439): FJ & JA Fry {Fry's Tours}, Tintagel (CO) 1/74; withdrawn by 6/84; West of England Transport Collection (as dealer), Winkleigh 10/84; T Wigley (dealer), Carlton for scrap 1/85.

176 GFJ (440): Blackbrooker (dealer), London SE20 12/73; Thamesmead Motor Services Ltd, London SE18 (LN) 35 1/74; withdrawn 1/77; 4th Shepshed Scouts, Shepshed (XLE) 10/77; withdrawn 5/84; P Paul Sykes Organisation Ltd (dealer), Barnsley 5/84; G Jones {Carlton Metals} (dealer), Carlton by 10/84.

1964

New Vehicles

AFJ 77B	AEC Reliance	2MU4RA5077	Harrington	2964	C36F	5/64	-/75
AFJ 78B	AEC Reliance	2MU4RA5078	Harrington	2965	C36F	5/64	-/75
AFJ 79B	AEC Reliance	2MU4RA4905	Harrington	2829	C41F	3/64	-/75
AFJ 80B	AEC Reliance	2MU4RA4906	Harrington	2830	C41F	3/64	-/75
AFJ 81B	AEC Reliance	2MU4RA4907	Harrington	2831	C41F	3/64	-/75
AFJ 82B	AEC Reliance	2MU4RA4908	Harrington	2832	C41F	3/64	-/75
AFJ 83B	AEC Reliance	2MU4RA4909	Harrington	2833	C41F	3/64	-/75
AFJ 84B	AEC Reliance	2MU4RA4910	Harrington	2834	C41F	3/64	-/76
AFJ 85B	AEC Reliance	2MU4RA5075	Harrington	2962	C41F	5/64	-/75
AFJ 86B	AEC Reliance	2MU4RA5076	Harrington	2963	C41F	5/64	-/75

Notes:

These vehicles were 7ft 6in wide.

AFJ 77B: Re-seated to C40F 4/66; to C41F 4/72; numbered 442 6/71; repainted in the white and ivy green livery 1972; repainted in NBC white coach livery 1974; renumbered 283 1/75.

AFJ 78B: Re-seated as C40F 4/66; to C41F 4/72; numbered 443 6/71; repainted in the white and ivy green livery 1972; renumbered 284 1/75.

AFJ 79B: Delivered 1963; numbered 444 6/71; repainted in the white and ivy green livery 1972; repainted in NBC white coach livery 1974; renumbered 285 1/75.

AFJ 80B: Delivered 1963; numbered 445 6/71; repainted in the white and ivy green livery 1972; renumbered 286 1/75.

AFJ 81B: Delivered 1963; numbered 446 6/71; repainted in the white and ivy green livery 1972; renumbered 287 1/75.

AFJ 82B: Delivered 1963; numbered 447 6/71; repainted in the white and ivy green livery 1971; repainted in NBC white coach livery 1974; renumbered 288 1/75.

AFJ 83B: Delivered 1963; numbered 448 6/71; repainted in the white and ivy green livery 1971; repainted in NBC white coach livery 1973; renumbered 289 1/75.

AFJ 84B: Delivered 1963; numbered 449 6/71; repainted in the white and ivy green livery 1972; loaned to Bristol Omnibus Co Ltd, Bristol (GL) 11/72 to 12/72; repainted in NBC white coach livery 1973; renumbered 290 1/75.

AFJ 85B: Delivered 1963; numbered 450 6/71; repainted in the white and ivy green livery 1972; repainted in NBC white coach livery 1974; renumbered 250 1/75.

AFJ 86B: Delivered 1963 and was numbered 451 6/71; repainted in the white and ivy green livery 1971; repainted in NBC white coach livery 1974; renumbered 251 1/75.

Disposals:

AFJ 77B (283): Midland Red Omnibus Co Ltd (as dealer), Birmingham (WM) 12/75; Paul Sykes Organisation Ltd (dealer), Barnsley 1/76; Mascot Motors Ltd, St Helier, Jersey (CI) 6 re-registered J 16654 2/76; Educational Holidays Guernsey Ltd {Island Coachways}, St Peter Port, Guernsey (CI) 9 re-registered 8229 5/81; Wacton Trading (dealer), Bromyard 12/84; Truscott, Roche for preservation 12/84; D Rundell, Falmouth for preservation 1/99; reverted to original registration AFJ 77B 4/99; Falmouth Coaches {King Harry}, Falmouth (CO) 7/02.

AFJ 78B (284): Midland Red Omnibus Co Ltd (as dealer), Birmingham (WM) 12/75; Paul Sykes Organisation Ltd (dealer), Barnsley 1/76; Mascot Motors Ltd, St Helier, Jersey (CI) 9 re-registered J 16845 2/76; RJ Courtanche, Jersey (CI) as a caravan 11/80; B Oddy, St Peters, Jersey as a caravan 6/83; presumed sold by 1/94.

AFJ 79B (285): RK & RE Webber {Webber Brothers}, Blisland (CO) 1/76; LJ Hubber {Streamline Coaches}, Newquay (CO) 2/78; RK & RE Webber {Webber Brothers}, Blisland (CO) 6/79; Educational Holidays Guernsey Ltd {Island Coachways}, St Peter Port, Guernsey (CI) re-registered 6768 7/81; WP Simon {Riduna Buses}, Alderney (CI) re-registered AY 58 c1983; noted unregistered and accident damaged at Torquay Docks on return from Alderney 1989; sold to unknown dealer, Peterborough but not collected; stored in yard of Torbay Seaways at Torre Station; P Platt, Exeter as spares for preservation project, being dismantled at Winkleigh 10/91.

AFJ 80B (286): Midland Red Omnibus Co Ltd (as dealer), Birmingham (WM) 12/75; Paul Sykes Organisation Ltd (dealer), Barnsley 1/76; Mascot Motors Ltd, St Helier, Jersey (CI) 8 re-

AFJ 81B (287): Dawlish Coaches Ltd {Tomlinson's}, Dawlish (DN) 11/75; Snell's Coaches Ltd, Newton Abbot (DN) 1/81; rebodied Duple C45F (142/5742) (this body was 7ft 6in wide) and re-registered STT 295X 9/81; Caetano (dealer), Heather 6/92; MJ Perry {Bromyard Omnibus}, Bromyard (HR) 58 10/92; AG Hazell, Northlew (DN) 9/93; Wacton Trading / Coach Sales (dealer), Bromyard 3/95; IR Phillips, Hereford (HR) 5/95; returned to Wacton Trading / Coach Sales (dealer), Bromyard 8/95; unknown owner, Milkwall by 7/00.

registered J 16841 2/76; Educational Holidays Guernsey Ltd {Island Coachways}, St Peter Port, Guernsey (CI) 1/81; not operated; WP Simon {Riduna Buses}, Alderney (CI) re-registered AY 305 c1981.

AFJ 82B (288): Midland Red Omnibus Co Ltd (as dealer), Birmingham (WM) 12/75; Paul Sykes Organisation Ltd (dealer), Barnsley 1/76; Mascot Motors Ltd, St Helier, Jersey (CI) 2 re-registered J 16590 1/76; Educational Holidays Guernsey Ltd {Island Coachways}, St Peter Port, Guernsey (CI) 8 re-registered 8228 7/81; WP Simon {Riduna Buses}, Alderney (CI) re-registered AY 91 3/84; re-imported through Torquay Docks 7/90; moved to Greenslade's yard in Exeter 7/90; West of England Transport Collection, Winkleigh for preservation 10/91; for sale by C Shears, Winkleigh and P Platt, Exeter; Wacton Trading / Coach Sales (dealer), Bromyard for scrap by 7/93 (probably 3/93).

AFJ 83B (289): Midland Red Omnibus Co Ltd (as dealer), Birmingham (WM) 12/75; Paul Sykes Organisation Ltd (dealer), Barnsley 1/76; Mascot Motors Ltd, St Helier, Jersey (CI) 4 re-registered J 16601 1/76; last licensed 5/77; used for spares.

AFJ 84B (290): Dawlish Coaches Ltd {Tomlinson's}, Dawlish (DN) 6/76; licensed 7/76; unidentified owner, Exeter as a caravan by 9/85; unidentified owner in the South West as a caravan c3/86; vandalised 2/87; sold for scrap.

AFJ 85B (250): Midland Red Omnibus Co Ltd (as dealer), Birmingham (WM) 12/75; Paul Sykes Organisation Ltd (dealer), Barnsley 1/76; Mascot Motors Ltd, St Helier, Jersey (CI) 15 re-registered J 16868 2/76; WP Simon {Riduna Buses}, Alderney (CI) re-registered AY 750 4/80; unidentified owner Torbay (reverted to original registration?) c6/89.

AFJ 86B (251): Midland Red Omnibus Co Ltd (as dealer), Birmingham (WM) 12/75; Paul Sykes Organisation Ltd (dealer), Barnsley 1/76; Mascot Motors Ltd, St Helier, Jersey (CI) 7 re-registered J 16706 2/76; Educational Holidays Guernsey Ltd {Island Coachways}, St Peter Port, Guernsey (CI) 10 re-registered 8230 1/81; Wacton Trading/Coach Sales (dealer), Bromyard 12/84; R Wilson, Bovey Tracey for preservation 12/84; reverted to orginal registration AFJ 86B by 5/88; D Sayer et al, Halifax for preservation 10/91; A & J Purvis, Seaburn for preservation 10/94; J Purvis, (alone), Seaburn for preservation 8/97; D Waymann, Oldham for preservation by 6/99; B Botley, Lee-on-Solent for preservation by 12/01; D Joseph, Ilford for preservation 6/11.

Vehicles acquired from Devon General Omnibus & Touring Co Ltd, Torquay (DN) 3/64

ROD 749	AEC Reliance	MU3RV640	Weymann	M7016	C37F	5/55	-/68
ROD 750	AEC Reliance	MU3RV641	Weymann	M7017	C37F	5/55	-/68

Previous History:
ROD 749: New as Devon General TCR749.
ROD 750: New as Devon General TCR750.

Disposals:
ROD 749: Lansdowne (dealer), Frating 2/68; Vines Luxury Coaches Ltd, Great Bromley (EX) 6/68; Luton Commercial Motors (dealer), Dunstable 9/68; MW Smaller {Mick Smaller's Luxury Coaches}, Barton-upon-Humber (LI) 1 11/68; withdrawn 11/70; subsequently used by Smaller as a non-psv at Anchor Steelworks, Scunthorpe.
ROD 750: Lansdowne (dealer), Frating 2/68; believed exported.

1965

New Vehicles

CFJ 894C	AEC Reliance	2U3RA5728	Duple (Northern)	164/2	C44F	7/65	-/75
CFJ 895C	AEC Reliance	2U3RA5730	Duple (Northern)	164/3	C44F	7/65	-/75
CFJ 896C	AEC Reliance	2U3RA5729	Duple (Northern)	164/4	C44F	7/65	-/75
CFJ 897C	AEC Reliance	2MU4RA5726	Duple (Northern)	162/1	C40F	6/65	-/75
CFJ 898C	AEC Reliance	2MU4RA5725	Duple (Northern)	162/2	C40F	6/65	-/75
CFJ 899C	AEC Reliance	2U3RA5727	Duple (Northern)	164/5	C44F	6/65	-/75

Notes:
CFJ 894C: Was 36ft long; repainted in the white and ivy green livery 1970; numbered 452 6/71; renumbered 252 1/75.
CFJ 895C: Was 36ft long; it was the first vehicle to receive in the white and ivy green livery 10/69; numbered 453 6/71; renumbered 253 1/75.
CFJ 896C: Was 36ft long; repainted in the white and ivy green livery 1970; numbered 454 6/71; repainted in NBC white coach livery 1974; renumbered 254 1/75.
CFJ 897C: Repainted in the white and ivy green livery 1970 and numbered 455 6/71; repainted in NBC white coach livery 1974; renumbered 255 1/75.
CFJ 898C: Repainted in the white and ivy green livery 1970 and numbered 456 6/71; repainted in NBC white coach livery 1974; renumbered 256 1/75.
CFJ 899C: Was 36 feet long; repainted in the white and ivy green livery 1970, numbered 457 6/71; renumbered 257 1/75.

Disposals:
CFJ 894C (252): Cannibalised for spares 9/75; DC Venner {Scarlet Coaches}, Minehead (SO) by 4/76; not operated.
CFJ 895C (253): Midland Red Omnibus Co Ltd (as dealer), Birmingham (WM) 4/76; Paul Sykes Organisation Ltd (dealer), Barnsley 4/76; W Irvine, Law (SC) 5/76; Kirkby (dealer), Glasgow 6/76; Newport Furnishers, Newport (XGT) 1976; World Wide Coaches (Scotland) Ltd, Lanark (SC) 11/76; rebodied Plaxton C46F (7711AC017S) and re-registered VGD 363R 5/77; JS Whiteford {Nationwide Coaches}, Lanark (SC) 3/78; H Lomas {Ladyline Coaches}, Key Green (CH) 8/88; G Jones, Knypersley (ST) 3/90.
CFJ 896C (254): Used for spares 9/75; used as a rest-room at Plympton garage by 11/75; body scrapped at Plymouth Friary goods yard 5/78.
CFJ 897C (255): Midland Red Omnibus Co Ltd (as dealer), Birmingham (WM) 12/75; Paul Sykes Organisation Ltd (dealer), Barnsley 1/76; J Galloway, Harthill (SC) 3/76; JD Peace, Kirkwall (OK) 6/77; still owned 7/84, scrapped by 12/86.
CFJ 898C (256): Midland Red Omnibus Co Ltd (as dealer), Birmingham (WM) 12/75; Paul Sykes Organisation Ltd (dealer), Barnsley 1/76; J Galloway, Harthill (SC) 3/76; W Irvine, Law (SC) 3/78; Gospel Hall, unknown location by 5/81.
CFJ 899C (257): Midland Red Omnibus Co Ltd (as dealer), Birmingham (WM) 12/75; Paul Sykes Organisation Ltd (dealer), Barnsley 1/76; Dawlish Coaches Ltd {Tomlinson's}, Dawlish (DN) 2/76; withdrawn 9/76; Dealers Vehicle Movements {Airport Mini Coach Service}, Exeter (DN) 10/76; WT, WR & SK Phillips {Bow Belle}, Crediton (DN) 1/78; World Wide Coaches (Scotland) Ltd, Lanark (SC) 2/78, not operated; JS Whiteford {Nationwide Coaches}, Lanark (SC) 3/78, not operated; still owned 1981; sold presumably for scrap by 1993.

1966

New Vehicles

FFJ 10D	AEC Reliance	2MU4RA6042	Harrington	3215	C40F	6/66	-/75
FFJ 11D	AEC Reliance	2MU4RA6043	Harrington	3216	C40F	6/66	-/75
FFJ 12D	AEC Reliance	2MU4RA6045	Harrington	3217	C40F	6/66	-/75
FFJ 13D	AEC Reliance	2MU4RA6046	Harrington	3218	C40F	6/66	-/75
FFJ 14D	AEC Reliance	2U3RA6145	Duple (Northern)	168/9	C49F	6/66	-/75
FFJ 15D	AEC Reliance	2U3RA6146	Duple (Northern)	168/10	C49F	6/66	-/75

Notes:
FFJ 10D: Numbered 458 6/71 repainted in the white and ivy green livery 1971; repainted in NBC white coach livery 1973; renumbered 258 1/75.
FFJ 11D: Numbered 459 6/71 repainted in the white and ivy green livery 1971; repainted in NBC white coach livery 1974; renumbered 259 1/75.
FFJ 12D: Numbered 460 6/71 repainted in the white and ivy green livery 1971; repainted in NBC white coach livery 1973; renumbered 260 1/75.
FFJ 13D: Had the last body built by Harrington; numbered 461 6/71; repainted in the white and ivy green livery 1971; repainted in NBC white coach livery 1974; renumbered 261 1/75.
FFJ 14D: Repainted in the white and ivy green livery 1970; numbered 462 6/71; renumbered 262 1/75; re-seated to C44F by 5/75.
FFJ 15D: Repainted in the white and ivy green livery 1970; numbered 463 6/71; repainted in NBC white coach livery 1974; renumbered 263 1/75; re-seated to C44F by 5/75.

Disposals:
- FFJ 10D (258): Paul Sykes Organisation Ltd (dealer), Barnsley 12/75; T Davies & Sons (Coach Hire) Ltd, Glyn Neath (WG) 1/76; licensed 2/76; withdrawn by 10/80.
- FFJ 11D (259): Paul Sykes Organisation Ltd (dealer), Barnsley 1/76; J Galloway, Harthill (SC) 3/76; withdrawn by 2/83.
- FFJ 12D (260): Paul Sykes Organisation Ltd (dealer), Barnsley 1/76; J Galloway, Harthill (SC) 3/76; withdrawn by 2/83.
- FFJ 13D (261): DC Venner {Scarlet Coaches}, Minehead (SO) 1/76; not operated; GE Nightingale, Budleigh Salterton (DN) 6/76; WS Yeates Ltd (dealer), Salisbury 7/78; unidentified owner for conversion to a transporter 11/78.
- FFJ 14D (262): DC Venner {Scarlet Coaches}, Minehead (SO) 1/76; licensed as C49F 6/76; HGJ Bruce and RRH Parker {Born's Coaches}, Okehampton (DN) 9/78; withdrawn 3/79; dumped at Whiddon Down 1/80.
- FFJ 15D (263): DC Venner {Scarlet Coaches}, Minehead (SO) 1/76; licensed as C49F 6/76; HGJ Bruce and RRH Parker {Born's Coaches}, Okehampton (DN) 9/78; withdrawn 3/79; re-instated 1/80; RRH Parker {Born's Coaches}, Okehampton 12/80; withdrawn by 10/84; operator ceased by 12/84.

Vehicles acquired from Devon General Omnibus & Touring Co Ltd, Torquay (DN) 3/66

XDV 850	AEC Reliance	MU3RV2075	Willowbrook	58102	C41F	5/58	-/68
XDV 851	AEC Reliance	MU3RV2076	Willowbrook	58108	C41F	5/58	-/68
XDV 852	AEC Reliance	MU3RV2077	Willowbrook	58104	C41F	5/58	-/68
XDV 853	AEC Reliance	MU3RV2078	Willowbrook	58109	C41F	5/58	-/68
XDV 854	AEC Reliance	MU3RV2079	Willowbrook	58103	C41F	5/58	-/68

Previous History:
XDV 850-854: New as Devon General 850-854.

Disposals:
- XDV 850: Lansdowne (dealer), Frating 11/68; Culling & Son (Norwich) Ltd, Norwich (NK) 5/71; withdrawn 10/74; Partridge (as dealer), Hadleigh 6/75; Green (dealer), Stock for scrap 4/76.
- XDV 851: Lansdowne (dealer), Frating 11/68; Vines Luxury Coaches Ltd, Great Bromley (EX) 5/69; Grenville Motors Ltd, Camborne (CO) 6/70; P Platt, Exeter for preservation 6/83; S Hookins, Bampton for preservation 12/83; P Platt, Broadclyst (or possibly Exeter) for preservation 9/05; S Blackman, Halifax for preservation 10/05; C Shears, Winkleigh for preservation by 8/07; R Gibbons, Hastings (or possibly Maidstone) to be used as spares for restoration of 253 BKM 9/10.
- XDV 852: Lansdowne (dealer), Frating 11/68; Vines Luxury Coaches Ltd, Great Bromley (EX) 6/69; licensed 4/71; Lansdowne (dealer), Frating 7/71.
- XDV 853: Lansdowne (dealer), Frating 11/68; Vines Luxury Coaches Ltd, Great Bromley (EX) and certified 10/70; not operated; Grenville Motors Ltd, Camborne (CO) 10/70; withdrawn 5/74.
- XDV 854: Lansdowne (dealer), Frating 11/68; Vines Luxury Coaches Ltd, Great Bromley (EX) 6/69; licensed 4/71; Lansdowne (dealer), Frating 7/71; Clapton Park Angling Society, London E9 (XLN) 8/73; unidentified owner, London E2 5/78; scrapped.

Vehicles acquired from Devon General Omnibus & Touring Co Ltd, Torquay (DN) 12/66

XDV 857	AEC Reliance	MU3RV2082	Willowbrook	58105	C41F	5/58	-/70
XDV 858	AEC Reliance	MU3RV2083	Willowbrook	58107	C41F	5/58	-/70
XDV 859	AEC Reliance	MU3RV2084	Willowbrook	58111	C41F	5/58	-/69
889 ADV	AEC Reliance	2MU3RV2348	Willowbrook	59365	C41F	5/59	-/70
890 ADV	AEC Reliance	2MU3RV2349	Willowbrook	59366	C41F	5/59	-/70
891 ADV	AEC Reliance	2MU3RV2350	Willowbrook	59367	C41F	5/59	-/70
892 ADV	AEC Reliance	2MU3RV2351	Willowbrook	59368	C41F	5/59	-/70

Previous History:
XDV 857-859: New as Devon General 857-859.
889-892 ADV: New as Devon General 889-892.

Notes:
These vehicles were 7ft 6in wide; licensed 4/67.

Disposals:
- XDV 857: W Norths (PV) Ltd (dealer), Sherburn in Elmet 1/70; Invicta Bridge, Hoveringham (XNG) 3/70; G Jones {Carlton Metals} (dealer), Carlton for scrap 2/78.
- XDV 858: W Norths (PV) Ltd (dealer), Sherburn in Elmet 1/70; DE & DS Bannatyne {Bannatyne Motors}, Blackwaterfoot (BU) 3/70; Allander Coaches Ltd, Milngavie (SC) 2/74; not operated; used for spares by 7/74; RW Dunsmore (dealer), Larkhall by 6/75.
- XDV 859: W Norths (PV) Ltd (dealer), Sherburn in Elmet 6/69; Allenways Ltd, Birmingham (WK) 6/69; North (dealer), Sherburn 1/71; sold 8/71.
- 889 ADV: W Norths (PV) Ltd (dealer), Sherburn in Elmet 12/70; Glen Tours (Baildon) Ltd, Baildon (WR) 28 9/71; licensed 12/71; Connor and Graham Ltd, Easington (ER) 47 5/73; withdrawn 11/75; CHC Phillips {Phillips Coach Co}, Shiptonthorpe (EY) by 5/78; not operated; Blackett (dealer), Butterknowle for scrap by 6/86.
- 890 ADV: Western National Omnibus Co Ltd, Exeter (DN) 437 7/70; renumbered 1237 7/71; withdrawn 5/80; G Sharman, Cobham for preservation 8/80; G Brazier, Staines for preservation by 10/90; M Gibbons, Weybridge for preservation c3/93; S Morris, Wiveliscombe for preservation by 8/96; Rexquote, Bishops Lydeard (SO) 4/97; moved to Norton Fitzwarren by 6/02; Quantock Motor Services, Wiveliscombe (SO) for preservation by 6/02; Cotton, Saltash for preservation 7/11.
- 891 ADV: W Norths (PV) Ltd (dealer), Sherburn in Elmet 12/70; DE & DS Bannatyne {Bannatyne Motors}, Blackwaterfoot (BU) 2/71; licensed 3/71; Grangemouth Celtic Amateur Football Supporters Club, Glasgow (XLK) 12/73; Allander Coaches Ltd, Milngavie (SC) 11/76, not operated.
- 892 ADV: W Norths (PV) Ltd (dealer), Sherburn in Elmet 12/70; Glen Tours (Baildon) Ltd, Baildon (WR) 26 6/71; withdrawn 8/73; S Twell (dealer), Ingham by 1/75.

1967

New Vehicles

HFJ 416E	AEC Reliance	6U3ZR6263	Plaxton	673058	C49F	6/67	-/76
HFJ 417E	AEC Reliance	6MU4R6737	Plaxton	672990	C40F	6/67	-/76
HFJ 418E	AEC Reliance	6MU4R6738	Plaxton	672991	C40F	6/67	-/76

Notes:
- HFJ 416E: Was 36ft long; rebuilt by Westcott Bros, Exeter, after sustaining severe accident damage 1969; numbered 480 6/71; repainted in the white and ivy green livery 1972; repainted in NBC white coach livery in 1974; renumbered 280 1/75.
- HFJ 417E: Repainted in the white and ivy green livery 1970; numbered 481 6/71; repainted in NBC white coach livery 1974; renumbered 281 1/75.
- HFJ 418E: Repainted in the white and ivy green livery 1971; numbered 482 6/71; repainted in NBC white coach livery 1974; renumbered 282 1/75.

Disposals:
- HFJ 416E (280): RK & RE Webber {Webber Brothers}, Blisland (CO) 6/76; not operated; MK Rowe, Dobwalls (CO) 7/76; I McGranaghan, Laneshaw Bridge (LA) 2/78; J & N Motors Ltd, Tredegar (GT) 3/79; sold by 11/79; parked at PR Waddon & Sons, Caerphilly (CS) between 11/79 and 2/80; unidentified owner, Broadwell (XOX) 2/82.
- HFJ 417E (281): RK & RE Webber {Webber Brothers}, Blisland (CO) 6/76; licensed 7/76; withdrawn 9/78; re-instated 11/78; withdrawn 4/79; C Pugsley, Yeo Vale (DN) 5/79; withdrawn by 4/84.
- HFJ 418E (282): RK & RE Webber {Webber Brothers}, Blisland (CO) 6/76; licensed 1/77; withdrawn 5/78; South Central Coaches (Dorchester) Ltd, Dorchester (DT) 6/79; withdrawn 10/80.

Vehicles acquired from Devon General Omnibus & Touring Co Ltd, Torquay (DN) 1/67

XDV 855	AEC Reliance	MU3RV2080	Willowbrook	58106	C41F	5/58	-/70
XDV 856	AEC Reliance	MU3RV2081	Willowbrook	58110	C41F	5/58	-/70

Previous History:
XDV 855-856: New as Devon General 855-856.

Notes:
These vehicles were 7ft 6in wide; first licensed to Greenslades 4/67.

Disposals:
- XDV 855: W Norths (PV) Ltd (dealer), Sherburn in Elmet 1/70; Cooper & Wood, Wakefield (XWR) 5/70; renamed Bacal Construction (Northern) by 11/70; unidentified owner, Coxhoe (GDM) as a mobile shop by 10/76.

XDV 856: W Norths (PV) Ltd (dealer), Sherburn in Elmet 1/70; Bacal Construction (Northern), Wakefield (XWY) 11/70; Warren & Taylor, Farnworth as a car transporter by 8/74; withdrawn 11/76.

1968

Vehicles acquired from Sheffield United Tours Ltd, Sheffield (WR) 1/68

1291 WE	AEC Reliance	2MU3RV2117 Plaxton	582375	C41F	-/59	-/69
1292 WE	AEC Reliance	2MU3RV2240 Plaxton	582416	C41F	-/59	-/69
1293 WE	AEC Reliance	2MU3RV2241 Plaxton	582417	C41F	-/59	-/69
1294 WE	AEC Reliance	2MU3RV2242 Plaxton	582419	C41F	5/59	-/69
1295 WE	AEC Reliance	2MU3RV2243 Plaxton	582418	C41F	-/59	-/69
1296 WE	AEC Reliance	2MU3RV2244 Plaxton	582421	C41F	-/59	-/69

Previous History:
　　1291 WE: New to Sheffield United 291 as C36F and was an entrant in the 1958 Nice coach rally; re-seated to C41F 1966.
　　1292-1296 WE: New to Sheffield United 292-296 as C36F; re-seated to C41F 1966.

Disposals:
　　1291 WE: W Norths (PV) Ltd (dealer), Sherburn in Elmet 12/69; TR Dowson, Bramham (WR) 7/70; licensed 8/70; withdrawn 7/72.
　　1292 WE: W Norths (PV) Ltd (dealer), Sherburn in Elmet 12/69; TR Dowson, Bramham (WR) 7/70; licensed 8/70; withdrawn after an accident 1/72.
　　1293 WE: Rear end damaged in an accident 5/69; stripped for spares, seats transferred to 542 CFJ 3/71; remains to Holmes (dealer), Exeter for scrap 3/71.
　　1294 WE: W Norths (PV) Ltd (dealer), Sherburn in Elmet 12/69; HEP Sherriff {Star Tours}, Gainsborough (LI) 1/70; withdrawn 12/75.
　　1295 WE: W Norths (PV) Ltd (dealer), Sherburn in Elmet 12/69; JG & L Hutchindon {Hutchinson Brothers}, Husthwaite (NR) 6/70; withdrawn 6/73.
　　1296 WE: W Norths (PV) Ltd (dealer), Sherburn in Elmet 12/69; W Walker, Hexthorpe (WR) 12/69; licensed 1/70; Camm (contractor), Chesterfield (XDE) as 40-seat 2/72; withdrawn by 8/76.

1969

New Vehicles

NFJ 619G	AEC Reliance	6U3ZR7212 Duple (Northern)	202/10	C49F	5/69	-/77
NFJ 620G	AEC Reliance	6U3ZR7215 Duple (Northern)	202/9	C49F	5/69	-/77
NFJ 621G	AEC Reliance	6U3ZR7211 Duple (Northern)	202/6	C44F	6/69	-/77
NFJ 622G	AEC Reliance	6U3ZR7213 Duple (Northern)	202/8	C44F	5/69	-/77
NFJ 623G	AEC Reliance	6U3ZR7214 Duple (Northern)	202/7	C44F	5/69	-/77

Notes:
　　NFJ 619G: Repainted in the white and ivy green livery 1970; numbered 490 6/71; repainted in NBC white coach livery 1973; renumbered 390 1/75.
　　NFJ 620G: Numbered 491 6/71; repainted in the white and ivy green livery 1972; repainted in NBC white coach livery 1974; renumbered 391 1/75.
　　NFJ 621G: Repainted in the white and ivy green livery 1970; allocated fleet number 492 6/71, not carried until repainted in NBC white coach livery 1974; renumbered 392 1/75.
　　NFJ 622G: Repainted in the white and ivy green livery 1970; numbered 493 6/71; repainted in NBC white coach livery in 1973; renumbered 393 1/75.
　　NFJ 623G: Repainted in the white and ivy green livery 1970; numbered 494 6/71; repainted in NBC white coach livery 1974; renumbered 394 1/75.

Disposals:
　　NFJ 619G (390): National Travel (South West) Ltd (GL) 175 6/77; withdrawn 11/77; Martin's Bus & Coach Sales Ltd (dealer), Middlewich 2/78; P & H Hamlett {PH Travel}, Middlewich (CH) 4/78; John Shaw & Son (Silverdale) Ltd, Silverdale (LA) 5/80; Mitchell's Mustella Coaches Ltd, Broxburn (CE) 4/82; Paul Sykes Organisation Ltd (dealer), Barnsley by 5/84.
　　NFJ 620G (391): National Travel (South West) Ltd (GL) 176 6/77; withdrawn 11/77; Martin's Bus & Coach Sales Ltd (dealer), Middlewich 2/78; P & H Hamlett {PH Travel}, Middlewich (CH) 4/78; PG Travel Ltd, Middlewich (CH) 4/80; returned to Martin's Bus & Coach Sales Ltd (dealer), Middlewich 1980; N Land, Batley as a transporter 3/81; S Evans, Radcliffe as a transporter by 4/83; K Riley, Ramsbottom as a transporter by 3/84.

NFJ 621G (392): National Travel (South West) Ltd (GL) 177 6/77; withdrawn 11/77; Martin's Bus & Coach Sales Ltd (dealer), Middlewich 2/78; A & JM Draper, Luton (BD) 2/78; withdrawn 12/82; Askin (dealer), Barnsley by 8/83.
NFJ 622G (393): National Travel (South West) Ltd (GL) 178 6/77; withdrawn 11/77; Martin's Bus & Coach Sales Ltd (dealer), Middlewich 2/78; A & JM Draper, Luton (BD) 2/78; withdrawn 12/82.
NFJ 623G (394): National Travel (South West) Ltd (GL) 179 6/77; withdrawn 11/77; Martin's Bus & Coach Sales Ltd (dealer), Middlewich 2/78; Lofty's Tours Ltd, Bridge Trafford (CH) as C49F 5/78; licensed 10/78; scrapped 1987.

Vehicles acquired from Devon General Omnibus & Touring Co Ltd, Torquay (DN) 5/69

934 GTA	AEC Reliance	2MU3RV3090	Willowbrook	60669	C41F	6/61	-/71
935 GTA	AEC Reliance	2MU3RV3091	Willowbrook	60670	C41F	6/61	-/71

Previous History:
934-935 GTA: New as Devon General 934-935.

Notes:
These vehicles were 7ft 6in wide.

935 GTA: Repainted in the white and ivy green livery 1971.

Disposals:
934 GTA: Western National Omnibus Co Ltd, Exeter (DN) 1238 7/71; withdrawn 10/73; C Pugsley, Yeo Vale (DN) 12/73; L Wadman {SW Coaches}, Throwleigh (DN) 5/74; withdrawn 8/77; Robison {Spreyton Garage}, Spreyton (XDN) for conversion to a caravan by 3/79; not carried out; sold 1983.

935 GTA: Western National Omnibus Co Ltd, Exeter (DN) 1239 7/71; withdrawn 10/73; C Pugsley, Yeo Vale (DN) 12/73; L Wadman {SW Coaches}, Throwleigh (DN) 5/74; licensed 6/74; believed sold by 5/94; M Sherwood {Grey Line Tours}, Paignton (DN) for preservation with operator by 1/96; Wright, Egmanton (NG) for preservation with operator 10/97; retained as preserved vehicle from 12/03; W Hulme, Yatton for preservation by 10/12.

1970

New Vehicles

RFJ 824H	AEC Reliance	6U3ZR7414	Plaxton	708901	C49F	8/70	-/77
RFJ 825H	AEC Reliance	6U3ZR7415	Plaxton	708902	C49F	6/70	-/77
RFJ 826H	AEC Reliance	6U3ZR7416	Plaxton	708903	C49F	6/70	-/77
RFJ 827H	AEC Reliance	6U3ZR7417	Plaxton	708904	C49F	8/70	-/77

Notes:
A fifth vehicle, RFJ 828H, was diverted to Devon General Omnibus & Touring Co Ltd, Torquay (DN) in 6/70. These were the first vehicles to be delivered new in the white and ivy green livery.

RFJ 824H: Numbered 495 6/71; repainted in NBC white coach livery 1974; renumbered 395 1/75; renumbered 195 and given "South West" fleetnames 4/77.

RFJ 825H: Numbered 496 6/71; repainted in NBC white coach livery 1974; renumbered 396 1/75; renumbered 196 and given "South West" fleetnames 4/77.

RFJ 826H: Numbered 497 6/71; while licensed as C49F, operated as C45F with tables for Exeter City Association Football Club during the 1970/1 and 1971/2 football seasons; repainted in NBC white coach livery 1974; renumbered 397 1/75; renumbered 197 and given "South West" fleetnames 4/77.

RFJ 827H: Numbered 498 6/71; repainted in NBC white coach livery 1974; renumbered 398 1/75; renumbered 198 and given "South West" fleetnames in 4/77.

Disposals:
RFJ 824H (195): National Travel (South West) Ltd (GL) 195 6/77; Martin's Bus & Coach Sales Ltd (dealer), Middlewich 1/78; Smith of Rainhill Ltd, Rainhill (MY) 1/78; Lawrenson's Travel Ltd, Bootle (MY) 2/80; WS Yeates Ltd (dealer), Loughborough by 8/81; DA Boardman {H & A Coaches}, Bolton (GM) 8/84; G Crompton {Graham Crompton Coaches}, Chorley (LA) by 1/86; NE, M & WR Robinson, Hindley (GM) by 5/87; JR Gray, Wigan (GM) for spares 9/88; broken up 4/89.

RFJ 825H (196): National Travel (South West) Ltd (GL) 196 6/77; Martin's Bus & Coach Sales Ltd (dealer), Middlewich 1/78; Smith of Rainhill Ltd, Rainhill (MY) 1/78; Lawrenson's Travel Ltd, Bootle (MY)

2/80; returned to Smith of Rainhill Ltd, Rainhill (MY) 1/82; not operated; WJ Lewis {Lewis Coaches}, Blaina (GT) 3/83; sold by 12/84.

RFJ 826H (197): National Travel (South West) Ltd (H) 197 6/77; Martin's Bus & Coach Sales Ltd (dealer), Middlewich 1/78; Smith of Rainhill Ltd, Rainhill (MY) 1/78; Lawrenson's Travel Ltd, Bootle (MY) 2/80; returned to Smith of Rainhill Ltd, Rainhill (MY) 1/82; not operated; WJ Lewis {Lewis Coaches}, Blaina (GT) 3/83; sold by 12/84.

RFJ 827H (198): National Travel (South West) Ltd (H) 198 6/77; Martin's Bus & Coach Sales Ltd (dealer), Middlewich 1/78; Smith of Rainhill Ltd, Rainhill (MY) 1/78; Lawrenson's Travel Ltd, Bootle (MY) 2/80; sold by 5/85; no further trace.

Vehicles acquired from Devon General Omnibus & Touring Co Ltd, Torquay (DN) 1/70

960 HTT	AEC Reliance	2MU3RV3934	Willowbrook	61764	C41F	5/62	-/73
961 HTT	AEC Reliance	2MU3RV3935	Willowbrook	61761	C41F	5/62	-/73
962 HTT	AEC Reliance	2MU3RV3936	Willowbrook	61765	C41F	5/62	-/73

Previous History:
960-962 HTT: New as Devon General 960-962.

Notes:
These vehicles were 7ft 6in wide.

960 HTT: Licensed 2/70; was the last vehicle in the buff and green livery, which it retained until withdrawal; numbered 422 6/71.
961 HTT: Licensed 2/70; numbered 423 6/71; repainted in the white and ivy green livery 1972.
962 HTT: Licensed 2/70; numbered 424 6/71; repainted in the white and ivy green livery 1972.

Disposals:
960 HTT (422): LJ & WB Ede {Roselyn Coaches}, Par (CO) 4/73; Tally Ho! Coaches Ltd, Kingsbridge (DN) 10/75; withdrawn 8/77; S Wren, Beddau and D Rockey, Exeter for preservation 11/77; kept at West of England Transport Collection, Winkleigh; S Wren, Pontypridd for preservation by 5/94.
961 HTT (423): Millbay Laundries, Plymouth (XDN) 3/73; West of England Transport Collection, Winkleigh for preservation 12/76; used for spares in resoration of 960 HTT 11/77; remains to Booth (dealer), Rotherham for scrap 1/78.
962 HTT (424): LJ & WB Ede {Roselyn Coaches}, Par (CO) 3/73; licensed 4/73; WG & CS Peake {El Peake}, Pontypool (GT) 8/75; WA Way & Sons (dealer), Cardiff by 10/78; Passenger Vehicle Spares (Barnsley) Ltd (dealer), Carlton 10/79.

Vehicles acquired from Devon General Omnibus & Touring Co Ltd, Torquay (DN) 7/70

941 GTA	AEC Reliance	2MU3RV3097	Willowbrook	60676	C37F	6/61	-/73
942 GTA	AEC Reliance	2MU3RV3098	Willowbrook	60677	C37F	6/61	-/72

Previous History:
941-942 GTA: New as Devon General 941-942.

Notes:
941-942 GTA: Repainted in the white and ivy green livery 1971; numbered 410-411 6/71.

Disposals:
941 GTA (410): Millbay Laundries, Plymouth (XDN) 3/73; West of England Transport Collection, Winkleigh for spares 1/77; RS Brown {Shaftesbury & District Motor Services}, Motcombe (DT) for spares 5/77.
942 GTA (411): Exeter City Architects Department, Exeter (XDN) V32/00 as a mobile office 12/72; plated as a goods vehicle 7/73; subsequently used as an immobile office; P Platt, Exeter for preservation 10/87; I Trotter & T Bartlett, Bruton for preservation 12/89; A Williams, Huddersfield for preservation 4/95; A Hardwick (dealer), Carlton for scrap 9/97.

Vehicle acquired from Western National Omnibus Co Ltd, Exeter (DN) 7/70

670 COD	Bristol SUS4A	157.012	ECW	11389	B30F	5/60	-/73

Previous History:
670 COD: New as Southern National Omnibus Co Ltd, Exeter (DN) 614; Western National Omnibus Co Ltd, Exeter (DN) 614 11/69.

Notes:
670 COD: Purchased for ferrying tours passengers from Sandy Bay to Exeter and Exmouth, but was only used as such in 1970 and later used on school contracts. It initially retained Tilling green livery, with the cream waistband overpainted in buff; repainted with white roof and window surrounds, with ivy green below and white fleetnames on the lower panels, towards the front in 10/70; numbered 402 6/71.

Disposal:
670 COD (402): Returned to Western National Omnibus Co Ltd, Exeter (DN) 614 9/73; Kinross Plant and Construction Co Ltd (contractor), Kinross (XTE) 2/80; Guernseybus, St Peter Port, Guernsey (CI) 143 12/82; AJS Salvage Co Ltd (dealer), Carlton 4/86.

Vehicles acquired from Devon General Omnibus & Touring Co Ltd, Torquay (DN) 10/70

937 GTA	AEC Reliance	2MU3RV3093	Willowbrook	60672	C41F	6/61	10/71
938 GTA	AEC Reliance	2MU3RV3094	Willowbrook	60673	C41F	6/61	10/71
939 GTA	AEC Reliance	2MU3RV3095	Willowbrook	60674	C41F	6/61	-/73
940 GTA	AEC Reliance	2MU3RV3096	Willowbrook	60675	C41F	6/61	-/73
963 HTT	AEC Reliance	2MU3RV3934	Willowbrook	61765	C41F	5/62	-/73

Previous History:
937-940 GTA: New as Devon General 937-940.
963 HTT: New as Devon General 963.

Notes:
These vehicles were 7ft 6in wide.
937 GTA: Retained the Grey Cars livery in which it was acquired; allocated fleet number 406 6/71, but never carried.
938 GTA: Repainted in the white and ivy green livery 1971; allocated fleet number 407 6/71, but never carried.
939 GTA: Numbered 408 6/71; repainted in the white and ivy green livery 1972.
940 GTA: Numbered 409 6/71; repainted in the white and ivy green livery 1972.
963 HTT: Numbered 425 6/71; repainted in the white and ivy green livery 1971.

Disposals:
937 GTA: Western National Omnibus Co Ltd, Exeter (DN) 1240 10/71; withdrawn 10/73; W Norths (PV) Ltd (dealer), Sherburn in Elmet 11/73; Simmons and Hawker Ltd, Feltham (XMX) 2/74; Windsor, Slough & Eton Athletic Club, Windsor (XBE) by 12/77; unidentified owner 5/81; left at premises of Rounds, Reading; sold to Lister (dealer), Bolton 8/87.
938 GTA: Western National Omnibus Co Ltd, Exeter (DN) 1241 10/71; withdrawn 7/73; Rundle (dealer), Plymouth for scrap after an accident 12/73.
939 GTA (408): J Hoare & Sons Ltd {The Ivy Coaches}, Ivybridge (DN) 3/73; Tally Ho! Coaches Ltd, Kingsbridge (DN) 3/76; withdrawn 8/76; Dudley Coles (contractor), Plymouth (XDN) 8/76; gone by 10/92.
940 GTA (409): J Hoare & Sons Ltd {The Ivy Coaches}, Ivybridge (DN) 2/73; Tally Ho! Coaches Ltd, Kingsbridge (DN) 3/76; withdrawn 9/76; E Beckett (dealer), Carlton 8/77.
963 HTT (425): LJ & WB Ede {Roselyn Coaches}, Par (CO) 4/73; HG Brown & G Davies {Truronian Coaches}, Truro (CO) 11/73; withdrawn 7/76; Cornwall County Council (Weare Comprehensive School), Saltash (XCO) 7/76; Willis (Central Garage) Ltd, Bodmin (CO) by 11/80; licensed, fitted with bus seats, 3/81; sold for scrap 1989.

1971

New Vehicles

300	UFJ 229J	Bristol RELH6L	4/392	Plaxton	713884	C44F	6/71	-/78
301	UFJ 230J	Bristol RELH6L	4/393	Plaxton	713885	C44F	7/71	-/78
302	UFJ 231J	Bristol RELH6L	4/394	Plaxton	713886	C44F	6/71	-/78
303	UFJ 232J	Bristol RELH6L	4/395	Plaxton	713887	C44F	6/71	-/78
304	UFJ 233J	Bristol RELH6L	4/396	Plaxton	713888	C44F	7/71	-/78
305	UUO 450J	Bristol RELH6L	4/328	Plaxton	713879	C47F	5/71	-/77
306	UUO 451J	Bristol RELH6L	4/329	Plaxton	713880	C47F	5/71	-/77
307	UUO 452J	Bristol RELH6L	4/330	Plaxton	713881	C47F	5/71	-/77
308	UUO 453J	Bristol RELH6L	4/331	Plaxton	713882	C47F	5/71	-/77
309	UUO 454J	Bristol RELH6L	4/332	Plaxton	713883	C47F	5/71	-/77

Notes:
These vehicles had roof-mounted destination boxes at the front, incorporating a three-track route number indicator.

UFJ 229-233J (300-304): Were the first vehicles in the fleet to carry fleet numbers from new.

UUO 450-454J (305-309): Ordered by Devon General Omnibus & Touring Co Ltd and allocated fleet numbers 450-454 in the Western National fleet when that operator took over the fleet of Devon General in 1/71; but delivered direct to Greenslades in Grey Cars white and grey livery.

UFJ 229J (300): Repainted in NBC white coach livery 1974.

UFJ 230J (301): Loaned to Bristol Omnibus Co Ltd, Bristol (GL) and painted in Bristol Greyhound livery 1/72; returned 5/72; repainted in NBC white coach livery 1974.

UFJ 231J (302): Repainted in NBC white coach livery 1972.

UFJ 232J (303): Repainted in NBC white coach livery 1974.

UFJ 233J (304): Repainted in NBC white coach livery 1974.

UUO 450J (305): Repainted in white and ivy green livery 1972; repainted in NBC white coach livery 1972; renumbered 606 and received "South West" fleetnames in 4/77.

UUO 451J (306): Repainted in white and ivy green livery 1972; repainted in NBC white coach livery 1972; loaned to Bristol Omnibus Co Ltd, Bristol (GL) from 11/72 until 5/73; renumbered 607 and received "South West" fleetnames 4/77.

UUO 452J (307): Repainted in white and ivy green livery in late 1971; repainted in NBC white coach livery 1972; loaned to Bristol Omnibus Co Ltd, Bristol (GL) from 11/72 until 5/73; renumbered 608 and received "South West" fleetnames 4/77.

UUO 453J (308): Loaned to Bristol Omnibus Co Ltd, Bristol (H) and painted in Bristol Greyhound livery 1/72; returned 2/72; repainted in NBC white coach livery 1972; renumbered 609 and received "South West" fleetnames 4/77.

UUO 454J (309): Although licensed to seat 47, it was fitted with 33 seats plus tables and other fittings for use by Torquay Association Football Club and Exeter City Association Football Club in 5/71, reverting to 47 seats for summer use between 8/71 and 5/74; repainted in white and ivy green livery in late 1971; repainted in NBC white coach livery 1972; renumbered 610 and received "South West" fleetnames in 4/77.

Disposals:
UFJ 229J (300): National Travel (South West) Ltd (GL) 400 3/78; Martin's Bus & Coach Sales Ltd (dealer), Middlewich at an unknown date; A Wild {A Ball & Son / Eagle Coaches}, Bristol (AV) 10/79; BE Ray {Bensway Travel}, Hartlepool (CD) 8/81; Michaels Travel Ltd, Croydon (LN) 59 re-registered 240 MT 1/84; re-registered HGC 233J 7/84; MJ Dean, Leatherhead (SR) re-registered SNJ 611 3/85; HPJ Miller {Arun Coaches}, Horsham (WS) by 3/88; re-registered ARU 80A 3/88; re-registered ARU 500A 12/88; D Woodmore {Crescent Coaches}, Paignton (DN) 4/89; re-registered IJI 5367 1/90; RJ Tree {City Centre Cars}, Cardiff (SC) 9/93; Wacton Trading / Coach Sales (dealer), Bromyard 5/94; MJ Perry, {Bromyard Omnibus}, Bromyard (HR) 72 as C49F 5/94; EJ Girling {Girlings of Plymouth}, Ivybridge (DN) 6/94; TP Jones {Vista Coachways}, Yatton (SO) 10/98; entered service, re-seated C51F and named "River Exe" 11/98; transferred to TP Jones {Vista Coachways}, Cleeve (SO) by 11/06; A Gray, Exeter for preservation 12/07.

UFJ 230J (301): National Travel (South West) Ltd (GL) 401 named "Elgar" 3/78; Martin's Bus & Coach Sales Ltd (dealer), Middlewich at an unknown date; A Wild {A Ball & Son/Eagle Coaches}, Bristol (AV) 10/79; given Plaxton Supreme IV front by 9/81; withdrawn by 11/87; sold (for scrap?) 11/87.

UFJ 231J (302): National Travel (South West) Ltd (GL) 402 named "Mozart" 3/78; Paul Sykes Organisation Ltd (dealer), Barnsley 6/79; Morris Brothers of Swansea Ltd, Swansea (WG) as C49F 9/79; JD Cleverly Ltd {Capitol Coaches}, Cwmbran (GT) 5/84; Ripley (dealer), Carlton 2/87.

UFJ 232J (303): National Travel (South West) Ltd (GL) 403 named "Strauss" 3/78; Paul Sykes Organisation Ltd (dealer), Barnsley 6/79; Morris Brothers of Swansea Ltd, Swansea (WG) as C49F 9/79; withdrawn by 1/84.

UFJ 233J (304): National Travel (South West) Ltd (GL) 404 named "Wagner" 3/78; withdrawn 8/79; Martin (dealer), Middlewich at an unknown date; PG Travel Ltd, Middlewich (CH) 8/80; Martin's Bus and Coach Sales Ltd {Martin's PG International}, Middlewich (CH) 8/82; Hulme Hall Educational Trust, Cheadle Hulme (GM) by 2/85; DBL & R Jones, Blaenau Ffestiniog (GD) by 4/86; used as a seat store by 4/87; Richardson, Port Llanrhaeadr as a transporter by 1987.

UUO 450J (606): National Travel (South West) Ltd (GL) 606 4/77; re-seated C44F 10/77; withdrawn by 6/79; Paul Sykes Organisation Ltd (dealer), Barnsley 6/79; K Askin (dealer), Barnsley 1979; Morris Brothers of Swansea Ltd, Swansea (WG) 9/79; licensed as C49F 2/80; JD Cleverly Ltd {Capitol Coaches}, Cwmbran (GT) 5/84; Ferry Marine Hotel, Beachley (XGL) 7/85; T Wigley (dealer), Carlton by 12/87.

UUO 451J (607): National Travel (South West) Ltd (GL) 607 4/77; re-seated to C46F at unknown date; withdrawn 7/79; Martin's Bus & Coach Sales Ltd (dealer), Middlewich at an unknown date; Rees and Williams Ltd {Tycroes and District}, Tycroes (DD) as C53F 1/81; JA Richards, Nantyglo (GT) at an unknown date; Burnley & Pendle Catholic Youth Society, Burnley (XLA) 5/83; P Cartmell, Burnley (LA) 12/89.

UUO 452J (608): National Travel (South West) Ltd (GL) 608 4/77; re-seated to C44F 10/77; withdrawn 12/79; Martin's Bus & Coach Sales Ltd (dealer), Middlewich at an unknown date; P & H Hamlett {PH Travel}, Middlewich (CH) 1/80; PG Travel Ltd, Middlewich (CH) 4/80; withdrawn 1/83; G & K Roberts, Old Colwyn (CL) 19 named "St Tudno" by 10/83; AJ Delaney {Avon Coach Hire}, Bristol (AV) by 5/86; sold by 6/90.

UUO 453J (609): National Travel (South West) Ltd (GL) 609 4/77; re-seated C44F 10/77; withdrawn 7/79; Martin's Bus & Coach Sales Ltd (dealer), Middlewich 12/79; Rees & Williams Ltd {Tycroes and District}, Tycroes (DD) by 4/80; licensed as C51F 6/80; Martin Bus & Coaches Sales Ltd (dealer), Middlewich 6/83; G & K Roberts, Old Colwyn (CL) 20 named "St David" by 9/83; Salvador Caetano (UK) Ltd (dealer), Northampton 1986; loaned to GW, JB & DG Summerson {The Eden}, West Auckland (DM) during 12/86; GH & KM Turner, Ulleskelf (NY) 7/87; Clevestone Transport Ltd, Hartlepool (CD) 11/87; North East Bus Breakers (dealer), Craghead at an unknown date; Bedlington & District, Ashington (ND) 11/88; W Norths (PV) Ltd (dealer), Sherburn in Elmet 11/91.

UUO 454J (610): National Travel (South West) Ltd (GL) 610 4/77; re-seated C44F 10/77; withdrawn 12/79; Martin's Bus & Coach Sales Ltd (dealer), Middlewich by 2/80; P & H Hamlett {PH Travel}, Middlewich (CH) 2/80; PG Travel Ltd, Middlewich (CH) 4/80; G Evans, Brynamman (WG) 10/80; entering service with a Plaxton Supreme IV front as C53F; sold 2/86; T Wigley (dealer), Carlton 4/87.

Vehicles acquired from Trent Motor Traction Co Ltd, Derby (DE) 1/71

YRC 43	AEC Reliance	2MU3RA3908	Harrington	2579	C37F	3/62	-/73
YRC 44	AEC Reliance	2MU3RA3909	Harrington	2580	C37F	5/62	-/73
YRC 46	AEC Reliance	2MU3RA3911	Harrington	2582	C37F	5/62	-/73

Previous History:
- YRC 43: New as Trent 43; renumbered 51 10/63.
- YRC 44: New as Trent 44; renumbered 52 3/64.
- YRC 46: New as Trent 46; renumbered 54 3/64.

Notes:
- YRC 43: Painted in white and ivy green when acquired; allocated fleet number 412 6/71, but never carried.
- YRC 44: Painted in white and ivy green when acquired; allocated fleet number 413 6/71, but never carried.
- YRC 46: Painted in white and ivy green when acquired; numbered 414 6/71.

Disposals:
- YRC 43: Returned to Trent Motor Traction Co Ltd, Derby (DE) for disposal 10/73; J Conlan & Sons Ltd (contractor), Bamber Bridge (XLA) 1/74; withdrawn and stored 11/77; Davidson & Son (dealer), Chorley 11/81; Tysons Contractors plc (contractor), Liverpool (XMY) 10/83; fitted with scaffolding platforms on the roof for use in installation of new lighting in the Mersey Tunnel; Mersey and Calder Bus Preservation Group, Burscough for spares 4/84; believed scrapped by 11/96.
- YRC 44: Returned to Trent Motor Traction Co Ltd, Derby (DE) for disposal 10/73; J Conlan & Sons Ltd (contractor), Bamber Bridge (XLA) 1/74; withdrawn and stored 11/77; Davidson & Son (dealer), Chorley 11/81; Tysons Contractors plc (contractor), Liverpool (XMY) 10/83; fitted with scaffolding platforms on the roof for use in installation of new lighting in the Mersey Tunnel; Ward and Galvin (dealer), Liverpool for scrap 4/84.
- YRC 46 (414): Returned to Trent Motor Traction Co Ltd, Derby (DE) for disposal 10/73; J Conlan & Sons Ltd (contractor), Bamber Bridge (XLA) 1/74; withdrawn and stored 11/77; Davidson & Son (dealer), Chorley 11/81; Tysons Contractors plc (contractor), Liverpool (XMY) 10/83; fitted with scaffolding platforms on the roof for use in installation of new lighting in the Mersey Tunnel; Ward and Galvin (dealer), Liverpool for scrap 4/84.

Vehicles acquired from Western National Omnibus Co Ltd, Exeter (DN) 5/71

964 HTT	AEC Reliance	2MU3RV3938	Willowbrook	61767	C41F	5/62	-/74
965 HTT	AEC Reliance	2MU3RV3939	Willowbrook	61762	C41F	5/62	-/74
966 HTT	AEC Reliance	2MU3RV3940	Willowbrook	61760	C41F	5/62	-/74
967 HTT	AEC Reliance	2MU3RV3941	Willowbrook	61763	C41F	5/62	-/74

DFJ 114 was new in 1937 to the Belcher fleet, a Bedford WTB with 25 seat Duple body, once again supplied with a canvas roof. The smartly attired driver stands proudly awaiting his charge of passengers. The coach survived only until 1942, having been transferred from Belchers to Greenslades in 1939. (David Cornforth, via Peter Tulloch)

Looking as though it had been bodied by Duple, JFJ 179 actually carries a body by Tiverton, one of five similar vehicles delivered in 1948. After five years service with Greenslades it passed to two other West Country operators. (Omnibus Society – Norris-Cull collection)

1950 saw the arrival of six Gurney Nutting bodied AEC Regal IIIs, as well as a single Leyland PS2/3 and a Bedford OB. Other similar coaches were delivered to associated fleets. The body on AEC Regal III KFJ 613 had a superficial resemblance to the classic Duple 'A' style body. (Omnibus Society – Norris-Cull collection – RHG Simpson)

Gurney Nutting were favoured again for a pair of 30ft long Maudslay Marathon IIIs in 1951, but the styling was very different, fully fronted and with central entrances. Both LFJ 804 and its sister, LFJ 801, were reseated to a more luxurious 26 seats for extended tours, before reverting to 35 seats. (Omnibus Society – Norris-Cull collection)

At the same time as the 30ft Maudslays were being delivered, Greenslades took delivery of a pair of unusual 30ft Leyland PS2/3s, LFJ 876 & 877. These introduced another coachbuilder to the company, having bodies built in Loughborough by Yeates. (Omnibus Society – Norris-Cull collection – RHG Simpson)

The bulk of the 1952 to 1954 deliveries consisted of petrol engined Bedfords with Duple bodies, though a pair of Gurney Nutting bodied Bedfords were delivered to the Belcher fleet. OFJ 791 is seen in London, possibly on hire to Royal Blue. (Omnibus Society – Norris-Cull collection – RHG Simpson)

ACN 682 was registered by the Gateshead dealer, Walton, and used by Associated Coachbuilders as a demonstrator, as seen here, before being purchased by Teign Cars of Teignmouth, passing to the main Greenslades fleet in 1954. (Omnibus Society – XLTM collection)

The start of a new purchasing policy saw the arrival in 1955 of a pair of AEC Reliances with Duple bodies, RFJ 380 and 381. RFJ 380 is seen here prepared to run on hire to Royal Blue on a service to Lyme Regis, Dorset. (Omnibus Society – Norris-Cull collection – RHG Simpson)

The other 1955 coaches could hardly have been more different. RFJ 395 was one of a pair of Commer Avenger IIIs with Devon Coachbuilders bodies transferred from older Commers operated by associate company, Belchers of Teignmouth. RFJ 395 is seen parked in the square in Tiverton. (Omnibus Society – DHD Spray)

One of three Leyland PS2/3s with Gurney Nutting bodies, KFJ 606 started life with Belcher, Teignmouth before being transferred firstly to Regent Coaches of Teignmouth, another associate company, in 1953 and then finally to Greenslades main fleet in 1955. (Omnibus Society – Norris-Cull collection – RHG Simpson)

The Bedford marque had one final fling in the Greenslades fleet before AEC Reliances took over completely. In 1956 no fewer than fourteen SBG models, all with Duple bodies, entered the fleet. Most had 41 seat bodies, like TFJ 436 seen here, but a few had either 28 or 36 seats. (Omnibus Society – DHD Spray)

South West meets South East, as VFJ 992, the next generation of AEC Reliances sits in front of a Maidstone & District coach in London. The Greenslades coach has worked up on hire to Royal Blue, a regular source of work for Greenslades coaches. (Omnibus Society – Norris-Cull collection – RHG Simpson)

For many years coaches were cascaded from the Grey Cars fleet to Greenslades, a tradition that started in 1958 with the transfer of the LTA batch of Duple bodied AEC Regal IIIs, as exemplified by LTA 624. The slight differences in styling between Duple and Gurney Nutting bodies, as on KFJ 611, can be seen here. (Omnibus Society – Norris-Cull collection – A Broughall)

Five AEC Reliances with Duple bodies joined the fleet in 1959, but XFJ 875 was not part of the original order from Greenslades. It had been ordered by Bowerman's Tours, a company acquired by Greenslades the previous year. (Omnibus Society – Norris-Cull collection – RHG Simpson)

A new source of bodies appeared with the 1960 delivery of the now customary AEC Reliances, Harrington. The Cavalier, and its successor the Grenadier, was to become a familiar sight in the Greenslades fleet over the next fifteen years. 556 AFJ was one of six Cavaliers taken into stock in 1960. (Omnibus Society – Norris-Cull collection – RHG Simpson)

After many years of operating Bedford SB models, Greenslades turned to their rival Ford for part of their new coach fleet in 1961. Three AEC Reliances were joined by four Ford 570E coaches with Duple bodies, two of which are seen here, 545 and 546 CFJ. (Omnibus Society – Norris-Cull collection)

1962 saw more innovation with the advent of the first 36ft long coaches and the deliveries in that year were split between four conventional 30ft long vehicles (567 to 570 EFJ) and three longer models (571 to 573 EFJ), of which 571 EFJ is seen here. (Omnibus Society - Peter Henson)

After more short Harrington bodied Reliances were delivered in 1963, the following year saw 7ft 6in wide versions of the Harrington Grenadier body on a batch of ten AEC Reliances for use on the narrow moorland roads in and around Devon. AFJ 77B (442) was the first of the batch and initially seated just 36 passengers. (Omnibus Society - Peter Henson)

Having taken a number of AEC Regal IVs from the Grey Car fleet, ROD 750 represented the first AEC Reliance to be downgraded and transferred to the Greenslades fleet. Weymann bodied ROD 750 rests alongside one of the Ford 570E Duple bodied coaches from the 1961 intake. (Omnibus Society – Norris-Cull collection – RHG Simpson)

The FFJ 10 to 13D batch of Harrington bodied Reliances were the last vehicles to be completed by Harrington before that company closed its doors for good. FFJ 10D is seen shortly after delivery being prepared for a tour duty. It was numbered 458 in 1971, when it also received the Ivy Green and White livery first adopted in October 1969. (Omnibus Society – Norris-Cull collection – RHG Simpson)

More AEC Reliances were received from Grey Cars in 1966 in the form of XDV and ADV registered Willowbrook coaches, of which XDV 854 was one. The Greenslades coach is seen on Royal Blue hire duty, this time working a service to Bournemouth, headquarters of Royal Blue. (Omnibus Society – Norris-Cull collection – RHG Simpson)

HFJ 418E (482 – not carried) was one of three Plaxton Panorama bodied coaches received in 1967, two of which, including this vehicle, were of shorter length. It is seen whilst on a Scottish tour duty, for which it was well suited with just 40 seats. Withdrawn in 1976 it joined its two sister coaches in the fleet of Webber Bros of Blisland, Cornwall. (Omnibus Society - Peter Henson)

No new coaches joined the fleet in 1968, but in 1969 five more AEC Reliances were purchased, this time carrying Duple (Northern) bodies. Once again a mixture of long and short models were chosen, with NFJ 621G (492 – not carried) being one of the shorter 44 seat coaches, seen here about to depart for Wales. (Omnibus Society - Peter Henson)

A most unusual arrival in 1970 was 670 COD (402), a Bristol SUS4A with ECW body. It initially retained its Tilling Green livery, but later in 1970 it was repainted into the Ivy Green and White livery and numbered 402. It spent much of its short life with Greenslades on school duties. (Omnibus Society - Peter Henson)

UFJ 229J (300) was the first of a batch of Bristol RELH6L coaches with Plaxton bodies. These coaches were delivered in Ivy Green and White and also carried fleet numbers from new. After sale in 1978 UFJ 229J had a very chequered history as can be seen under its disposal details. It is currently preserved. (Omnibus Society - Peter Henson)

Showing a destination which reveals its past history, YRC 46 (414) was the first second hand Harrington bodied Reliance purchased, one of three that arrived from Trent. After a two year stay at Greenslades the coach was returned to Trent for disposal. (Omnibus Society - Peter Henson)

More Harrington bodied AEC Reliances were to follow, 1 RDV being another Grey Cars coach. This coach, however, arrived in May 1971 when the entire Grey Cars operation was transferred to the control of Greenslades. Numbered 431, the number was not carried initially. 1 RDV was a 7ft 6in wide model. (Geoffrey Morant, courtesy Richard Morant)

The Grey Cars fleet acquired in 1971 also contained five Duple bodied Bedford SB5s, all of them new to Court Garages (Torquay) Ltd, which was a Devon General subsidiary company. CXF 257G was allocated fleet number 487, but later renumbered 387. The coach was bought by a company in Jersey on withdrawal. (Omnibus Society - Peter Henson)

In 1970 five AEC Reliances were due to have been delivered, but one was diverted to the Grey Cars fleet. RFJ 828H (499) was that coach, but it eventually joined its stablemates when the Grey Cars fleet was transferred to Greenslades control in 1971. (Geoffrey Morant, courtesy Richard Morant)

By 1972 good quality second-hand AEC Reliances were proving more difficult to locate, therefore YTX 322H (406) was the first of many Leyland Leopards purchased by Greenslades, in this case coming from Western Welsh. (Geoffrey Morant, courtesy Richard Morant)

More Bristol RELH6L coaches with Plaxton Panorama Elite bodies arrived in 1973. BFJ 311L (311), now with matching fleet and registration numbers, was one of a batch of five similar coaches. Another coach seen on an extended tour, these coaches were the first delivered in National White livery. (Omnibus Society – Norris-Cull collection – RHG Simpson)

A return to Bedford coaches was heralded in 1974, with eight Bedford YRTs and two VAS5s, all carrying Duple bodies. The Bedford VAS5s were 7ft 6in wide coaches, continuing the policy of having narrow coaches for some of Devon and Cornwall's narrower roads. PFJ 352M (352) is seen wearing the National White livery. (Geoffrey Morant, courtesy Richard Morant)

968 HTT	AEC Reliance	2MU3RV3942	Willowbrook	61768	C41F	5/62	-/73
1 RDV	AEC Reliance	2MU3RV4971	Harrington	2850	C41F	4/64	-/75
2 RDV	AEC Reliance	2MU3RV4972	Harrington	2851	C41F	4/64	-/75
3 RDV	AEC Reliance	2MU3RV4973	Harrington	2852	C41F	4/64	-/75
4 RDV	AEC Reliance	2MU3RV4974	Harrington	2853	C41F	4/64	-/75
5 RDV	AEC Reliance	2MU3RV4975	Harrington	2854	C41F	4/64	-/75
6 RDV	AEC Reliance	2MU3RV4976	Harrington	2855	C41F	4/64	-/75
7 RDV	AEC Reliance	2MU3RV4977	Harrington	2856	C41F	4/64	-/75
8 RDV	AEC Reliance	2MU3RV4978	Harrington	2857	C41F	4/64	-/75
EOD 24D	AEC Reliance	2U3RA6023	Harrington	3207	C49F	3/66	-/75
EOD 25D	AEC Reliance	2U3RA6024	Harrington	3208	C49F	4/66	-/75
EOD 26D	AEC Reliance	2U3RA6025	Harrington	3209	C49F	4/66	-/75
EOD 27D	AEC Reliance	2U3RA6026	Harrington	3210	C49F	4/66	-/75
EOD 28D	AEC Reliance	2U3RA6027	Harrington	3211	C49F	5/66	-/75
EOD 29D	AEC Reliance	2U3RA6028	Harrington	3212	C49F	5/66	-/75
EOD 30D	AEC Reliance	2U3RA6029	Harrington	3213	C49F	5/66	-/75
EOD 31D	AEC Reliance	2U3RA6030	Harrington	3214	C49F	5/66	-/75
HOD 32E	AEC Reliance	2U3RA6454	Duple (Northern)	175/8	C49F	4/67	-/76
HOD 33E	AEC Reliance	2U3RA6455	Duple (Northern)	175/9	C49F	4/67	-/76
HOD 34E	AEC Reliance	2U3RA6456	Duple (Northern)	175/7	C49F	4/67	-/76
HOD 35E	AEC Reliance	2U3RA6457	Duple (Northern)	175/6	C49F	4/67	-/76
HOD 36E	AEC Reliance	2U3RA6458	Duple (Northern)	175/5	C49F	4/67	-/76
HOD 37E	AEC Reliance	2U3RA6459	Duple (Northern)	175/4	C49F	4/67	-/76
HOD 38E	AEC Reliance	2U3RA6460	Duple (Northern)	175/3	C49F	4/67	-/76
HOD 39E	AEC Reliance	2U3RA6461	Duple (Northern)	175/2	C49F	4/67	-/76
JTA 763E	Bedford SB5	7802536	Duple	1213/2	C41F	5/67	-/74
JTA 764E	Bedford SB5	7802556	Duple	1213/1	C41F	4/67	-/74
JTA 765E	Bedford SB5	7803235	Duple	1213/3	C41F	5/67	-/74
CXF 256G	Bedford SB5	9T466343	Duple	1224/24	C41F	4/69	-/76
CXF 257G	Bedford SB5	9T466109	Duple	1224/25	C41F	4/69	-/76
RFJ 828H	AEC Reliance	6U3ZR7418	Plaxton	708905	C49F	6/70	-/77

Previous History:
These vehicles comprised the entire Grey Cars fleet of Devon General, which had been taken over by Western National in January 1971, together with the rest of the Devon General fleet. They retained their Devon General fleet numbers with Western National.

    964-968 HTT: Were 7ft 6in wide; new as Devon General 964-968 HTT.
    1-8 RDV: Were 7ft 6in wide; new as Devon General 1-8.
    EOD 24-31D: New as Devon General 24-31.
    HOD 32-39E: New as Devon General 32-39.
    JTA 763E: Was 7ft 6in wide; new to Court Garages (Torquay) Ltd, Torquay (DN), which was a Devon General subsidiary from 10/66; absorbed into the main fleet and allocated fleet number 493 10/70, but never carried..
    JTA 764E: Was 7ft 6in wide; new to Court Garages (Torquay) Ltd, Torquay (DN), which was a Devon General subsidiary from 10/66; absorbed into the main fleet and allocated fleet number 494 10/70, but never carried.
    JTA 765E: Was 7ft 6in wide; new to Court Garages (Torquay) Ltd, Torquay (DN), which was a Devon General subsidiary from 10/66; absorbed into the main fleet and allocated fleet number 495 10/70, but never carried.
    CXF 256G: Was 7ft 6in wide; new to Court Garages (Torquay) Ltd, Torquay (DN), which was a Devon General subsidiary from 10/66; absorbed into the main fleet and allocated fleet number 496 10/70, but never carried.
    CXF 257G: Was 7ft 6in wide; new to Court Garages (Torquay) Ltd, Torquay (DN), which was a Devon General subsidiary from 10/66; absorbed into the main fleet and allocated fleet number 497 in 10/70, but never carried.
    RFJ 828H: New as Devon General 499, having been a diverted order from Greenslades.

Notes:
    964 HTT: Numbered 426 6/71 and received black fleet number plates; repainted in white and ivy green livery 1972.
    965 HTT: Numbered 427 6/71 and received black fleet number plates; repainted in white and ivy green livery 1972.

966 HTT: Numbered 428 6/71 and received black fleet number plates; repainted in white and ivy green livery 1972; repainted in NBC white coach livery 1974.
967 HTT: Numbered 429 6/71 but did not carry that number until grey transfer numbers were applied in 1974; repainted in white and ivy green livery 1972.
968 HTT: Numbered 430 6/71 and received black fleet number plates; repainted in white and ivy green livery 1972.
1 RDV: Acquired in the revised Grey Cars livery of white with slate grey waistband and numbered 431 6/71, but did not carry that number until grey transfer numbers were applied in 1974; repainted in white and ivy green livery 1972; repainted in NBC white coach livery 1974; allocated new fleet number 291 1/75, but never carried.
2 RDV: Acquired in the revised Grey Cars livery of white with slate grey waistband and numbered 432 6/71, but did not carry that number until grey transfer numbers were applied in 1974; repainted in white and ivy green livery 1972; repainted in NBC white coach livery 1974; allocated new fleet number 292 1/75, but never carried.
3 RDV: Acquired in the revised Grey Cars livery of white with slate grey waistband; numbered 433 6/71 and received black fleet number plates; repainted in white and ivy green livery 1972; renumbered 293 1/75.
4 RDV: Acquired in the revised Grey Cars livery of white with slate grey waistband; numbered 434 6/71 and received black fleet number plates; repainted in white and ivy green livery 1972; repainted in NBC white coach livery 1974; allocated new fleet number 294 1/75, but never carried.
5 RDV: Acquired in the revised Grey Cars livery of white with slate grey waistband, numbered 435 6/71 and received black fleet number plates; repainted in white and ivy green livery in 1972, repainted in NBC white coach livery in 1973; allocated new fleet number 295 1/75, but never carried.
6 RDV: Acquired in the revised Grey Cars livery of white with slate grey waistband; numbered 436 6/71 and received black fleet number plates; repainted in white and ivy green livery 1971; repainted in NBC white coach livery 1974; allocated new fleet number 296 1/75, but never carried.
7 RDV: Acquired in the revised Grey Cars livery of white with slate grey waistband; numbered 437 6/71 and received black fleet number plates; repainted in white and ivy green livery 1972; allocated new fleet number 297 1/75, but never carried.
8 RDV: Acquired in the revised Grey Cars livery of white with slate grey waistband; numbered 438 6/71 and received black fleet number plates; repainted in white and ivy green livery 1972; allocated new fleet number 298 1/75, but never carried.
EOD 24D: was numbered 464 6/71 and received black fleet number plates; repainted in white and ivy green livery 1972; renumbered 264 1/75.
EOD 25D: Acquired in the revised Grey Cars livery of white with slate grey waistband, numbered 465 6/71 and received black fleet number plates; repainted in white and ivy green livery 1972; renumbered 265 1/75.
EOD 26D: Numbered 466 6/71 and received black fleet number plates; repainted in white and ivy green livery 1971; repainted in NBC white coach livery 1974; renumbered 266 1/75.
EOD 27D: Acquired in the revised Grey Cars livery of white with slate grey waistband, numbered 467 6/71, but did not carry that number until grey transfer numbers were applied 1974; repainted in white and ivy green livery 1972; repainted in NBC white coach livery 1974; renumbered 267 1/75.
EOD 28D: Numbered 468 6/71 and received black fleet number plates; repainted in white and ivy green livery 1972; renumbered 266 1/75.
EOD 29D: Numbered 469 6/71 and received black fleet number plates; repainted in white and ivy green livery 1971; renumbered 269 1/75.
EOD 30D: Acquired in the revised Grey Cars livery of white with slate grey waistband; numbered 470 6/71 and received black fleet number plates; repainted in white and ivy green livery 1972; renumbered 270 1/75.
EOD 31D: Acquired in the revised Grey Cars livery of white with slate grey waistband; numbered 471 6/71 and received black fleet number plates; repainted in white and ivy green livery 1972; renumbered 271 1/75.
HOD 32E: Acquired in the revised Grey Cars livery of white with slate grey waistband; numbered 472 6/71 and received black fleet number plates; repainted in white and ivy green livery 1972; repainted in NBC white coach livery 1974; renumbered 272 1/75.
HOD 33E: Acquired in the revised Grey Cars livery of white with slate grey waistband; numbered 473 6/71 and received black fleet number plates; repainted in white and ivy green livery 1972; repainted in NBC white coach livery 1973; renumbered 273 1/75.
HOD 34E: Acquired in the revised Grey Cars livery of white with slate grey waistband; numbered 474 6/71 and received black fleet number plates; repainted in white and ivy green livery 1972; repainted in NBC white coach livery 1974; renumbered 274 1/75.
HOD 35E: Acquired in the revised Grey Cars livery of white with slate grey waistband; numbered 475 6/71 and received black fleet number plates; repainted in white and ivy green livery 1972; repainted in NBC white coach livery 1974; renumbered 275 1/75.

HOD 36E: Acquired in the revised Grey Cars livery of white with slate grey waistband; numbered 476 6/71 and received black fleet number plates; repainted in white and ivy green livery 1972; repainted in NBC white coach livery 1974; renumbered 276 1/75.
HOD 37E: Acquired in the revised Grey Cars livery of white with slate grey waistband; numbered 477 6/71 and received black fleet number plates; repainted in white and ivy green livery 1972; repainted in NBC white coach livery 1973; renumbered 277 1/75.
HOD 38E: Acquired in the revised Grey Cars livery of white with slate grey waistband; numbered 478 6/71 and received black fleet number plates; repainted in white and ivy green livery 1972; repainted in NBC white coach livery 1974; renumbered 278 1/75.
HOD 39E: Acquired in the revised Grey Cars livery of white with slate grey waistband; numbered 479 6/71 and received black fleet number plates; repainted in NBC white coach livery 1972; renumbered 279 1/75.
JTA 763E: Acquired in the revised Grey Cars livery of white with slate grey waistband; numbered 483 and received black fleet number plates; repainted in white and ivy green livery 1972.
JTA 764E: Acquired in the revised Grey Cars livery of white with slate grey waistband; numbered 484, but did not carry that number until grey transfer numbers were applied 1974; repainted in white and ivy green livery 1972; repainted in NBC white coach livery 1974.
JTA 765E: Acquired in the revised Grey Cars livery of white with slate grey waistband; numbered 485 and received black fleet number plates; repainted in white and ivy green livery 1972.
CXF 256G: Acquired in the revised Grey Cars livery of white with slate grey waistband; numbered 486, but did not carry that number until grey transfer numbers were applied 1974; repainted in white and ivy green livery 1972; repainted in NBC white coach livery 1974; renumbered 386 1/75.
CXF 257G: Acquired in the revised Grey Cars livery of white with slate grey waistband; numbered 487 and received black fleet number plates; repainted in white and ivy green livery 1972; renumbered 387 1/75.
RFJ 828H: Acquired in the revised Grey Cars livery of white with slate grey waistband; numbered 499 6/71 and received black fleet number plates; repainted in white and ivy green livery 1971; renumbered 399 6/71; renumbered 199 and given "South West" fleetnames 4/77.

Disposals:
964 HTT (426): Blackbrooker (dealer), London SE11 9/74; G Jones {S Jones & Son}, Bancyfelin (CR) 1974; D Lansdown {CH Lansdown & Sons}, Tockington (GL) 4/75; withdrawn 8/76; Haywards Heath Grammar School, Haywards Heath (XWS) 1976; IE Thomas, West Ewell (SR) 2/78; JC Retallick & RC Kernutt {Surreyways}, Godalming (SR) 7/78; not operated; moved to Guildford (SR) 12/79.
965 HTT (427): Dawlish Coaches Ltd {Tomlinson's}, Dawlish (DN) 10/74; having been on loan from 8/74; licensed 11/74; withdrawn 1/77; Mitchell's (Perranporth) Ltd, Perranporth (CO) 6/77.
966 HTT (428): Blackbrooker (dealer), London SE11 9/74.
967 HTT (429): Blackbrooker (dealer), London SE11 9/74; G Jones {S Jones & Son}, Bancyfelin (CR) 1974; Moseley (Gloucester) Ltd (dealer), Cinderford 4/75; LE Evans, Yate (GL) 5/75; withdrawn 2/76; RS Brown {Shaftesbury & District Motor Services}, Motcombe (DT) 3/76; licensed 5/76; becoming M Light & RS Brown {Shaftesbury & District Motor Services, Motcombe (DT) 10/77; withdrawn 9/79; RS Brown, Motcombe (XDT) 9/80; P Morley, Dunster for preservation 10/81; S Gilkes, Chiselhurst as spares for preserved vehicle 1/86; remains to T Wigley (dealer), Carlton for scrap 2/87.
968 HTT (430): RK & RE Webber {Webber Brothers}, Blisland (CO) 5/73; WT Moyle, Newquay (CO) 3/75; withdrawn 8/78.
1 RDV: DE Allmey, Eastcote (LN) 5/75; withdrawn 12/79; loaned to P Platt, Exeter for preservation from 12/79; repainted in Grey Cars livery 1981; moved to Crediton 3/01; moved to Exeter by 8/04; moved to Dawlish Warren 9/11.
2 RDV: FJ & JA Fry {Fry's Tours}, Tintagel (CO) 4/75; withdrawn by 3/83; West of England Transport Collection, Winkleigh (P Platt, Exeter) for spares 10/84; R Greet, Broadhempston for preservation 5/04.
3 RDV (293): AO Sherrin, Carhampton (SO) 7/75; withdrawn 7/78; P Baird {Prestwood Travel}, Prestwood (BK) 9/78; withdrawn by 9/84; sold for scrap by 2/85.
4 RDV: DC Venner {Scarlet Coaches}, Minehead (SO) 7/75; DE Allmey, Pinner (LN) 11/77; withdrawn 6/81; Dawlish Coaches Ltd {Tomlinson's}, Dawlish (DN) re-registered TSV 850 4/85; reverted to original registration 4 RDV 1/94; R Huckle, Sutton Coldfield for preservation 1/94; B Haywood & K Prosser {A-Line}, Bedworth (WK) by 12/94; P Platt, Crediton for preservation 3/04; R Greet, Broadhempstead for preservation 5/04.
5 RDV: RK & RE Webber {Webber Brothers}, Blisland (CO) 4/75; Educational Holidays Guernsey Ltd {Island Coachways}, St Peter Port, Guernsey (CI) re-registered 6769 5/82; Wacton Trading / Coach Sales (dealer), Bromyard 12/84; Truscott, Roche for preservation 12/84; D Rundle,

Falmouth for preservation 1/99; Falmouth Coaches {King Harry}, Falmouth (CO) 7/02; converted to recovery vehicle by 12/03; re-registered YCV 365B 10/05.

6 RDV: RK & RE Webber {Webber Brothers}, Blisland (CO) for spares 4/75; scrapped at Blisland by 5/78.

7 RDV: SEJ Ridler {Dulverton Motors}, Dulverton (SO) 5/75; licensed 7/75; T Greenslade, Bathealton (XSO) c7/80; sold by 10/92; R Warren, Martock for preservation 3/02.

8 RDV: SEJ Ridler {Dulverton Motors}, Dulverton (SO) 5/75; licensed 7/75; Dawlish Coaches Ltd {Tomlinson's}, Dawlish (DN) 7/80; re-registered BDV 175B by 8/88; SC Glover, Exeter as a mobile caravan 8/88.

EOD 24D (264): P Sykes (dealer), Barnsley 12/75; RI Davies & Son Ltd, Tredegar (MH) 3/76; Stonnis, Tredegar (MH) 2/77; JN Baker Ltd, Weston-Super-Mare (SO) 5/77; withdrawn 7/77; Wilkins Coaches (Cymmer) Ltd, Cymmer (WG) 9/77; disused by 7/82; scrapped at Pantdu 3/83.

EOD 25D (265): P Sykes (dealer), Barnsley 12/75; J Nicholls, Tredegar (GT) 1/76; withdrawn 8/76; Arlington Motor Co Ltd (dealer), Potters Bar by 12/78; RA Jefferiss {R & J Coaches}, Southall (LN) for spares 1979; DE Allmey, Eastcote (LN) for spares 1979; remains to Wombwell Diesels Co Ltd (dealer), Wombwell for scrap 3/79.

EOD 26D (266): P Sykes (dealer), Barnsley 12/75; RI Davies & Son Ltd, Tredegar (GT) 2/76; DM Nicholls {Broad Oak Coaches}, Garway (HR) 11/76; withdrawn 2/78; Vincent Greenhous (Hereford) (dealer) 8/78; Eardington Tours Ltd {Bridgnorth Coach Co}, Eardington (SH) by 12/78; licensed 4/79; W Hall, Rock End (ST) 4/80; Martin's Bus & Coach Sales Ltd (dealer), Middlewich for scrap 5/83.

EOD 27D (267): P Sykes (dealer), Barnsley 12/75; RI Davies & Son Ltd, Tredegar (GT) 2/76; Stonnis, Tredegar (GT) 2/77; JN Baker Ltd, Weston-Super-Mare (SO) 5/77; withdrawn 7/77; Wilkins Coaches (Cymmer) Ltd (WG) 9/77; disused by 7/82; scrapped at Pantdu 3/83.

EOD 28D (268): P Sykes (dealer), Barnsley 12/75; RI Davies & Son Ltd, Tredegar (GT) 3/76; Stonnis, Tredegar (GT) 2/77; JN Baker Ltd, Weston-Super-Mare (SO) 5/77; withdrawn 7/77; CE Smith, Ingham (LI) 12/78; withdrawn 4/80.

EOD 29D (269): P Sykes (dealer), Barnsley 12/75; RI Davies & Son Ltd, Tredegar (GT) 2/76; Stonnis, Tredegar (GT) 2/77; Wilkins Coaches (Cymmer) Ltd, Cymmer (WG) 9/77; withdrawn 1982.

EOD 30D (270): P Sykes (dealer), Barnsley 12/75; RI Davies & Son Ltd, Tredegar (GT) 2/76; Stonnis, Tredegar (GT) 2/77; Wilkins Coaches (Cymmer) Ltd, Cymmer (WG) 9/77; withdrawn 1982.

EOD 31D (271): P Sykes (dealer), Barnsley 2/76; RI Davies & Son Ltd, Tredegar (GT) 3/76; WA & J Howells Ltd, Ynysddu (GT) 5/76; licensed 8/76; A Ward {Webster's Coaches}, Hognaston (DE) 16 4/77; Barraclough (dealer), Carlton 11/79.

HOD 32E (272): Midland Red Omnibus Co Ltd (as dealer), Birmingham (WM) 4/76; Paul Sykes Organisation Ltd (dealer), Barnsley 4/76; Doagh Flaxing and Spinning Co Ltd, Doagh (XAM) 6/76; sold for scrap by 6/84.

HOD 33E (273): Midland Red Omnibus Co Ltd (as dealer), Birmingham (WM) 4/76; Paul Sykes Organisation Ltd (dealer), Barnsley 4/76; Morlais Services Ltd, Merthyr Tydfil (MG) 6/76; withdrawn 4/78; Mrs IFK Tanner & M Allpress, Sibford Gower (OX) 8/78; withdrawn 11/80; J Sykes (dealer), Carlton 10/83; Diamond Drum Majorettes, Royston (XSY) 1984; J Sykes (dealer), Carlton for scrap 9/85.

HOD 34E (274): Midland Red Omnibus Co Ltd (as dealer), Birmingham (WM) 4/76; Paul Sykes Organisation Ltd (dealer), Barnsley 4/76; A Simpson, Keswick (CA) 5/76; Moseley (dealer), Durham 6/78; hired to Gardiner Brothers, Spennymoor (DM) 6/78; withdrawn late 1978; S & N Motors Ltd (dealer), Bishopbriggs 8/79; J Cosgrove {Tay Valley Coaches}, Invergowrie (TE) 10/79; unidentified private owner, Dundee 11/79; Thompson (dealer), Carnoustie by 5/81.

HOD 35E (275): Midland Red Omnibus Co Ltd (as dealer), Birmingham (WM) 4/76; Paul Sykes Organisation Ltd (dealer), Barnsley 4/76; W Irvine, Law (SC) 5/76; Paul Sykes Organisation Ltd (dealer), Barnsley 10/76; Askin (dealer), Barnsley for scrap 4/78.

HOD 36E (276): Midland Red Omnibus Co Ltd (as dealer), Birmingham (WM) 4/76; Paul Sykes Organisation Ltd (dealer), Barnsley 4/76; Morlais Services Ltd, Merthyr Tydfil (MG) 6/76; withdrawn 4/78; Harris Coaches (Pengam) Ltd, Fleur-de-Lys (SG) 4/78; although licensed it was not operated by Harris and the purchase was not completed, the vehicle returning to Morlais 5/78; Mrs IFK Tanner & M Allpress, Sibford Gower (OX) 8/78; withdrawn 9/79; re-instated by Tanner, Sibford Gower (OX) 4/80; Kiss of Life public house, Wath (XNY) by 11/83; Jones (dealer), Carlton by 12/84.

HOD 37E (277): In use as a seat store by Greenslades by 4/76; GE Haywood {George's Coaches}, Coventry (WM) 6/76; withdrawn 10/76; Paul Sykes Organisation Ltd (dealer), Barnsley 11/76; TH, E & EB Jones {TH Jones & Son / Caelloi Holidays}, Pwllheli (GD) 9/78; withdrawn 9/80; Ripley (dealer), Carlton by 3/84.

HOD 38E (278): Midland Red Omnibus Co Ltd (as dealer), Birmingham (WM) 4/76; Paul Sykes Organisation Ltd (dealer), Barnsley 4/76; W Irvine, Law (SC) 5/76; Worldwide Coaches (Scotland) Ltd, Lanark (SC) 6/76; JS Whiteford {Nationwide Coaches}, Lanark (SC) 3/78; not operated; still owned 1981; sold (for scrap?) by 1993.

HOD 39E (279): Midland Red Omnibus Co Ltd (as dealer), Birmingham (WM) 4/76; Paul Sykes Organisation Ltd (dealer), Barnsley 4/76; James Gibson & Sons {Gibson's Motor Service}, Moffat (DG) 5/76; withdrawn after an accident 1/77; IE Thomas, West Ewell (SR) 1978; chassis rebuilt and given new chassis number ETS1078 10/78; rebodied Plaxton C53F (7911AC018S) and re-registered CPM 520T 6/79; Workforce (dealer), London E1 4/87; Zarb, Birkirkara (O-M) 4/87; re-registered Y 0883 by 10/88; re-registered JCY 883 c1996.

JTA 763E (483): Dawlish Coaches Ltd {Tomlinson's}, Dawlish (DN) 11/74; Waverley Coaches Ltd, St Brelade, Jersey (CI) 3 re-registered J 29255 3/76; PJ Powell, St Helier, Jersey (CI) 4/89; Wacton Trading / Coach Sales (dealer), Bromyard for scrap 7/94.

JTA 764E (484): A & AR Turner, Chulmleigh (DN) 1/75; Wacton Trading / Coach Sales (dealer), Bromyard for scrap 1/85.

JTA 765E (485): A & AR Turner, Chulmleigh (DN) 1/75; withdrawn 1/85; re-instated by 10/85; Moseley (dealer), Taunton by 8/86; JW Pugsley {Blue Embassy Coaches}, Atherington (DN) by 10/86; P Stark, A Harris & T Doe {Country Bus Service}, Atherington (DN) 6/88; Wacton Trading / Coach Sales (dealer), Bromyard 8/88.

CXF 256G (386): DC Venner {Scarlet Coaches}, Minehead (SO) 8/76; not operated; BJ Redwood {Redwood Services}, Hemyock (DN) 11/76; A & R Millman, Buckfastleigh (DN) 1/80; withdrawn 7/80; BJD Whitehead {Flashes Coaches}, Newent (GL) 2/81; Wacton Trading / Coach Sales (dealer), Bromyard 3/82; Executors of AO Sherrin, Carhampton (SO) 4/82; Autojade Ltd {Exe Line}, Tiverton (DN) by 6/84.

CXF 257G (387): Mascot Motors Ltd, St Helier, Jersey (CI) 25 re-registered J 51937 7/76; Waverley Coaches Ltd, St Brelade, Jersey (CI) 4 c1983; renumbered 13 by 11/91; renumbered 19 by 5/98; withdrawn 4/04; Glen Hamel, St Clement, Jersey (XCI) as farm bus 2007; Amazin Adventure Park, St Peter, Jersey as static children's party bus by 1/10; P Talbot {Jersey Bus Tours}, St Helier, Jersey (CI) c1/13; not operated; M Wyles, Hinckley for preservation 4/13.

RFJ 828H (199): National Travel (South West) Ltd (GL) 199 6/77; withdrawn 11/77; Martin's Bus & Coach Sales Ltd (dealer), Middlewich 2/78; Smith of Rainhill Ltd, Rainhill (MY) 2/78; withdrawn 8/78.

Numbering Scheme 1971

This was drawn up in May 1971 and put into effect from June 1971. Metal fleet number plates, painted black with polished metal numerals, were used until March 1974; by which date all existing vehicles, except 429, 431-432, 467, 484, 486 and 492 had been numbered. From March 1974 standard NBC style number transfers in silver grey were used on all new and acquired vehicles.

Fleet Numbers	Registration Numbers	Fleet Numbers	Registration Numbers
300-304	UFJ 229-233J	441	974 FFJ
305-309	UUO 450-454J	442-451	AFJ 77-86B
396-401	554-559 AFJ	452-457	CFJ 894-899C
402	670 COD	458-463	FFJ 10-15D
403-405	540-542 CFJ	464-471	EOD 24-31D
406-411	937-942 GTA	472-479	HOD 32-39E
412-414	YRC 43, 44, 46	480-482	HFJ 416-418E
415-421	567-573 EFJ	483-485	JTA 763-765E
422-430	960-968 HTT	486-487	CXF 256-257G
431-438	1-8 RDV	490-494	NFJ 619-623G
439-440	175-176 GFJ	495-499	RFJ 824-828H

Vehicles acquired from Western Welsh Omnibus Co Ltd, Cardiff (GG) 10/71

390	ABO 144B	AEC Reliance	2MU3RA5069	Harrington	2903	C40F	2/64	-/73
391	ABO 145B	AEC Reliance	2MU3RA5070	Harrington	2904	C40F	2/64	-/73
392	ABO 146B	AEC Reliance	2MU3RA5071	Harrington	2905	C40F	2/64	-/73
393	ABO 147B	AEC Reliance	2MU3RA5072	Harrington	2906	C40F	3/64	-/73
394	ABO 147B	AEC Reliance	2MU3RA5073	Harrington	2907	C40F	3/64	-/73
395	ABO 147B	AEC Reliance	2MU3RA5074	Harrington	2908	C40F	3/64	-/73

Previous History:
ABO 144B (390): New to Western Welsh 144 as C36F; re-seated to C38F, then C40F acquired via Western National Omnibus Co, as dealer.
ABO 145B (391): New to Western Welsh 145 as C36F; re-seated to C38F, then C40F acquired via Western National Omnibus Co, as dealer.
ABO 146B (392): New to Western Welsh 146 as C36F; re-seated to C38F, then C40F acquired via Western National Omnibus Co, as dealer.

ABO 147B (393): New to Western Welsh 147 as C36F; re-seated to C38F, then C40F acquired via Western National Omnibus Co, as dealer.
ABO 148B (394): New to Western Welsh 148 as C36F; re-seated to C38F, then C40F acquired via Western National Omnibus Co, as dealer.
ABO 149B (395): New to Western Welsh 149 as C36F; re-seated to C38F, then C40F acquired via Western National Omnibus Co, as dealer.

Notes:
ABO 146B (392): Fleet number never carried.
ABO 149B (395): Fleet number never carried.

Disposals:
ABO 144B (390): RK & RE Webber {Webber Brothers}, Blisland (CO) 4/74; Dawlish Coaches Ltd {Tomlinson's}, Dawlish (DN) 6/77; withdrawn 1/81; rebodied Duple C45F (242/5725) (7ft 6in wide) and re-registered WDV 505X 4/82; Loverings (Combe Martin) Ltd, Combe Martin (DN) 5/86; DJ Isaac {Dene Valley Coaches}, Barnstaple (DN) 4/89; E Crabtree {EMC Tours & Travel}, Bradford (WY) 5/91; R Kirk & J Shufflebotham, Liversedge (WY) by 11/91; HG Kinsman & Son Ltd, Bodmin (CO) 4/92; entered service 6/92.
ABO 145B (391): Sadler, New Waltham (LI) 11/73; W Hall, Rock End (ST) 7/75; W Hall Junior, Rock End (ST) 3/85; W Hall Junior & Mrs A Hall, Rock End (ST) 10/85; withdrawn c1986; Morris, Hook (XHA) by 6/86; B Catchpole, Halling for preservation by 11/87; re-seated to C36F by 6/91; P Willson, Sidcup for preservation 5/03; sold to an unknown buyer for preservation 5/11.
ABO 146B: FJ & JA Fry {Fry's Tours}, Tintagel (CO) 4/74; West of England Transport Collection (as dealer), Winkleigh 10/84; T Wigley (dealer), Carlton for scrap 1/85.
ABO 147B (393): RK & RE Webber {Webber Brothers}, Blisland (CO) 10/73; MK Rowe, Dobwalls (CO) 6/76 withdrawn 7/78; Willis (Central Garage) Ltd, Bodmin (CO) for spares 9/78; repainted in 1981; noted derelict in yard 9/82; Mitchell's (Perranporth) Ltd, Perranporth (CO) for preservation by 10/86; returned to Willis, Bodmin (CO) 12/87; B Catchpole, Halling for preservation 9/90; R & C Gibbons, Maidstone for preservation 11/91; W Smith, Cwmbran for preservation by 5/97; C Jones, Chepstow for preservation by 8/12.
ABO 148B (394): FR Piper, Scarborough (NY) 2/75; TW Campling, Filey (EY) 3/76; unidentified owner, Northern Ireland by 7/78.
ABO 149B: RK & RE Webber {Webber Brothers}, Blisland (CO) 10/73; Street's Coachways Ltd, Bickington (DN) 11/78; RK & RE Webber {Webber Brothers}, Blisland (CO) 4/79; Okeridge Motor Services Ltd, Okehampton (DN) 1/80; withdrawn 4/80; re-instated by 8/82; T Wigley (dealer), Carlton 9/83.

1972

Vehicles acquired from Western Welsh Omnibus Co Ltd, Cardiff (GG) 1/72

| 406 | YTX 322H | Leyland PSU3A/4R | 7001906 | Plaxton | 709108 | C49F | 7/70 | -/74 |
| 407 | YTX 323H | Leyland PSU3A/4R | 7002030 | Plaxton | 709109 | C49F | 7/70 | -/74 |

Previous History:
YTX 322H (406): New as Rhondda Transport Co Ltd, Porth (GG) 322; Western Welsh 2322 1/71; allocated new fleet number 107, but never carried; acquired via Western National Omnibus Co. and delivered to Exeter still in Rhondda livery.
YTX 323H (407): New as Rhondda Transport Co Ltd, Porth (GG) 323; Western Welsh 2323 1/71; renumbered 108 11/71; acquired via Western National Omnibus Co.

Notes:
YTX 322H (406): Licensed 2/72; repainted in NBC white coach livery 1973.
YTX 323H (407): Licensed 2/72; loaned to Bristol Omnibus Co Ltd, Bristol (GL) from 2/72 until 5/72; during which time it carried Bristol Greyhound livery; repainted in NBC white coach livery 1974.

Disposals:
YTX 322H (406): National Travel (South West) Ltd {Black and White}, Cheltenham (GL) 230 10/74; National Travel (West) Ltd, Cheltenham (GL) 8/81; withdrawn 11/82; re-instated by 7/83; withdrawn by 11/83; Transport and General Workers' Union, Birmingham (XWM) 11/83; re-seated to C41F by 12/86; still owned 5/87; Linkfast Ltd, Hadleigh (EX) by 7/89; sold by 3/95.
YTX 323H (407): National Travel (South West) Ltd {Black and White}, Cheltenham (GL) 231 10/74; National Travel (West) Ltd, Cheltenham (GL) 8/81; withdrawn 11/82; re-instated by 7/83; loaned to City of Oxford Motor Services Ltd, Oxford (OX) from 1/9/83 to at least 11/4/84; National Travel (South West) Ltd {Black and White}, Cheltenham (GL) 231 6/84; MJ Key {K & M Travel},

Worcester (HW) 9/84; re-seated to C47F 1989; Rover, Bromsgrove (HW) 4/90; Wacton Trading / Coach Sales (dealer), Bromyard (7/90?); scrapped 2/91.

1973

New Vehicles

310	BFJ 310L	Bristol RELH6L	4/557	Plaxton	733196	C46F	5/73	-/78
311	BFJ 311L	Bristol RELH6L	4/558	Plaxton	733198	C46F	5/73	-/78
312	BFJ 312L	Bristol RELH6L	4/559	Plaxton	733197	C46F	5/73	-/78
313	BFJ 313L	Bristol RELH6L	4/560	Plaxton	733199	C46F	5/73	-/78
314	BFJ 314L	Bristol RELH6L	4/561	Plaxton	733200	C46F	6/73	-/78
315	NTT 315M	AEC Reliance	6MU4R24729	Duple	277/2303	C41F	8/73	-/78

Notes:

BFJ 310-314L (310-314): Were the first vehicles delivered in NBC white coach livery and had front destination equipment similar to 300-309 of 1971.

BFJ 311L (311): Re-seated to C42F 2/77.

BFJ 312L (312): Re-seated to C38F 1/77; to C42F 5/78.

BFJ 313L (313): Re-seated to C42F 2/77.

BFJ 314L (314): Used by Exeter City Association Football Club as C36F for the 1974/75 season; as C32F for the 1975/76 season; re-seated to C42F 2/77.

NTT 315M (315): Ordered by A Timpson & Sons Ltd, London SE6 (LN) and had destination boxes below the windscreen. It was the last vehicle to receive a fleet number plate and was delivered in NBC white coach livery.

Disposals:

BFJ 310L (310): National Travel (South West) Ltd (GL) 510 3/78; Martin's Bus & Coach Sales Ltd (dealer), Middlewich 1980; PG Travel Ltd, Middlewich (CH) as C53F 9/80; J Boyd, Glasgow (SW) 11/82; sold by 5/86; G & D Walker {Tower Bus Co}, Wigton (CA) by 10/86; R & CA Daglish, Kirkland (CA) by 1/90; sold by 1/93.

BFJ 311L (311): National Travel (South West) Ltd (GL) 511 3/78; Martin's Bus & Coach Sales Ltd (dealer), Middlewich 1980; Bryn Alyn Communities Ltd, Cefn-y-Bedd (CL) 6/80; AS Simpson Junior {Alyn Coaches}, Buckley (CL) 6/84; still owned 7/87; unknown (dealer), Barnsley by 12/90.

BFJ 312L (312): National Travel (South West) Ltd (GL) 312 3/78; licensed 7/78; Martin's Bus & Coach Sales Ltd (dealer), Middlewich 1980; Holmeswood Coaches Ltd, Holmeswood (LA) as C41F 7/80; sold by 4/92.

BFJ 313L (313): National Travel (South West) Ltd (GL) 313 3/78; Martin's Bus & Coach Sales Ltd (dealer), Middlewich 1980; Mrs A Wild {A Ball & Son / Eagle Coaches}, Bristol (GL) 12/80; re-registered 671 XYA by 9/84; Nu-Venture Coaches Ltd, Aylesford (KT) by 11/85; JN McEwen, Amisfield (DG) 5/87; AG Dickson, Dumfries (DG) by 4/88; returned to JM McEwen, Amisfield (DG) by 6/89; JS Sturrock, Methilhill (FE) 7/89; re-registered GHH 31L 7/89; M Spencer, Leven (FE) by 2/91; unidentified dealer by 12/93.

BFJ 314L (314): National Travel (South West) Ltd (GL) 314 3/78; Martin's Bus & Coach Sales Ltd (dealer), Middlewich 1980; PG Travel Ltd, Middlewich (CH) as C53F 5/80; ME Taylor {Westerbus}, Badbea (HI) by 5/81; Mackenzie and MacLennan {Westerbus}, Gairloch (HI) 1/85; Autoparts (dealer), Dundee 5/86; D Stewart, Dalmuir (SC) 12/86, not operated; Rennie's of Dunfermline Ltd, Dunfermline (FE) 1/87; licensed 7/87; sold 5/88; scrapped 7/88.

NTT 315M (315): National Travel (South West) Ltd (GL) 411 3/78, Martin's Bus & Coach Sales Ltd (dealer), Middlewich 1980; ME Taylor {Westerbus}, Badbea (HI) by 5/81; I Campbell, Linlithgow (CE) by 5/87; not operated; transferred to Campbell and Gardiner, Linlithgow (CE) 11/89; unknown owner by 8/90; scrapped by 1/04.

Vehicles acquired from Black and White Motorways Ltd, Cheltenham (GL) 10/73

396	AAD 247B	AEC Reliance	2MU4RA5152	Harrington	2892	C41F	-/64	-/74
397	AAD 248B	AEC Reliance	2MU4RA5153	Harrington	2893	C41F	-/64	-/74
398	AAD 249B	AEC Reliance	2MU4RA5154	Harrington	2894	C41F	-/64	-/74
399	AAD 250B	AEC Reliance	2MU4RA5155	Harrington	2895	C41F	-/64	-/74
400	AAD 251B	AEC Reliance	2MU4RA5156	Harrington	2896	C41F	-/64	-/74

Previous History:

AAD 247-251B (396-400): New as Black and White A247-251.

Notes:
    AAD 247-251B (396-400): Licensed by Greenslades 4/74.

Disposals:
    AAD 247B (396): Blackbrooker (dealer), London SE11 12/74; FJ & JA Fry {Fry's Tours}, Tintagel (CO) 1/75; West of England Transport Collection (as dealer), Winkleigh 10/84; Wigley (dealer), Carlton 10/84.
    AAD 248B (397): Blackbrooker (dealer), London SE11 12/74; Gourd's Coaches (Bishopsteignton) Ltd {Gourd's of Devon}, Newton Abbot (DN) 12/74; becoming Devonways Travel Ltd, Newton Abbot (DN) 6/75; Edwards Coaches Ltd, Joy's Green (GL) 11/76; Dean Forest Coaches Ltd, Joy's Green (GL) 2/82; Wacton Trading / Coach Sales (dealer), Bromyard 4/82; Hollybush Royal Tartanaires Jazz Band, Cwmbran (XGT) 4/82; Hollybush Royal Imperials Jazz Band, Cwmbran (XGT) 5/83; Wacton Trading / Coach Sales (dealer), Bromyard 3/84; AJS Salvage Co Ltd (dealer), Carlton for scrap 3/84.
    AAD 249B (398): Blackbrooker (dealer), London SE11 12/74; Gourd's Coaches (Bishopsteignton) Ltd {Gourd's of Devon}, Newton Abbot (DN) 12/74; becoming Devonways Travel Ltd, Newton Abbot (DN) 6/75; withdrawn 6/77; Air Training Corps (2443 Squadron), Okehampton (XDN) 6/77; unidentified pop group, Preston as a caravan by 4/83; P Lloyd (dealer), Cundy Cross for scrap 2/84.
    AAD 250B (399): Blackbrooker (dealer), London SE11 12/74; Gourd's Coaches (Bishopsteignton) Ltd {Gourd's of Devon}, Newton Abbot (DN) 12/74; becoming Devonways Travel Ltd, Newton Abbot (DN) 6/75; Edwards Coaches Ltd, Joy's Green (GL) 3/77; Dean Forest Coaches Ltd, Joy's Green (GL) 2/82; Blackett (dealer), Butterknowle 12/83.
    AAD 251B (400): Blackbrooker (dealer), London SE11 12/74; Gourd's Coaches (Bishopsteignton) Ltd {Gourd's of Devon}, Newton Abbot (DN) 5/75; not operated; scrapped by 7/82.

1974

New Vehicles

360	OOD 360M	Bedford YRT	DW450941	Duple	417/3066	C53F	4/74	-/78
361	OOD 361M	Bedford YRT	DW450944	Duple	417/3067	C53F	4/74	-/78
362	OOD 362M	Bedford YRT	DW452433	Duple	417/3068	C53F	5/74	-/78
363	OOD 363M	Bedford YRT	DW452429	Duple	417/3069	C53F	5/74	-/78
364	OOD 364M	Bedford YRT	DW452431	Duple	417/3070	C53F	5/74	-/78
365	OOD 365M	Bedford YRT	DW452425	Duple	417/3071	C53F	5/74	-/78
366	OOD 366M	Bedford YRT	DW452434	Duple	417/3072	C53F	5/74	-/78
367	OOD 367M	Bedford YRT	DW452460	Duple	417/3073	C53F	5/74	-/78
351	PFJ 351M	Bedford VAS5	DW451223	Duple	411/1001	C29F	6/74	-/78
352	PFJ 352M	Bedford VAS5	DW451228	Duple	411/1002	C29F	6/74	-/78

Notes:
These vehicles were delivered in NBC white coach livery, as were all subsequent additions to the fleet.

PFJ 351-352M (351-352): Were 7ft 6in wide.

Disposals:
    OOD 360M (360): Western National Omnibus Co Ltd, Exeter (DN) 2200 4/78; licensed 5/78; Southern Vectis Omnibus Co Ltd, Newport (IW) 400 3/80; withdrawn by 9/82; Ensign Bus Co Ltd (dealer), Purfleet 11/82; Shaw's Coaches Ltd, Barnsley (SY) 2/83; Drapeweb Ltd {Terry Shaw's Coaches}, Barnsley (SY) by 10/85; withdrawn 1986.
    OOD 361M (361): Western National Omnibus Co Ltd, Exeter (DN) 2201 4/78; licensed 5/78; Southern Vectis Omnibus Co Ltd, Newport (IW) 401 3/80; withdrawn by 6/83; converted to publicity and exhibition vehicle PC1 for Isle of Wight Tourist Board 6/83; to service 11/83; still owned by Southern Vectis; Hinsley, Trevallyn Hotel, Sandown (XIW) as an exhibition vehicle 9/87; sold upon closure of the hotel 1991; MJ Wellington, Sandown (XIW) by 5/91; withdrawn 10/91; People Seekers, Hornchurch (XLN) 1/92; Wacton Trading/Coach Sales (dealer), Bromyard by 5/96.
    OOD 362M (362): Western National Omnibus Co Ltd, Exeter (DN) 2202 4/78; licensed 5/78; Southern Vectis Omnibus Co Ltd, Newport (IW) 402 3/80; withdrawn by 9/82; Ensign Bus Co Ltd (dealer), Purfleet 11/82; Avon Coaches Ltd, Romford (LN) 3/83; withdrawn 9/85; disused on premises 1/87.
    OOD 363M (363): Western National Omnibus Co Ltd, Exeter (DN) 2203 4/78; licensed 5/78; Southern Vectis Omnibus Co Ltd, Newport (IW) 404 3/80; WH Colbourne & RJ Pulham {Town & Country

Coaches}, Newton Abbot (DN) re-registered 697 UYD 11/87; entered service 12/87; unknown owner, Paignton as a mobile home by 4/94.

OOD 364M (364): Western National Omnibus Co Ltd, Exeter (DN) 2204 4/78; licensed 5/78; Southern Vectis Omnibus Co Ltd, Newport (IW) 404 3/80; WH Colbourne & RJ Pulham {Town & Country Coaches}, Newton Abbot (DN) re-registered 627 UYB 11/87; entered service 12/87; DJ Fletcher {B & D Travel}, Offerton (GM) 10/89; PSV Products (dealer), Ardwick re-registered CNB 354M 12/91; Manchester Minibus Ltd {Bee Line Buzz Co}, Stockport (GM) as an ancillary vehicle 12/91; Midland Red (North) Ltd (ST) TV54 as a driver trainer 5/93; Passenger Vehicle Spares (Barnsley) Ltd (dealer), Carlton for scrap 4/95.

OOD 365M (365): Western National Omnibus Co Ltd, Exeter (DN) 2205 4/78; licensed 5/78; Southern Vectis Omnibus Co Ltd, Newport (IW) 405 3/80; withdrawn by 9/82; Ensign Bus Co Ltd (dealer), Purfleet 11/82; Shaw's Coaches Ltd, Barnsley (SY) 3/83; Drapeweb Ltd {Terry Shaw's Coaches}, Barnsley (SY) by 10/85; withdrawn 1986.

OOD 366M (366): Western National Omnibus Co Ltd, Exeter (DN) 2206 4/78; licensed 5/78; Southern Vectis Omnibus Co Ltd, Newport (IW) 116 3/80; Shamrock and Rambler Coaches Ltd, Bournemouth (DT) 3121 5/85; re-registered 649 TAE 6/85, allocated fleet number 3149, but not carried; Tourist Coachways Ltd, London SW14 (LN) 6/86, licensed 7/87; sold 12/92.

OOD 367M (367): Western National Omnibus Co Ltd, Exeter (DN) 2207 4/78; licensed 5/78; Southern Vectis Omnibus Co Ltd, Newport (IW) 117 3/80; withdrawn 9/83; loaned to Shamrock and Rambler Coaches Ltd, Bournemouth (DT) 9/83; purchased 5/84; numbered 3122 6/84; named "Bluebell" c1/85; renumbered 3126 6/85; withdrawn 7/85; LPC (dealer), Hounslow by 5/86; RD Woollon, Cranford (LN) 8/86; re-registered YSV 598 10/86; Dunstan & Bruckshaw, Davenport (GM) 98 8/88; Walker (dealer), Audenshaw 1/90; Norwest Holst (contractor) by 4/92; ADT Auctions (dealer), Manchester 4/92; Eastern Health and Social Services Board (XNI) re-registered XXI 4976 by 12/93; North and West Belfast Health and Social Services Trust (XNI) 4/94; sold to unknown buyer at auction 6/96.

PFJ 351M (351): Western National Omnibus Co Ltd, Exeter (DN) 1249 4/78; licensed 5/78; withdrawn 1/80; JK & KN Wilby, Hibaldstow (LI) 8/80; Arlington Motor Co Ltd (dealer), Potters Bar 7/83; Wacton Trading / Coach Sales (dealer), Bromyard 8/83; Wiltshire County Council (Lackham College), Laycock (XWI) 8/83; Educational Holidays Guernsey Ltd {Island Coachways}, St Peter Port, Guernsey (CI) re-registered 3989 2/90; to service 3/90; G Blacker {Needabus}, Pitsea (EX) reverting to original registration PFJ 351M 11/92; named "Carol Anne" by 5/93; GH Brailey, Canvey Island (EX) 12/94; sold by 4/99.

PFJ 352M (352): National Travel (South West) Ltd (H) 352 3/78; Martin's Bus & Coaches Sales Ltd (dealer), Weaverham 1978; G Lightfoot {GL Travel}, Winsford (CH) 7/78; A Farrugia {Fargo Transport}, Bracknell (BE) 6/84; EC Hanks {Eddie's}, Mablethorpe (LI) 6/87; Wacton Trading / Coach Sales (dealer), Bromyard 4/90; Clarendon Coaches Ltd, St Helier, Jersey (CI) 4/90; not operated; returned to Wacton Trading / Coach Sales (dealer), Bromyard 6/90; MJ Perry, Bromyard (HR) 1/91; Northwick, Worcester (XWO) 5/91; KC Shorthouse {KCS Coaches}, Droitwich (WO) by 9/92.

Vehicle acquired from DC Venner {Scarlet Coaches}, Minehead (SO) 3/74

| 316 | AAX 259J | Bristol LHL6L | LHL-181 | Plaxton | 713367 | C53F | -/71 | -/77 |

Previous History:
AAX 259J (316): New to CG Hill & Sons Ltd, Tredegar (MH); from whom it was acquired 3/73.

Notes:
AAX 259J (316): Had the distinction of being the only Bristol LHL in any NBC fleet.

Disposals:
AAX 259J (316): Devonways Travel Ltd, Newton Abbot (DN) 11/77; becoming Devonways Travel (1982) Ltd, Kingskerswell (DN) by 1/83; Davies, Chilton Trinity (XSO) by 11/83; Wacton Trading / Coach Sales (dealer), Bromyard 1/85.

Vehicle acquired from National Travel (South West) Ltd, Cheltenham (GL) 10/74

| 330 | ADG 330K | Bristol RELH6G | 4/359 | Plaxton | 723899 | C47F | 2/72 | -/78 |

Previous History:
ADG 330K (330): New as Black and White Motorways Ltd, Cheltenham (GL) 330; from whom it was acquired as fleet number 330 2/74; but had originally been ordered by Western National Omnibus Co Ltd, Exeter (DN).

Disposal:
    ADG 330K (330): National Travel (South West) Ltd (GL) 330 3/78; allocated fleet number 493 but retained fleet number 330; Paul Sykes Organisation Ltd (dealer), Barnsley 1982; North West Coachlines, Kirkham (LA) 5/82; withdrawn 3/83; F Armstrong {AC Coaches}, Linlithgow (CE) 5/83; Tony Andrews (PSV Sales) (dealer), Stair 12/83; Queen City Ltd {Burford Travel}, Burford (OX) 9/84; HPJ Miller {Arun Coaches}, Horsham (WS) by 9/85; re-registered ARU 99A by 3/88; re-registered NRX 149K by 8/89; sold by 9/90; AL, J, CP & JI Bailey {Axe Valley Coaches}, Biddisham (SO) by 5/91, not operated; scrapped by 8/92.

Vehicles acquired from National Travel (South West) Ltd, Cheltenham (GL) 10/74

331	ADG 331K	Bristol RELH6G	4/353	Plaxton	723900	C47F	5/72	-/78
332	ADG 332K	Bristol RELH6G	4/361	Plaxton	723901	C47F	5/72	-/78

Previous History:
    ADG 331-332K (331-332): New as Black and White Motorways Ltd, Cheltenham (GL) 331-332; from whom they were acquired as fleet numbers 331-332 in 2/74; had originally been ordered by Western National Omnibus Co Ltd, Exeter (DN).

Disposal:
    ADG 331K (331): National Travel (South West) Ltd (GL) 331 3/78; allocated fleet number 494 but retained fleet number 331; JL Elliott {T Robinson}, Appleby (CA) 10/79; A Wills and Co Ltd, Uppingham (XRD) 7/81; sold 6/86; Vanguard Coaches Ltd, Bulkington (WK) for spares 2/87; unidentified dealer, Woolston for scrap 3/87; body scrapped, chassis returned to Vanguard 3/87 for spares, and broken up by them 11/87.

    ADG 332K (332): National Travel (South West) Ltd (GL) 332 3/78; allocated fleet number 495 but retained fleet number 332; A Ward {Webster's Coaches}, Hognaston (DE) 6/80; GR Clements {North Somerset Coaches}, Nailsea 19 (SO) 4/82; GO Mace, Cheltenham (GL) 3/83; Queen City {Burford Travel}, Burford (OX) 7/84; Wealden Omnibuses (dealer), Nettlestead by 3/85.

1975

Renumbering Scheme 1975

In January 1975 the fleet was renumbered as part of the National Travel (South West) Ltd fleet. Greenslades vehicles were allocated number 250-399, although some vehicles never actually carried these numbers (see notes).

New Numbers	Old Numbers	Registration Numbers
250-251	450-451	AFJ 85-86B
252-257	452-457	CFJ 894-899C
258-263	458-463	FFJ 10-15D
264-271	464-471	EOD 24-31D
272-279	472-479	HOD 32-39E
280-282	480-482	HFJ 416-418E
283-290	442-449	AFJ 77-84B
291-298	432-438	1-8 RDV
300-304	No change	UFJ 229-233J
305-309	No change	UUO 450-454J
310-314	No change	BFJ 310-314L
315	No change	NTT 315M
316	No change	AAX 259J
330-332	No change	ADG 330-332K
351-352	No change	PFJ 351-352M
360-367	No change	OOD 360-367M
386-387	486-487	CXF 256-257G
390-394	490-494	NFJ 619-623G
395-399	495-499	RFJ 824-828H

New Vehicles:

317	JFJ 497N	Bristol LH6L	LH-1060	Plaxton	7510BC007S	C45F	6/75	-/78
318	JFJ 498N	Bristol LH6L	LH-1063	Plaxton	7510BC008S	C45F	7/75	-/78
319	JFJ 499N	Bristol LH6L	LH-1064	Plaxton	7510BC009S	C45F	7/75	-/78
320	JFJ 500N	Bristol LH6L	LH-1068	Plaxton	7510BC010S	C45F	7/75	-/78
321	JFJ 501N	Bristol LH6L	LH-1069	Plaxton	7510BC011S	C45F	7/75	-/78

322	JFJ 502N	Bristol LH6L		LH-1114	Plaxton	7510BC012S	C45F	7/75	-/78
323	JFJ 503N	Bristol LH6L		LH-1115	Plaxton	7510BC013S	C45F	7/75	-/78
324	JFJ 504N	Bristol LH6L		LH-1116	Plaxton	7510BC014S	C45F	8/75	-/78
325	JFJ 505N	Bristol LH6L		LH-1117	Plaxton	7510BC015S	C45F	8/75	-/78
326	JFJ 506N	Bristol LH6L		LH-1119	Plaxton	7510BC016S	C45F	7/75	-/78
327	JFJ 507N	Bristol LH6L		LH-1120	Plaxton	7510BC017S	C45F	7/75	-/78
328	JFJ 508N	Bristol LH6L		LH-1121	Plaxton	7510BC018S	C45F	8/75	-/78

Notes:
These vehicles were the first Plaxton bodied Bristol LH6L vehicles to be built to a width of 7ft 6in.

Disposals:
JFJ 497N (317): Western National Omnibus Co Ltd, Exeter (DN) 1332 4/78; licensed 5/78; Western National Ltd, Truro (CO) 1332 1/83; Guernseybus, St Peter Port, Guernsey (CI) 158 re-registered 31908 9/93; States of Guernsey and leased to Educational Holidays Guernsey Ltd {Island Coachways}, St Peter Port, Guernsey (CI) 158 11/00; C Billington (dealer/preservationist), Maidenhead 3/01; stored at Fifield; Rexquote {Quantock Motor Services}, Bishops Lydeard (SO) 11/01; not operated; used for spares from 12/02; sold for scrap 12/02.

JFJ 498N (318): Western National Omnibus Co Ltd, Exeter (DN) 1333 4/78; licensed 5/78; Western National Ltd, Truro (CO) 1333 1/83; Guernseybus, St Peter Port, Guernsey (CI) 159 re-registered 31909 5/92; States of Guernsey and leased to Educational Holidays Guernsey Ltd {Island Coachways}, St Peter Port, Guernsey (CI) 157 11/00; C Billington (dealer/preservationist), Maidenhead 3/01; stored at Winkleigh; Exeter LH Group for preservation 10/01; Partridge, Saltash as spares for preservation project 9/05; T Wigley & Son (Bus) Ltd (dealer), Carlton for scrap 4/06.

JFJ 499N (319): Western National Omnibus Co Ltd, Exeter (DN) 1334 4/78; licensed 5/78; North Devon Ltd {Red Bus}, Barnstaple (DN) 1334 1/83; Guernseybus, St Peter Port, Guernsey (CI) 166 re-registered 31906 3/85; entered service 5/85; re-registered 31916 and re-seated to C45F 7/90; States of Guernsey and leased to Educational Holidays Guernsey Ltd {Island Coachways}, St Peter Port, Guernsey (CI) 166 11/00; C Billington (dealer/preservationist), Maidenhead 3/01.

JFJ 500N (320): Western National Omnibus Co Ltd, Exeter (DN) 1335 4/78; licensed 5/78; North Devon Ltd {Red Bus}, Barnstaple (DN) 1335 1/83; Guernseybus, St Peter Port, Guernsey (CI) 167 3/85; re-registered 31918; entered service 4/85; re-registered 31917 7/90; States of Guernsey and leased to Educational Holidays Guernsey Ltd {Island Coachways}, St Peter Port, Guernsey (CI) 167 11/00; C Billington (dealer/preservationist), Maidenhead 3/01; stored at Fifield; Rexquote {Quantock Motor Services}, Bishops Lydeard (SO) 11/01; not operated; C Shears, Winkleigh for preservation 12/02; T Partridge, Saltash for preservation 9/05; T Wigley & Son (Bus) Ltd (dealer), Carlton by 10/07.

JFJ 501N (321): Western National Omnibus Co Ltd, Exeter (DN) 1336 4/78; licensed 5/78; Devon General Ltd, Exeter (DN) 336 1/83; Guernseybus, St Peter Port, Guernsey (CI) 168 3/85, re-registered 31919; entered service 6/85; re-registered 31918 and re-seated to C45F 7/90; States of Guernsey and leased to Educational Holidays Guernsey Ltd {Island Coachways}, St Peter Port, Guernsey (CI) 168 11/00; C Billington (dealer/preservationist), Maidenhead 3/01; stored at Fifield; Rexquote {Quantock Motor Services}, Bishops Lydeard (SO) 11/01, not operated; unknown private owner, Semington, Somerset by 11/02.

JFJ 502N (322): Western National Omnibus Co Ltd, Exeter (DN) 1337 4/78; licensed 5/78; Devon General Ltd, Exeter (DN) 337 1/83; Guernseybus, St Peter Port, Guernsey (CI) 169 3/85, re-registered 31907; entered service 7/85; re-registered 31919 7/90; States of Guernsey and leased to Educational Holidays Guernsey Ltd {Island Coachways}, St Peter Port, Guernsey (CI) 169 11/00; Billington (dealer/preservationist), Maidenhead 3/01; Mrs B Cainey {Mike's Travel}, Thornbury (GL) 4/01; allocated fleet number 19, but not carried; not operated; T Ward, Woodside, Gloucestershire for preservation 9/09.

JFJ 503N (323): National Travel (South West) Ltd (GL) 323 6/78; Western National Omnibus Co Ltd, Exeter (DN) 323 5/81; Devon General Ltd, Exeter (DN) 323 1/83; Guernseybus, St Peter Port, Guernsey (CI) 160 re-registered 31910 2/85; entered service 4/85; scrapped by 12/99.

JFJ 504N (324): National Travel (South West) Ltd (GL) 324 7/78; Western National Omnibus Co Ltd, Exeter (DN) 324 5/81; Devon General Ltd, Exeter (DN) 324 1/83; withdrawn 9/84; Guernseybus, St Peter Port, Guernsey (CI) 161 re-registered 31911 2/85; entered service 4/85; States of Guernsey and leased to Educational Holidays Guernsey Ltd {Island Coachways}, St Peter Port, Guernsey (CI) 161 11/00; C Billington (dealer/preservationist), Maidenhead 3/01; stored at Winkleigh; reverted to original registration by 9/03; J Pratt, Exeter for preservation by 9/04; T Partridge, Saltash for preservation 3/05; Woods (dealer), Crediton for scrap 9/05.

JFJ 505N (325): National Travel (South West) Ltd (GL) 325 7/78; Western National Omnibus Co Ltd, Exeter (DN) 325 5/81; Devon General Ltd, Exeter (DN) 325 1/83; Guernseybus, St Peter Port,

Guernsey (CI) 162 re-registered 31912 2/85; entered service 4/85; States of Guernsey and leased to Educational Holidays Guernsey Ltd {Island Coachways}, St Peter Port, Guernsey (CI) 162 11/00; C Billington (dealer/preservationist), Maidenhead 3/01; stored at Fifield; reverted to original registration JFJ 505N with unidentified owner, Birmingham for preservation by 6/02; unidentified owner for conversion to exhibition unit, Weymouth by 10/03; unidentified owner at unknown location 6/05.

JFJ 506N (326): National Travel (South West) Ltd (GL) 326 6/78; Western National Omnibus Co Ltd, Exeter (DN) 326 5/81; Devon General Ltd, Exeter (DN) 326 1/83; Guernseybus, St Peter Port, Guernsey (CI) 163 re-registered 31913 3/85; entered service 4/85; States of Guernsey and leased to Educational Holidays Guernsey Ltd {Island Coachways}, St Peter Port, Guernsey (CI) 163 11/00; C Billington (dealer/preservationist), Maidenhead 3/01; Chelveston Preservation Group 4/01; B Heginbotham, Irthlingborough for preservation by 12/01; reverted to original registration JFJ 506N by 12/01; B Smith, Kettering for preservation by 1/11.

JFJ 507N (327): National Travel (South West) Ltd (GL) 327 6/78; Western National Omnibus Co Ltd, Exeter (DN) 327 5/81; Devon General Ltd, Exeter (DN) 327 1/83; Guernseybus, St Peter Port, Guernsey (CI) 164 re-registered 12723 11/84; entered service 12/84; re-registered 31914 7/90; States of Guernsey and leased to Educational Holidays Guernsey Ltd {Island Coachways}, St Peter Port, Guernsey (CI) 164 11/00; C Billington (dealer/preservationist), Maidenhead 3/01; stored at Winkleigh; J Pratt & M Locke, Torquay for preservation and reverted to original registration JFJ 507N by 7/02; K & J Stafford, Bedford for preservation 5/04.

JFJ 508N (328): National Travel (South West) Ltd (GL) 328 6/78; Western National Omnibus Co Ltd, Exeter (DN) 328 5/81; Devon General Ltd, Exeter (DN) 328 1/83; Guernseybus, St Peter Port, Guernsey (CI) 165 12/84, re-registered 12727; entered service 1/85; re-registered 31915 7/90; States of Guernsey and leased to Educational Holidays Guernsey Ltd {Island Coachways}, St Peter Port, Guernsey (CI) 165 11/00; C Billington (dealer/preservationist), Maidenhead 3/01; stored at Winkleigh; Gray, Andrews and Allen, South Devon for preservation 1/02.

Vehicles acquired from Wessex National Ltd, Bristol (GL) 11/75

250	140 DBO	Leyland PSU3/3R	L00319	Duple (Northern)	137/2	C49F	4/63	-/76
252	142 DBO	Leyland PSU3/3R	L00320	Duple (Northern)	137/3	C49F	5/63	-/76

Previous History:
140 DBO (250): New as Western Welsh Omnibus Co Ltd, Cardiff (GG) 140; Black and White Motorways Ltd, Cheltenham (GL) 140 9/71; from whom it was acquired 11/74; licensed 1/75.
142 DBO (252): New as Western Welsh Omnibus Co Ltd, Cardiff (GG) 142; Black and White Motorways Ltd, Cheltenham (GL) 142 9/71; from whom it was acquired 11/74; licensed 1/75.

Notes:
142 DBO (252): Renumbered 251 by 2/76.

Disposals:
140 DBO (250): Creamline Services (Tonmawr) Ltd, Tonmawr (WG) 9/76; withdrawn 9/78, but still owned 8/80.
142 DBO (251): Hope and Anchor Sea Fishing Club, Hanley (XST) by 8/77; still in use 4/88.

Vehicles on loan from National Travel (South West) Ltd, Cheltenham (GL)

252	DDG 252C	Leyland PSU3/3R	L23632	Harrington	3093	C47F	4/65	
253	DDG 253C	Leyland PSU3/3R	L23633	Harrington	3094	C47F	4/65	
254	DDG 254C	Leyland PSU3/3R	L23683	Harrington	3095	C47F	4/65	
255	DDG 255C	Leyland PSU3/3R	L23692	Harrington	3096	C47F	4/65	
256	DDG 256C	Leyland PSU3/3R	L23693	Harrington	3097	C47F	4/65	

Notes:
DDG 252C (252): This vehicle was numbered 252 in the National Travel (South West) fleet and was on loan from 11/75 until 5/76; although officially renumbered 152 this was never carried.
DDG 253C (253): This vehicle was numbered 253 in the National Travel (South West) fleet and was on loan from 11/75 until 7/76; renumbered 153 1976.
DDG 254C (254): This vehicle was numbered 254 in the National Travel (South West) fleet and was on loan from 11/75 until 5/76; although officially renumbered 154 this was never carried.
DDG 255C (255): This vehicle was numbered 255 in the National Travel (South West) fleet and was on loan from 11/75 until 7/76; renumbered 155 1976.
DDG 256C (256): This vehicle was numbered 256 in the National Travel (South West) fleet and was on loan from 11/75 until 7/76; although officially renumbered 156 this was never carried.

Vehicles acquired from National Travel (South East) Ltd, London SE6 (LN) 11/75

333	JYT 606K	AEC Reliance	6MU4R7947	Plaxton	728783	C41F	5/72	-/78
334	JYT 607K	AEC Reliance	6MU4R7948	Plaxton	728788	C41F	5/72	-/78
335	JYT 608K	AEC Reliance	6MU4R7949	Plaxton	728785	C41F	5/72	-/78
336	JYT 609K	AEC Reliance	6MU4R7950	Plaxton	728786	C41F	5/72	-/78
337	JYT 610K	AEC Reliance	6MU4R7951	Plaxton	728784	C41F	5/72	-/78
338	JYT 611K	AEC Reliance	6MU4R7952	Plaxton	728787	C41F	5/72	-/78

Previous History:
  JYT 606K (333): New to A Timpson & Sons Ltd, London SE6 (LN); National Travel (South East) Ltd 1/74; re-seated to C43F before entering service 4/76.
  JYT 607-609K (334-336): New to A Timpson & Sons Ltd, London SE6 (LN); National Travel (South East) Ltd 1/74; re-seated to C43F before entering service.
  JYT 610K (337): New to A Timpson & Sons Ltd, London SE6 (LN); National Travel (South East) Ltd 1/74; re-seated to C43F before entering service 5/76.
  JYT 611K (338): New to A Timpson & Sons Ltd, London SE6 (LN); National Travel (South East) Ltd 1/74; re-seated to C43F before entering service 4/76.

Disposals:
  JYT 606K (333): Martin's Bus & Coach Sales Ltd (dealer), Middlewich 6/78; R Mayers {Thomas Coaches}, Cheadle Heath (GM) 9/78; R Askin (dealer), Barnsley by 1/79; Garelochhead Coach Services Ltd, Garelochhead (SC) 152 7/79; withdrawn 9/80; R Bullock and Co (Transport) Ltd, Cheadle (GM) 2/81; withdrawn 1984.
  JYT 607K (334): Martin's Bus & Coach Sales Ltd (dealer), Middlewich 6/78; G Lightfoot {GL Travel}, Winsford (CH) 6/78; licensed 10/78; withdrawn 1/81; WS Yeates Ltd (dealer), Loughborough 1981; R Catterall, Southam (WK) 3/82; transferred to Portrest Ltd, Southam (WK) 8/86; still owned 5/87.
  JYT 608K (335): Martin's Bus & Coach Sales Ltd (dealer), Middlewich 6/78; CD Preece, Buxton (DE) 6/78; licensed 8/78; JJ Priest {Cliff's Coaches}, Buxton (DE) 3/80; withdrawn by 3/83; JW Ritchie {Charter Coach}, Buxton (DE) for spares by 7/83; derelict on premises by 11/84; scrapped after 10/85.
  JYT 609K (336): Martin's Bus & Coach Sales Ltd (dealer), Middlewich 6/78; R Mayers {Thomas Coaches}, Cheadle Heath (GM) 9/78; R Askin (dealer), Barnsley by 1/79; Garelochhead Coach Services Ltd, Garelochhead (SC) 153 7/79; withdrawn 9/80; R Bullock and Co (Transport) Ltd, Cheadle (GM) 2/81; Church of God of Prophecy, Moss Side (XGM) 9/85; withdrawn 5/86; Belgrade Morris Dancers, Adlington (XCH) 2/87.
  JYT 610K (337): Martin's Bus & Coach Sales Ltd (dealer), Middlewich 6/78; Prospect Coach Group Ltd, Lye (WM) 8/78; E & AR Morgan, Sedgley (WM) by 1981; Prospect Coaches (West) Ltd, Lye (WM) as a burnt out wreck 11/85; still there 5/87.
  JYT 611K (338): Martin's Bus & Coach Sales Ltd (dealer), Middlewich 6/78; Garelochhead Coach Services Ltd, Garelochhead (SC) 70 7/79; withdrawn 9/80; R Bullock and Co (Transport) Ltd, Cheadle (GM) 2/81; Globe Luxury Coaches Ltd, Barnsley (SY) by 4/84; Extracar Ltd, Borehamwood (HT) 8/85; Plustrans Ltd, Gillingham (KT) 3/86; R Boardman & SD Wilson {Blue Bus Service}, Eccles (GM) 8/87; sold (for scrap?) 4/88.

1976

New Vehicles

368	NFJ 368P	Bedford YMT	FW453599	Plaxton	7611TC101	C53F	5/76	-/78
369	NFJ 369P	Bedford YMT	FW453506	Plaxton	7611TC102	C53F	5/76	-/78
370	NFJ 370P	Bedford YMT	FW453573	Plaxton	7611TC103	C53F	5/76	-/78
371	NFJ 371P	Bedford YMT	FW453646	Plaxton	7611TC104	C53F	5/76	-/78
372	NFJ 372P	Bedford YMT	FW453588	Plaxton	7611TC105	C53F	6/76	-/78
373	NFJ 373P	Bedford YMT	FW453595	Plaxton	7611TC106	C53F	5/76	-/78
374	NFJ 374P	Bedford YMT	FW453873	Plaxton	7611TC107	C53F	5/76	-/78
375	NFJ 375P	Bedford YMT	FW453835	Plaxton	7611TC108	C53F	5/76	-/78
376	NFJ 376P	Bedford YMT	FW453946	Plaxton	7611TC109	C53F	6/76	-/78
377	NFJ 377P	Bedford YMT	FW453714	Plaxton	7611TC110	C53F	5/76	-/78

Notes:
  These vehicles were licensed, in error, to National Travel (South West) Ltd until 6-7/77.

Disposals:

NFJ 368P (368): National Travel (South West) Ltd (GL) 368 5/78; Arlington Motor Co Ltd (dealer), Potters Bar 1/79; Sampsons Coaches and Travel Ltd, Hoddesdon (HT) 93 1/79; named "Sampson's Adventurer"; rebuilt with Plaxton Suprene IV front by 3/82; withdrawn 1/88.

NFJ 369P (369): National Travel (South West) Ltd (GL) 369 5/78; Arlington Motor Co Ltd (dealer), Potters Bar 1/79; Sampsons Coaches and Travel Ltd, Hoddesdon (HT) 94 1/79; named "Sampson's Invader"; Carlone Ltd, Forest Green (SR) 10/88; Alan Wilson (PSV) Ltd (dealer), Ratby by 8/92.

NFJ 370P (370): National Travel (South West) Ltd (GL) 370 5/78; Arlington Motor Co Ltd (dealer), Potters Bar 1/79; Sampsons Coaches and Travel Ltd, Hoddesdon (HT) 95 1/79; named "Sampson's Moonraker"; withdrawn 1/88.

NFJ 371P (371): National Travel (South West) Ltd (GL) 371 5/78; Arlington Motor Co Ltd (dealer), Potters Bar 1/79; Sampsons Coaches and Travel Ltd, Hoddesdon (HT) 96 1/79; named "Sampson's Trafalgar"; Fleetville Bus and Coach Co Ltd {T & J Coaches/A-Z Travel}, Hoddesdon (HT) c6/86; returned to Sampsons Coaches and Travel Ltd, Hoddesdon (HT) 11/86; withdrawn 7/88.

NFJ 372P (372): National Travel (South West) Ltd (GL) 372 6/78; Arlington Motor Co Ltd (dealer), Potters Bar 1/79; Sampsons Coaches and Travel Ltd, Hoddesdon (HT) 97 1/79; named "Sampson's Pathfinder"; withdrawn 1/88.

NFJ 373P (373): National Travel (South West) Ltd (GL) 373 5/78; Arlington Motor Co Ltd (dealer), Potters Bar 1/79; Sampsons Coaches and Travel Ltd, Hoddesdon (HT) 98 1/79; named "Sampson's Telstar"; withdrawn 7/88.

NFJ 374P (374): National Travel (South West) Ltd (GL) 374 6/78; Arlington Motor Co Ltd (dealer), Potters Bar 1/79; AC Travel Ltd, Northfleet (KT) 9/79; returned to Arlington Motor Co Ltd (dealer), Potters Bar 6/80; Transauto Self-Drive Services Ltd, High Wycombe (BK) 3/81; Havering Corps of Drums, Hornchurch (XLN) 9/83; re-registered RTK 808 1989; Spraggon Self Drive, Hornchurch (XLN) 1989; transferred to Smith Self Drive, Hornchurch (XLN) by 4/89; re-registered OJN 470P by 7/90; withdrawn by 11/02.

NFJ 375P (375): National Travel (South West) Ltd (GL) 375 5/78; Arlington Motor Co Ltd (dealer), Potters Bar 1/79; AC Travel Ltd, Northfleet (KT) 2/79; returned to Arlington Motor Co Ltd (dealer), Potters Bar by 8/81; DG & JH Heaps {Davian Coaches}, Enfield (LN) 3/82; Burke, Claretuam (EI) re-registered 76 GIO 4/87.

NFJ 376P (376): National Travel (South West) Ltd (GL) 376 6/78; Arlington Motor Co Ltd (dealer), Potters Bar 1/79; Sampsons Coaches and Travel Ltd, Hoddesdon (HT) 99 1/79; Fleetville Bus and Coach Co Ltd {T & J Coaches / A-Z Travel}, Hoddesdon (HT) 11/85; last licensed 8/98; exported to an unknown country.

NFJ 377P (377): National Travel (South West) Ltd (GL) 377 6/78; Arlington Motor Co Ltd (dealer), Potters Bar 1/79; Sampsons Coaches and Travel Ltd, Hoddesdon (HT) 100 1/79; named "Sampson's Liberator"; Wealdon PSV Sales (dealer), Five Oak Green by 8/90.

Vehicles acquired from National Travel (South West) Ltd, Cheltenham (GL)

200	CHA 83C	Leyland PSU3/4R	L41010	Duple (Northern)	163/10	C49F	7/65	-/77
255	CHA 94C	Leyland PSU3/4R	L41441	Duple (Northern)	163/21	C49F	8/65	-/76
205	CHA 95C	Leyland PSU3/4R	L41443	Duple (Northern)	163/22	C49F	8/65	n/a
257	CHA 96C	Leyland PSU3/4R	L41442	Duple (Northern)	163/23	C49F	8/65	-/77
258	CHA 98C	Leyland PSU3/4R	L41444	Duple (Northern)	163/25	C49F	9/65	-/76
262	CHA 99C	Leyland PSU3/4R	L41595	Duple (Northern)	163/26	C49F	9/65	-/76
260	CHA 100C	Leyland PSU3/4R	L41598	Duple (Northern)	163/27	C49F	9/65	-/76
263	CHA 104C	Leyland PSU3/4R	L41686	Duple (Northern)	163/31	C49F	9/65	-/77
210	CHA 105C	Leyland PSU3/4R	L41793	Duple (Northern)	163/32	C49F	9/65	-/77
211	CHA 106C	Leyland PSU3/4R	L41793	Duple (Northern)	163/33	C49F	9/65	-/76
264	CHA 116C	Leyland PSU3/4R	L41909	Duple (Northern)	163/43	C49F	10/65	-/77
265	CHA 122C	Leyland PSU3/4R	L42450	Duple (Northern)	163/49	C49F	10/65	-/77

Previous History:

CHA 83C (200): New as Birmingham and Midland Motor Omnibus Co Ltd {Midland Red}, Smethwick (WM) 5783; Midland Red Omnibus Co Ltd, Birmingham (WM) 5783 3/74; from whom it was acquired 1/76; entering service 2/76.

CHA 94C (255): New as Birmingham and Midland Motor Omnibus Co Ltd {Midland Red}, Smethwick (WM) 5794, Midland Red Omnibus Co Ltd, Birmingham (WM) 5794 3/74; from whom it was acquired 12/75; entering service 1/76.

CHA 95C (205): New as Birmingham and Midland Motor Omnibus Co Ltd {Midland Red}, Smethwick (WM) 5795; Midland Red Omnibus Co Ltd, Birmingham (WM) 5795 3/74; from whom it was acquired 12/75; entering service 2/76.

CHA 96C (257): New as Birmingham and Midland Motor Omnibus Co Ltd {Midland Red}, Smethwick (WM) 5796; Midland Red Omnibus Co Ltd, Birmingham (WM) 5796 3/74; from whom it was acquired 1/76; entering service 5/76.
CHA 98C (258): New as Birmingham and Midland Motor Omnibus Co Ltd {Midland Red}, Smethwick (WM) 5798; Midland Red Omnibus Co Ltd, Birmingham (WM) 5798 3/74; from whom it was acquired 3/76; entering service 5/76.
CHA 99C (262): New as Birmingham and Midland Motor Omnibus Co Ltd {Midland Red}, Smethwick (WM) 5799; Midland Red Omnibus Co Ltd, Birmingham (WM) 5799 3/74; from whom it was acquired 3/76; entering service 5/76.
CHA 100C (260): New as Birmingham and Midland Motor Omnibus Co Ltd {Midland Red}, Smethwick (WM) 5800; Midland Red Omnibus Co Ltd, Birmingham (WM) 5800 3/74; from whom it was acquired 3/76; entering service 5/76.
CHA 104C (263): New as Birmingham and Midland Motor Omnibus Co Ltd {Midland Red}, Smethwick (WM) 5804; Midland Red Omnibus Co Ltd, Birmingham (WM) 5804 3/74; from whom it was acquired 3/76; not operated.
CHA 105C (210): New as Birmingham and Midland Motor Omnibus Co Ltd {Midland Red}, Smethwick (WM) 5805; Midland Red Omnibus Co Ltd, Birmingham (WM) 5805 3/74; from whom it was acquired 12/75; entering service 1/76.
CHA 106C (211): New as Birmingham and Midland Motor Omnibus Co Ltd {Midland Red}, Smethwick (WM) 5806; Midland Red Omnibus Co Ltd, Birmingham (WM) 5806 3/74; from whom it was acquired 12/75; entering service 1/76.
CHA 116C (264): New as Birmingham and Midland Motor Omnibus Co Ltd {Midland Red}, Smethwick (WM) 5816; Midland Red Omnibus Co Ltd, Birmingham (WM) 5816 3/74; from whom it was acquired 3/76; not operated.
CHA 122C (265): New as Birmingham and Midland Motor Omnibus Co Ltd {Midland Red}, Smethwick (WM) 5822; Midland Red Omnibus Co Ltd, Birmingham (WM) 5822 3/74; from whom it was acquired 3/76; not operated.

Notes:
CHA 83C (200): Acquired and licensed 6/76; allocated fleet number 254, but never carried; initially Black and White fleetnames were retained; Greenslades fleetnames applied by 11/76.
CHA 94C (255): Acquired 6/76; licensed 7/76; initially, Black and White fleetnames were retained; South West names applied by 11/76.
CHA 95C (205): Acquired 6/76; licensed 7/76; allocated fleet number 256, but never carried; received Greenslades fleetnames, but was never operated, although remained licensed until 3/77.
CHA 96C (257): Acquired and licensed 6/76 with South West fleetnames.
CHA 98C (258): Acquired 6/76; licensed 7/76 with South West fleetnames.
CHA 99C (262): Acquired and licensed 7/76 with South West fleetnames; allocated fleet number 208; but never carried; renumbered 259 in 1976.
CHA 100C (260): Acquired 6/76; licensed 7/76 with South West fleetnames.
CHA 104C (263): Acquired 5/76; licensed 7/76 with South West fleetnames; renumbered 261 7/76.
CHA 105C (210): Acquired and licensed 6/76; allocated fleet number 262, but never carried; operated without fleetnames.
CHA 106C (211): Acquired and licensed 5/76; allocated fleet number 263, but never carried; operated without fleetnames.
CHA 116C (264): Acquired 5/76; licensed 9/76 with South West fleetnames.
CHA 122C (265): Acquired 5/76; licensed 8/76 with South West fleetnames.

Disposals:
CHA 83C (200): W Norths (PV) Ltd (dealer), Sherburn in Elmet 5/77; Heyfordian Travel Ltd {Cherwell Valley}, Upper Heyford (OX) 10/77; licensed as C51F 2/78; withdrawn 1982; C Meynell (dealer), Carlton 7/82.
CHA 94C (255): Paul Sykes Organisation Ltd (dealer), Barnsley 5/77; LC, SJ & AC Munden {Crown Coaches}, Bristol (GL) 6/77; becoming LC Munden & Son Ltd {Crown Coaches}, Bristol (GL) at an unknown date; withdrawn 8/80; rebuilt, rebodied Plaxton C49F (8111LC046/S) and re-registered FTC 2W 5/81; numbered 7 3/95; unidentified owner use not known, Midsomer Norton by 9/98.
CHA 95C (205): Used for spares from 7/76; Paul Sykes Organisation Ltd (dealer), Barnsley 5/77; A Barraclough (dealer), Carlton for scrap 6/77.
CHA 96C (257): Martin's Bus & Coach Sales Ltd (dealer), Middlewich 6/77; Mustafa, London SE5 (XLN) by 5/79; exported to Cyprus re-registered TAH 144 as C40F c6/81; believed sold 1982.
CHA 98C (258): Paul Sykes Organisation Ltd (dealer), Barnsley 5/77; LC, SJ & AC Munden {Crown Coaches}, Bristol (GL) 5/77; becoming LC Munden & Son Ltd {Crown Coaches}, Bristol (GL) at an unknown date; withdrawn 7/79; in use as a storeshed by 9/80.

CHA 99C (259): Paul Sykes Organisation Ltd (dealer), Barnsley 5/77; Fergus & Haynes (contractor), London E4 (XLN) L4 5/77; used in Wester Ross; withdrawn 1977; believed sold to Howard Doris (contractor) for use as a static hut at Kishorn 6/78.
CHA 100C (260): Paul Sykes Organisation Ltd (dealer), Barnsley 5/77; Fergus & Haynes (contractor), London E4 (XLN) L5 5/77; used in Wester Ross; withdrawn after an accident 1977; scrapped 1978.
CHA 104C (261): Paul Sykes Organisation Ltd (dealer), Barnsley 5/77; Baird (dealer), Climping, Littlehampton 6/77; Training Ship "Explorer", Havant (XHA) 6/77; returned to Paul Sykes Organisation Ltd (dealer), Barnsley 5/80; RK & RE Webber {Webber Brothers}, Blisland (CO) for spares 5/80.
CHA 105C (210): Martin's Bus & Coach Sales Ltd (dealer), Middlewich 6/77; AB Cooper, Stockton Heath (CH) 8/77; not operated in acquired condition; rebuilt, rebodied Plaxton C51F (7811LCM080S) and re-registered BNF 151T with new chassis number JWF 1 in 12/78; JW Fieldsend Ltd, Salford (GM) 12/81; IRH McLeod & D North {Garforth Coachways}, Allerton Bywater (WY) by 5/82; Wigley (dealer) Carlton for scrap by 11/93.
CHA 106C (211): Paul Sykes Organisation Ltd (dealer), Barnsley 5/77; LC, SJ & AC Munden {Crown Coaches}, Bristol (GL) 5/77; becoming LC Munden & Son Ltd {Crown Coaches}, Bristol (GL) at an unknown date; withdrawn 11/78; rebuilt, rebodied Plaxton C51F (7911LC007/S) and re-registered WHT 825T 4/79; re-registered 837 XHW 1/87; Matthews TravelLtd, Cwmbran (GT) 8/88; Hartlepool Transport ITD (CD) 106 7/90; re-registered DEF 822T 5/94; North East Bus Breakers (dealer) for scrap 7/95
CHA 116C (264): Paul Sykes Organisation Ltd (dealer), Barnsley 5/77; RK & RE Webber {Webber Brothers}, Blisland (CO) 5/77; withdrawn by 6/83.
CHA 122C (265): Paul Sykes Organisation Ltd (dealer), Barnsley 5/77; LC, SJ & AC Munden {Crown Coaches}, Bristol (GL) 5/77; becoming LC Munden & Son Ltd {Crown Coaches}, Bristol (GL) at an unknown date; withdrawn at an unknown date; not traced further.

Vehicles on loan from National Travel (South West) Ltd, Cheltenham (GL)

257	DDG 257C	Leyland PSU3/3R	L23558	Duple (Northern)	163/57	C47F	6/65
258	DDG 258C	Leyland PSU3/3R	L23559	Duple (Northern)	163/56	C47F	6/65
259	DDG 259C	Leyland PSU3/3R	L23560	Duple (Northern)	163/55	C47F	6/65
260	DDG 260C	Leyland PSU3/3R	L23561	Duple (Northern)	163/51	C47F	6/65
261	DDG 261C	Leyland PSU3/3R	L23631	Duple (Northern)	163/54	C47F	6/65

Notes:
DDG 257-260C (257-260): These vehicles were numbered 257-260 in the National Travel (South West) fleet and were on loan during 1976, being returned 7/76; renumbered 157-160 1976.
DDG 261C (261): This vehicle was numbered 261 in the National Travel (South West) fleet and was on loan during 1976, being returned 7/76; although officially renumbered 161 this was never carried.

Vehicle acquired from Wessex National Ltd, Bristol (GL) 5/76

| 471 | VHT 912H | Bedford VAM70 | 9T470729 | Duple | 1226/223 | C45F | 3/70 | -/77 |

Previous History:
VHT 912H (471): New to Wessex Coaches Ltd, Bristol (GL); from whom it was acquired 8/74.

Notes:
VHT 912H (471): Allocated new fleet number 299, but never carried.

Disposal:
VHT 912H (471): Paul Sykes Organisation Ltd (dealer), Barnsley 2/77; LS Panton {Mayflower Bus Services}, Kingston (O-JA) 12/78.

Vehicles acquired from Ribble Motor Services Ltd, Preston (LA) 6/76

340	KCK 381H	Leyland PSU4A/4R	903893	Plaxton	709076	C36F	4/70	-/78
341	KCK 990H	Leyland PSU4A/4R	903728	Plaxton	709066	C36F	4/70	-/78
342	KCK 991H	Leyland PSU4A/4R	903922	Plaxton	709067	C36F	4/70	-/78
343	KCK 994H	Leyland PSU4A/4R	903699	Plaxton	709070	C36F	4/70	-/78

Previous History:
KCK 381H: New as Ribble 1000.
KCK 990-991H: New as Ribble 990-991.
KCK 994H: New as Ribble 994.

Notes:
    KCK 381H (340): Re-seated to C41F 3/77.
    KCK 990H (341): Re-seated to C43F 3/77.
    KCK 991H (342): Re-seated to C41F 1/77.
    KCK 994H (343): Re-seated to C28F c9/76; to C41F 3/77.

Disposals:
    KCK 381H (340): National Travel (South West) Ltd (GL) 340 6/78; Martin's Bus & Coach Sales Ltd (dealer), Middlewichby 6/81; Parfitt's Motor Services Ltd, Rhymney Bridge (CS) 4/82; rebuilt with a Supreme IV front 5/86; re-registered JEP 609 12/87; GD Handy, Merthyr Tydfil (MG) 9/89; re-registered NIJ 6060 5/90; Abacus, Cardiff (SG) 10/94; re-registered LIL 7077 10/95; F Lawrance, Colchester for preservation 10/95; reverted to original registration KCK 381H 11/95; T Andrews, Havant for preservation by 10/98; AJ & MB Bailey {Portsmouth Coaches}, Portsmouth (HA) by 7/01; M Nash (dealer), Weybridge by 10/01; G Beattie, Reading for preservation 2/02.
    KCK 990H (341): National Travel (South West) Ltd (GL) 341 6/78; W Norths (PV) Ltd (dealer), Sherburn in Elmet 10/81; Independent Coachways (Leeds) Ltd, Horsforth (WY) 11/81; Ballykinler Social Club, Ballykinler (XDO) 3/83; Roman Catholic Church, Tyrella (XDO) by 6/91.
    KCK 991H (342): National Travel (South West) Ltd (GL) 342 6/78; W Norths (PV) Ltd (dealer), Sherburn in Elmet 10/81; DW Cook, Warmsworth (SY) by 12/81; Sherburn High School, Sherburn in Elmet (XNY) 2/82; Balby Carr High School, Doncaster (XSY) by 11/85 (probably by 7/84); returned to Norths (PV) Ltd (dealer), Sherburn in Elmet 7/88.
    KCK 994H (343): National Travel (South West) Ltd (GL) 343 6/78; Martin's Bus & Coach Sales Ltd (dealer), Middlewich at an unknown date; Allander Coaches Ltd, Milngavie (SC) 8/80; sold for scrap by 7/82, after an accident in 6/82.

Vehicles acquired from National Travel (South East) Ltd, London SE6 (LN) 6/76

329	ELU 599J	AEC Reliance	6MU4R7575	Plaxton	712829	C41F	4/71	-/78
339	ELU 600J	AEC Reliance	6MU4R7576	Plaxton	712830	C41F	4/71	-/78

Previous History:
    ELU 599J (329): New to A Timpson & Sons Ltd, London SE6 (LN); from whom it was acquired 1/74.
    ELU 600J (339): New to A Timpson & Sons Ltd, London SE6 (LN); from whom it was acquired 1/74.

Notes:
    ELU 599J (329): Re-seated to C43F before entering service in 7/76.
    ELU 600J (339): Licensed by Greenslades in 7/76;r ebuilt by Booker, Newton Abbot following extensive fire damage in 1976 and re-entered service 1/77; re-seated to C43F 2/77.

Disposals:
    ELU 599J (329): National Travel (South West) Ltd (GL) 406 named 'Devon' 3/78; Paul Sykes Organisation Ltd (dealer), Barnsley 6/79; WH Shaw & Son Ltd, Diggle (XGM) as C41F 1/80; West End Garage (dealer), Slaithwaite 12/83; AE Goodwin, Wythenshawe (GM) 4/84, not operated; Pearson & Son Ltd (dealer), Heywood 5/84; St Cyprian's Church, Stanley, Liverpool (XMY) 6/84; sold for scrap 6/86.
    ELU 600J (339): National Travel (South West) Ltd (GL) 407 named 'Cornwall' 3/78; Martin's Bus & Coach Sales Ltd (dealer), Middlewich 12/79; TH, E & EB Jones {TH Jones & Son / Caelloi Holidays}, Pwllheli (GD) 5/80; RG Owen {Nefyn Coaches}, Nefyn (GD) 4/81; F Woolley, Llanedwen (AY) by 4/84; WC Goodsir, Holyhead (CN) by 6/84; returned to F Woolley, Llanedwen (AY) by 4/85; unidentified owner, Nefyn as a mobile snack bar by 4/85.

1977

New Vehicles

378	STA 378R	Bedford YMT	GW454318	Duple	717/2551	C53F	7/77	-/78
379	STA 379R	Bedford YMT	GW454045	Duple	717/2552	C53F	7/77	-/78
380	STA 380R	Bedford YMT	GW454053	Duple	717/2553	C53F	7/77	-/78
381	STA 381R	Bedford YMT	GW454245	Duple	717/2554	C53F	7/77	-/78
382	STA 382R	Bedford YMT	GW454030	Duple	717/2555	C53F	7/77	-/78

Notes:
    STA 378R (378): Re-seated to C49F 3/78: to C53F 4/79.
    STA 379R (379): Re-seated to C49F 3/78: to C53F 4/79.

STA 380R (380): Re-seated to C49F 3/78: to C53F 4/79.
STA 381R (381): Re-seated to C49F 3/78: to C53F 4/79.
STA 382R (382): Re-seated to C49F 3/78: to C53F 4/79.

Disposals:
STA 378R (378): National Travel (South West) Ltd (GL) 378 6/78; withdrawn 2/80; IJ Lucas, Kingsley (ST) 38 5/80; chassis scrapped 6/85; body transferred to Leyland PSU3A/4R LJX 817H, which was then re-registered Q364 FVT 6/85.
STA 379R (379): National Travel (South West) Ltd (GL) 379 6/78; withdrawn 2/80; Smith (Shenington) Ltd, Alcester (WK) 5/80; Kenmargra Coaches Ltd, Linthwaite (WY) 10/80; MS Mountford, Crumpsall (GM) 10/88; Hughes, Llandudno (CN) 7/89; sold 10/93.
STA 380R (380): National Travel (South West) Ltd (GL) 380 6/78; withdrawn 2/80; WA & R Cheyne {Cheyne's Coaches}, Daviot (GN) 4/80; DJ & SI Cheyne, Turriff (GN) 8/94; SA & M Robertson, Alford (GN) 11/99.
STA 381R (381): National Travel (South West) Ltd (GL) 381 6/78; withdrawn 2/80; JW Carnell Ltd, Sutton Bridge (HD) 6/80; unknown owner as café on the A134 (XNK) by 9/00.
STA 382R (382): National Travel (South West) Ltd (GL) 382 6/78; withdrawn 2/80; JG Wilson {Robert Wilson}, Carnwath (SC) 3/80; Kenmargra Coaches Ltd, Linthwaite (WY) by 5/83; MS Mountford, Crumpsall (GM) 10/88; Hughes, Llandudno (CN) 7/89; withdrawn 9/94; scrapped on site.

Vehicle acquired from National Travel (South West) Ltd, Cheltenham (GL) 4/77

| 344 | RCY 55H | AEC Reliance | 8U3ZR7193 | Duple (Northern) | 202/11 | C44F | 8/69 | -/77 |

Previous History:
RCY 55H: New to South Wales Transport Co Ltd, Swansea (CW) 1055; renumbered 174 11/70; from whom it was acquired 12/76.

Disposal:
RCY 55H (344): Unidentified owner (Martin?) unknown location and date; JK, PER & EK Baker, Biddulph (ST) 4/79; O'Connor, Little Island, Cork (EI) 6/81; sold by 4/90.

SUBSIDIARY OPERATORS

H Belcher 87 Lancaster Street, Birmingham (WK) (from c1922)
H Belcher 14 Teignmouth Street, Teignmouth
(operations also commenced in Teignmouth 1923; moved to Teignmouth summer 1923, Birmingham operation ceased).
H & EA Belcher Ltd (from 6/4/32)   **Empress Coaches**   14, Wellington Street, Teignmouth
H & EA Belcher (Teignmouth) Ltd (from 12/39)   Teignmouth

Business acquired by Greenslades in 1/32 and a new company H & EA Belcher Ltd, was formed in 4/32. The title was changed to H & EA Belcher (Teignmouth) Ltd in 12/39, however the company had no vehicles licensed to it between 10/39 and 12/47. The sister subsidiary Miller & Son (Exmouth) Ltd was absorbed in 4/53 with their former vehicles being licensed to Belcher, who also operated from Exmouth. Vehicles remaining in the Belcher fleet were transferred to the main Greenslades fleet in 1/55 with the company subsequently being wound up.

Livery: Pre-1932: Not known.
         Post-1932: Same as Greenslades, but with Empress fleetnames.

Reg	Chassis	Chassis No	Body	Body No	Type	New	Acq	Wdn
TA 6356	Lancia Tetraiota	417	?		Ch14	5/23	5/23	1/29
OB 5297	?	?	?		Ch14	-/17	-/23	-/23
OE 3645	Talbot	?	?		Ch14	-/19	-/23	-/28
FR 4666	Lancia Tetraiota	15	?		Ch20	5/22	2/25	4/30
TT 8232	Lancia Pentaiota	1199	?		Ch20	5/26	5/26	by -/37
N 7939	Rolls-Royce	?	?		Car7	-/--	by8/27	by9/29
LX 6167	Rolls-Royce	?	?		Car7	-/19	by6/28	c-/32
K 7866	Lancia Di Kappa 16 30hp	?	?		Ch12	-/21	3/29	-/30
DV 1082	Lancia Torino	2743	Duple	1586	C26F	5/29	5/29	8/38
DV 3145	Daimler	31341	?		Car7	12/29	12/29	by12/38
TK 5760	Daimler	?	?		Car	1/31	-/--	-/--
DV 5419	BAT Cruiser	3X153	?		C20-	5/30	5/30	-/--
DV 8411	BAT Cruiser	3X178	Torquay MC		C20-	3/31	3/31	5/36
DV 9548	Bedford WLG	113380	?		C14F	6/31	6/31	6/36
OD 2488	Morris Viceroy	240Y	?		C20F	5/32	5/32	10/39
AFJ 783	Bedford WTL	876072	Duple	5082	C25R	5/35	5/35	5/39
AFJ 782	Bedford WTL	875342	Duple	5081	C25R	6/35	6/35	5/39
FJ 8351	Morris Director	075RP	Duple	2861	C14F	6/32	6/36	10/39
AUO 454	Dodge PLB	1028	Thurgood	557	C20R	6/35	5/37	10/39
DFJ 46	Bedford WTB	111152	Tiverton		C20F	5/37	5/37	10/39
DFJ 47	Bedford WTB	111307	Tiverton		C20F	5/37	5/37	10/39
DFJ 114	Bedford WTB	111501	Duple	8893	C25F	6/37	6/37	10/39
HFJ 834	Bedford OB	58801	Duple	43362	C29F	12/47	12/47	4/53
HFJ 835	Bedford OB	63622	Duple	43364	C29F	12/47	12/47	4/53
KFJ 606	Leyland PS2/3	494660	Gurney Nutting		C33F	3/50	3/50	2/53
MFJ 609	Leyland PSU1/13	520442	Burlingham	4926	C28C	4/52	4/52	2/53
MFJ 900	Bedford SB	9121	Gurney Nutting	1307	C36F	7/52	7/52	3/53
MFJ 901	Bedford SB	8359	Gurney Nutting	1308	C36F	7/52	7/52	4/53
AUO 334	Leyland KP2	2953	Tiverton		C20F	6/35	4/53	12/54
BJY 703	Guy Vixen	CFNLP14877	Mumford		C20F	5/39	4/53	4/54
HDV 415	Bedford OB	55413	Whitson	5794	C27F	8/47	4/53	1/54
KTA 388	Commer Commando	17A0920	Harrington	385	C29F	8/48	4/53	9/53
LTA 185	Guy Vixen	LLV41247P	Devon Coachbuilders		FC24F	7/49	4/53	*
LOD 266	Commer Avenger	23A0313	Devon Coachbuilders		C31F	5/50	4/53	*
MTA 173	Commer Avenger	23A0536	Devon Coachbuilders		C31F	7/50	4/53	*
NDV 263	Bedford SB	9009	Duple	1020/19	C33F	5/52	4/53	*

Previous History:
K 7866: Original operator not known; Peruvian Embassy, London SW1 (XLN) by 11/22; FA Briggs, London SE1 (LN) 5/24; Higgs, London SE (LN) 11/25; subsequently with private owners, as a car, passing to Belcher in 11/28; relicensed as Ch14 3/29.
N 7939: Probably acquired from private owner.
DV 3145: New to Hammonds, Exmouth.
FJ 8351: New to Greenslades Tours Ltd, Exeter (DN).
FR 4666: New to F & C Smith, Blackpool (LA).
LX 6167: Probably acquired from private owner.

OB 5297: New to H Belcher, Birmingham (WK), moving to Teignmouth by 3/23.
OE 3645: New to H Belcher, Birmingham (WK), moving to Teignmouth by 3/23.
TK 5760: Believed new to a private owner.
AFJ 782: New to Greenslades Tours Ltd, Exeter (DN).
AUO 334: New to Miller & Son (Exmouth) Ltd (DN); from whom it was acquired.
AUO 454: New to Regent Coaches (Teignmouth) Ltd, Teignmouth (DN); from whom it was acquired.
BJY 703: New to Miller & Son (Exmouth) Ltd (DN); from whom it was acquired.
HDV 415: New to Miller & Son (Exmouth) Ltd (DN); from whom it was acquired.
KTA 388: New to Miller & Son (Exmouth) Ltd (DN); from whom it was acquired.
LOD 266: New to Miller & Son (Exmouth) Ltd (DN); from whom it was acquired.
LTA 185: New to Miller & Son (Exmouth) Ltd (DN); from whom it was acquired.
MTA 173: New to Miller & Son (Exmouth) Ltd (DN); from whom it was acquired.
NDV 263: New to Miller & Son (Exmouth) Ltd (DN); from whom it was acquired.

Disposals:

K 7866: Mumford & Sons Ltd (dealer), Plymouth 1/31; W Hockin Anderton (CO) 7/31; Skinner & Sons, Millbrook (CO) 9/31 withdrawn last licensed 8/32; JA Watson, Gunnislake (CO) 10/32 withdrawn last licensed 5/33.
N 7939: Not traced.
DV 1082: Greenslades Tours Ltd, Exeter (DN) 10/39; not operated; scrapped.
DV 3145: CW & WHM Terraneau, South Molton (DN) by 12/38.
DV 5419: AJ Rowsell {Otter Coaches}, Ottery St Mary (DN) c1939; J Cutler {Pride of Nailsea}, Nailsea (SO) at an unknown date; last licensed to Warren (dealer?), Nailsea 5/44.
DV 8411: Withdrawn after an accident and sold for scrap.
DV 9548: Greenslades Tours Ltd, Exeter (DN) 6/36; not operated.
FJ 8351: Waterman Bros {Pines Services}, Spaxton (SO) by 9/42; JA Edwards, Winchester (GHA) as a lorry at an unknown date; last licensed 12/46.
FR 4666: Tickle & Sons, Torrington (DN) 4/30; last licensed by 11/37.
LX 6167: Not traced.
OB 5297: Not traced.
OD 2488: Greenslades Tours Ltd, Exeter (DN) 10/39.
OE 3645: Not traced.
TA 6356: W Lowrie {Express Motor Tours}, Plymouth (DN) 1929; last licensed 9/34.
TK 5760: Not traced.
TT 8232: JH Clarke {Tally Ho!}, East Allington (DN) 1937; F Willmott & Son Ltd, Plymouth for scrap at an unknown date; last licensed 3/37.
AFJ 782: Lamboll and Ingham {Ruby Cars}, Paignton (DN) 5/39; AA Woodbury, Wellington (SO) 10/39; WJ Redwood, Hemyock (DN) 7/50; Batten and Thorne Ltd, Tiverton (DN) 7/50; withdrawn 12/52; SA Kingdom {Tivvy Coaches}, Tiverton (DN) 5/53; withdrawn 5/55; D Leach, Great Yarmouth (GNK) as a van at an unknown date; last licensed 6/59.
AFJ 783: G Street {Quantock Coaches}, Watchet (SO) 5/39; Quantock Hauliers Ltd, Watchet (SO) 8/42; HK Blunn, Castle Bromwich (WK) 4/44; CN Pullin, Newport (MH) 4/46; Rogers & Son (dealer), Chipping Sodbury for scrap at an unknown date.
AUO 334: SK Hill, Stibb Cross (DN) 12/54 withdrawn 1/57; LCW Motor Services Ltd, Llandeilo (CR) at an unknown date; Arlington Motor Co Ltd (dealer), Cardiff for scrap 11/59.
AUO 454: Greenslades Tours Ltd, Exeter (DN) 10/39; not operated.
BJY 703: Royal Signals, Denbury (XDN) 4/54.
DFJ 46: Greenslades Tours Ltd, Exeter (DN) 10/39.
DFJ 47: Greenslades Tours Ltd, Exeter (DN) 10/39.
DFJ 114: Greenslades Tours Ltd, Exeter (DN) 10/39.
HDV 415: Reed's Garage, Honiton (DN) 1/54; withdrawn 4/69.
HFJ 834: Regent Coaches (Teignmouth) Ltd, Teignmouth (DN) 4/53.
HFJ 835: Regent Coaches (Teignmouth) Ltd, Teignmouth (DN) 4/53.
KFJ 606: Regent Coaches (Teignmouth) Ltd, Teignmouth (DN) 2/53.
KTA 388: Heard's Garages Ltd {Torrie Coaches}, Torrington (DN) 9/53; last licensed 7/65.
MFJ 609: Greenslades Tours Ltd, Exeter (DN) 2/53.
MFJ 900-901: Greenslades Tours Ltd, Exeter (DN) 2/53.

Vehicles marked with an asterisk (*) passed to Greenslades 1/55.

WH & J Miller {Miller & Sons}
Miller & Son (Exmouth) Ltd (from 1935)   Miller's Tours   Strand Garage, The Strand, Exmouth

Livery: Cream and brown.

Business acquired by H & EA Belcher (Teignmouth) Ltd 4/53.

Fleet No.	Make	Chassis No.	Body	Body Type	New	Acquired	Disposed
T 3928	Dennis Subsidy 4 ton	?	Dennis	Ch27	3/14	3/14	-/17
DB 5134	Dennis	?	?	Ch28	5/19	5/19	by12/19
T 7180	Karrier	2829	?	Ch32	8/19	8/19	2/26
T 8754	Guy (30 cwt?)	723	?	C20-	6/20	6/20	by -/27
TA 804	Karrier K3	5103	?	C32-	3/21	3/21	by12/31
TA 6422	Karrier C	20106	?	?	5/23	5/23	-/--
TT 414	SPA	8698	?	C20-	6/24	6/24	9/34
TT 8371	Karrier ZX	32013	?	-20-	6/26	6/26	by3/39
UO 2039	Guy J	J4681	Guy	T18	4/27	4/27	9/37
UO 2040	Guy J	J4682	Guy	T18	4/27	4/27	9/37
UO 2380	Karrier H	1054	?	C19-	5/27	5/27	6/33
UO 7044	Graham Bros	GB4880	?	C14F	6/28	6/28	-/34
DV 1939	Graham Dodge	D202478	Mumford	C14F	7/29	7/29	-/35
DV 5649	Dennis Dart	75715	Mumford	C20-	6/30	6/30	9/36
OD 6003	Bedford WLB	108988	Mumford	C20-	6/33	6/33	-/34
OD 6025	Commer Centaur	46207	Mumford	C20-	6/33	6/33	9/49
OD 9617	Dodge PLB	107	Mumford	C20R	5/34	5/34	7/48
DV 1293	Reo Sprinter	FA11128	?	C14F	6/29	-/34	-/39
AUO 334	Leyland KP2	2953	Tiverton	C20F	6/35	6/35	*
BOD 8	Commer PN4	63516	Mumford	C20F	5/36	5/36	6/50
CTT 943	Dennis Arrow Minor	255033	Mumford	C24F	6/37	6/37	4/52
BJY 703	Guy Vixen	CFNLP14877	Mumford	C20F	5/39	5/39	*
HDV 415	Bedford OB	55413	Whitson 5794	C27F	8/47	9/47	*
KTA 388	Commer Commando	17A0920	Harrington 385	C29F	8/48	8/48	*
LTA 185	Guy Vixen	LLV41247P	Devon Coachbuilders	FC24F	7/49	7/49	*
LOD 266	Commer Avenger	23A0313	Devon Coachbuilders	C31F	5/50	5/50	*
MTA 173	Commer Avenger	23A0534	Devon Coachbuilders	C31F	7/50	7/50	*
NDV 263	Bedford SB	9009	Duple 1020/19	C33F	5/52	5/52	*

Previous History:
    DV 1293: New to A Harris, Exmouth (DN); from whom it was acquired.

Notes:
    T 7180: Re-seated to C28- 1921-1922.
    T 8754: Re-seated to C18- 1921-1922.
    TA 804: Re-seated to C29- 1921-1922
    OD 6025: Re-seated to C16- at an unknown date.
    UO 2039: Re-seated to T20 at an unknown date.
    UO 2040: Re-seated to T20 at an unknown date.
    UO 2380: Re-seated to C20- at an unknown date.

Disposals:
    T 3928: No further operator.
    T 7180: Witheridge Transport Co, Witheridge (DN) 2/26; Jones WF, Longwell Green, Bristol (GGL) as a lorry, last licensed 3/33
    T 8754: SC Wiltshire, Bristol (GGL) as a lorry at an unknown date; last licensed 3/31.
    DV 1293: AE Chenneouk, Topsham (GDN) as a lorry at an unknown date; last licensed 9/44.
    DV 1939: Willmott, Plymouth (DN) at an unknown date; withdrawn 7/38; TW Billingshurst, Saltash (CO) at an unknown date; Western National Omnibus Co Ltd, Exeter (DN) 3788 6/39; not operated.
    DV 5649: GB Carter {Rambler Coaches}, Weston-Super-Mare (SO) at an unknown date; LC Bawden, Puriton (SO) at an unknown date; AE Banwell {Regent Coaches}, Biddisham (SO) at an unknown date. Last owner LC Bawdon; last licensed 9/46.
    OD 6003: J Hoare & Sons Ltd {The Ivy Coaches}, Ivybridge (DN) 1934; last licensed 11/51; withdrawn 5/54.
    OD 6025: Last licenced to Miller 9/49; scrapped 9/49.
    OD 9617: E Saunders, Winkleigh (DN) 8/48; last licensed 9/54; withdrawn 7/55.
    TA 804: Hearn, Mountnessing (GEX) as a lorry at an unknown date; last licensed 12/31.

TA 6422: Hayne, Exmouth (GDN) as a van at an unknown date; last licensed 12/35.
TT 414: No further operator.
TT 8371: WJ Carter, Royston (GHT?) as a lorry at an unknown date; last licensed 3/39; scrapped.
UO 2039: Last licenced 9/37; scrapped 3/39.
UO 2040: Last licenced 9/37; scrapped 3/39.
UO 2380: France and Rossiter {Teignmouth Motor Car Co}, Teignmouth (DN) as C20- at an unknown date; Devon General Omnibus & Touring Co Ltd, Torquay (DN) 9/35; not operated; last licensed 9/35; scrapped.
UO 7044: AE Townsend, Torquay (DN) 1933; CA Gayton, Ashburton (DN) 1934; last licensed 3/42.
BOD 8: WHA Reece, Sidmouth (DN) 6/50; withdrawn 5/53; BE Robinson (showman), Otterton at an unknown date; last licensed 9/54.
CTT 943: GE Nightingale, Budleigh Salterton (DN) 5/52 withdrawn 3/53; DC Venner, Witheridge (DN) 9/53; withdrawn 7/55; scrapped.

Vehicles marked with an asterisk (*) passed to H & EA Belcher (Teignmouth) Ltd 4/53.

W Milton — Milton's Services — High Street, Crediton
Executors of William Milton deceased (AR Garnish & FM Milton) from 1930 — High Street, Crediton
Milton's Services (Crediton) Ltd from 12/31

Greenslade's acquired the business of the Executors of William Milton deceased, AR Garnish & FM Milton in 12/31. The limited company was set up jointly by Greenslades and the business was operated as a subsidiary. Some of the vehicles were absorbed into the main fleet by 4/36 with the remainder being sold by 7/38; although the Witheridge goods fleet remained licensed to this company, though this is outside to scope of this publication.

Livery: Light and dark blue

Reg	Make	Chassis	Body	Fleet	Seats	In	Acq	Out
T 9743	Garford Overland RUBM	936	Dowell		-20-	-/18	11/21	3/27
Y 1035	Belsize 14/16hp	?	?		-14-	-/20	-/21	-/21
T 6396	Willys Overland	2049C	?	?		-/18	-/--	-/27
UO 1276	Graham Dodge	A584568	?		B20-	2/27	2/27	6/31
FJ 2074	Leyland C1 Special	19162	Westcott		C20-	5/22	12/31	-/34
FJ 5607	Graham Dodge	A587848	?		B14F	4/28	4/28	11/33
DV 1698	Chevrolet LQ	54385	Strachan		C24D	7/29	7/29	12/31
FH 4762	Dennis F	80010	GRCW		C26-	5/27	-/33	by11/35
FJ 8005	Dennis Lancet	170012	Duple	2715	B32R	12/31	12/31	4/36
FJ 8350	Morris Director	067RP	Duple	2910	B20F	6/32	6/32	4/36
FJ 9060	Dennis Lancet	170318	Duple	3381	C32R	5/33	6/33	4/36
FJ 9581	Dennis Ace	200026	Duple	4067	B20F	3/34	3/34	7/38

Previous History:
T 9743: New to Sellers, Exmouth as a van with 6 seats; from whom it was acquired and bodied as above.
Y 1035: New to Keynton & Lind {Exeter & District Express Delivery}, Exeter (GDN) as goods; fitted with the body listed; from an unknown manufacturer prior to entering service.
FH 4762: New to Davis & Sons {Westgate}, Gloucester (GL); from whom it was acquired.
FJ 2074: New to Greenslades; from whom it was acquired.
FJ 9060: New to Greenslades; from whom it was acquired.

Notes:
DV 1698 : Had an extended chassis with an additional rear axle.
FJ 2074: Rebodied when transferred to Milton's.
FJ 9060: Had a canvas roof which folded back from the front bulkhead to the waistrail at the rear; there was no rear dome in the body; re-seated to C30R then back to C32R at unknown dates.

Disposals:
T 9743: No further operator; scrapped (1929?).
Y 1035: Moxey (Sellers & Co), Exmouth (GDN) (1921?).
DV 1698: Dependance Motor Transport Ltd, London (LN) at an unknown date; last licensed 9/34.
FH 4762: Greenslades Tours Ltd, Exeter (DN) 11/35.
FJ 2074: BJ Elston, Honiton as a goods vehicle 1934; last licenced 12/38.
FJ 5607: Greenslades Tours Ltd, Exeter (DN) 12/31.
FJ 8005: Greenslades Tours Ltd, Exeter (DN) 4/36.

FJ 8350: HJ Reed, Bassingbourn (CM) 4/36 withdrawn 7/37; HS Theobald & Son, Long Melford (SK) 12/37 withdrawn 12/39; CJ Wilkes-Wiffen {Wiffen's Coaches}, Finchingfield (EX) at an unknown date, not operated; last licensed 12/39.
FJ 9060: Greenslades Tours Ltd, Exeter (DN) 4/36.
FJ 9581: Newbury and District Motor Services Ltd, Newbury (BE) 66 7/38; CMW Brock, Aylesbury at an unknown date; last licensed 9/51.
UO 1276: No further operator.

WH Broadbeer & Sons   **Regent Coaches**   **25 Regent Street, Teignmouth**
Regent Coaches (Teignmouth) Ltd (from 6/36)   **later 14, Wellington Street**

The original company was acquired by Greenslades and the limited company formed in 6/36. It was absorbed by Greenslades in 1/55.

Reg	Make	Chassis	Body mk	Body no	Body	New	Acq	Disp
FX 7174	Austin	?	?		Ch11	-/--	2/27	-/32
DV 982	Chevrolet LQ	52800	?		C20-	5/29	5/29	7/35
TT 7987	Overland	BM2093	?		Car6	4/26	-/--	12/32
TT 8819	Buick	109150	?		Car8	7/26	-/30	c-/33
DV 8410	Chevrolet LQ	69014	?		C14-	3/31	3/31	9/34
JY 454	Morris Director	077RP	Mumford		C18-	7/32	7/32	11/39
OD 6288	Commer Corinthian	56002	?		C20F	7/33	7/33	6/36
AUO 454	Dodge PLB	1028	Thurgood	557	C20R	6/35	6/35	5/37
DFJ 113	Bedford WTB	111528	Duple	8891	C25F	6/37	6/37	3/49
FFJ 997	Bedford OWB	16748	Duple	34021	B32F	11/43	11/43	11/49
HFJ 150	Bedford OB	38386	Duple	43202	C29F	3/47	3/47	1/50
HFJ 151	Bedford OB	38485	Duple	43190	C29F	3/47	3/47	10/49
JFJ 259	Bedford OB	76613	Duple	46960	C29F	6/48	6/48	*
JFJ 867	Bedford OB	92701	Duple	46961	C29F	3/49	3/49	*
KFJ 608	Leyland PS2/3	494737	Gurney Nutting		C33F	3/50	3/50	*
KFJ 683	Bedford OB	121961	Duple	46963	C29F	5/50	5/50	*
KFJ 606	Leyland PS2/3	494660	Gurney Nutting		C33F	3/50	2/53	*
MFJ 552	Bedford SB	5495	Duple	1006/448	C33F	3/52	2/53	*
HFJ 834	Bedford OB	58801	Duple	43362	C29F	12/47	4/53	*
HFJ 835	Bedford OB	63622	Duple	43364	C29F	12/47	4/53	*

Previous History:
FX 7174: Acquired from an unknown operator.
TT 7987: Acquired from an unknown (probably private) owner.
TT 8819: New to Lamboll and Ingham {Ruby Cars}, Torquay (DN); Brook and Amos Ltd, Galashiels (SS) at an unknown date; from whom it was acquired.
HFJ 834: New to H & EA Belcher, Teignmouth (DN); from whom it was acquired.
HFJ 835: New to H & EA Belcher, Teignmouth (DN); from whom it was acquired.
KFJ 606: New to H & EA Belcher, Teignmouth (DN); from whom it was acquired.
MFJ 552: New to Greenslades Tours Ltd, Exeter (DN); from whom it was acquired.

Disposals:
DV 982: WH Kestel, Bodmin (CO) 7/35; Blake, Delabole (CO) 1942; WH Morris, Padstow (GCO) as goods at an unknown date; last licensed 6/44.
DV 8410: FJ Allin, Hatherleigh (DN) 9/34; SJ Hookway, Meeth (DN) at an unknown date, WH Lee, Meddon, Hartland (DN) 6/48; withdrawn 10/49.
FX 7174: No further trace.
JY 454: Greenslades, Exeter (DN) 11/39; JH Clark {Tally Ho! Coaches}, East Allington (DN) 6 as C20- 1940; withdrawn 9/50.
OD 6288: Greenslades Tours Ltd, Exeter (DN) 6/36.
TT 7987: No further trace.
TT 8819: Ravenhill, Shaldon (DN) at an unknown date; last licensed 6/36.
AUO 454: H & EA Belcher, Teignmouth (DN) 5/37.
DFJ 113: FG & EG Trathen {FG Trathen & Son}, Yelverton (DN) 3/49; withdrawn 2/54; Dudley Coles Ltd (contractor), Plymouth (XDN) at an unknown date; last licensed 11/59.
FFJ 997: DC Venner, Witheridge (DN) 11/49; WH Hobbs {Golden Hind Coaches}, Uffculme (DN) 1/54 withdrawn 6/56; WJ Down {Otter Coaches}, Ottery St Mary (DN) at an unknown date; L Arscott & Son (Chagford) Ltd (DN) at an unknown date, not operated; SJ Hookway, Meeth (DN) for spares at an unknown date; last licensed to Arscott 11/57.

HFJ 150: JP Kemble, Bratton Fleming (DN) 9/50; believed to AJ Orchard {White Hart Tours}, Bratton Fleming (DN) at an unknown date; until c6/66.
HFJ 151: A & SJ Stevens {W Stevens & Sons / The Harrier}, Modbury (DN) 11 11/50; private owner, Hampshire 2/64; Bexleyheath Transport Co Ltd (KT) for spares 2/65; scrapped at an unknown date; registration void 10/73.

Vehicles marked with an asterisk (*) passed to Greenslades 1/55.

VEHICLES OF ACQUIRED OPERATORS

Abbott & Searle
WJ Abbott
WJ Abbott (Exmouth) Ltd (from 1934)

Abbott's Blue Bus Service

31 Victoria Road, Exmouth
2/3 Johnson's Place, Exmouth

Livery: Light and dark blue.

Business acquired by Greenslades 11/39.

TT 5882	Chevrolet R	6065T	?		C14F	10/25	10/25	5/28
TT 7391	Chevrolet R	7416T	Dowell?		C14F	3/26	3/26	-/29
UO 1973	Chevrolet LM	15732	?		C14F	4/27	4/27	-/30
TX 1506	S & D Freighter	43:59	Hickman?		B20R	-/24	9/27	9/35
UO 6681	Chevrolet LO	40534	Sherston & Dunsford?		C14F	5/28	5/28	1/32
PR 2802	S & D Freighter	48:44	?		B20R	6/24	-/29	9/35
DV 4498	Chevrolet LQ	52937	?		C18F	3/30	3/30	11/39
OD 9497	Dodge	KB149	Thurgood	517	C20F	5/34	5/34	9/39
CN 3967	Gilford 166 OT	10629	Darland-Mason		B26F	5/29	10/34	by-/39
RU 4802	Studebaker	?	?		C20-	-/27	-/34	-/36
DL 5576	ADC 416	416731	Dodson		B32D	-/28	5/35	2/38
AOD 358	Albion PK115	25009D	Tiverton		C31-	4/36	4/36	9/39
YD 4649	Morris Dictator	100H	Midland Counties		B32F	6/32	-/36	9/38
UX 6621	Chevrolet U	65541	?		-14-	4/30	4/38	11/38
JX 501	Albion PH49	15004H	ECOC	2908	B20F	3/33	9/38	*
DDV 662	Albion PK115	25023L	Tiverton		C30F	1/39	1/39	c9/39

Previous History:

CN 3967: New to Smith's Safeway Services Ltd, Middlesbrough (NR); United Automobile Services Ltd, Darlington (DM) B100 in 9/32; from whom it was acquired.

DL 5576: New to Dodson Brothers Ltd, Cowes (IW) 28; Southern Vectis Omnibus Co Ltd, Newport (IW) 28 in 3/29; renumbered 303 in 1932; from whom it was acquired.

JX 501: New to Hebble Motor Services Ltd, Halifax (WR) 94; from whom it was acquired.

PR 2802: New to R Parsons, Swanage (DT); Hants & Dorset Motor Services Ltd, Bournemouth (DT) 1927-1928; from whom it was acquired.

RU 4802: Acquired from an unknown operator.

TX 1506: Believed to have been new as an unregistered Shelvoke & Drewry demonstrator; Price's Motors, Dinas Powis (GG) for whom it was first registered 7/26; Thomas White & Co (Cardiff and Barry) Ltd (GG) 7/27; from whom it was acquired.

UX 6621: New to FG Sadler, Stanton Lacy (SH); S Smith, Bitterley (SH) 5/35; FW Dowell {Orange and Black Coaches}, Branscombe (DN) c1936; Southern National Omnibus Co Ltd, Exeter (DN) 3658 in 5/36; from whom it was acquired.

YD 4649: New to EJ Dunn, Taunton (SO) 24; Western National Omnibus Co Ltd, Exeter (DN) 3442 in 6/33; from whom it was acquired.

Disposals:

CN 3967: No further operator.

DL 5576: Gorman, Exeter use and date unknown; registration void 2/38.

DV 4498: Moir & Davies, Bovey Tracey (GDN) as a lorry 11/39; last licensed 12/42.

OD 9497: E Last & Sons, Woburn Sands at an unknown date; A Harris, Wavendon at an unknown date; last licensed 12/48.

PR 2802: Unidentified dealer, Honiton for scrap at an unknown date.

RU 4802: Not traced.

TT 5882: F Passmore, Bideford (DN) by 2/28; Mumford (dealer), Plymouth at an unknown date; scrapped.

TT 7391: D Evans, Truro (GDN) as a lorry at an unknown date; last licensed 2/35.

TX 1506: Unidentified dealer, Honiton for scrap 1938.

UO 1973: JH Shaddick, Exmouth (DN) at an unknown date; withdrawn 12/30.

UO 6681: CE Heard, Burlescombe (DN) at an unknown date; A Heard, Ashbrittle (GSO) as a lorry at an unknown date; last licensed 12/39.

UX 6621: AFC & WH Greenslade {F Greenslade & Sons}, Dulverton (SO) at an unknown date; withdrawn 7/50.

YD 4649: Unidentified showman at an unknown date.

AOD 358: War Department (GOV) 1940; re-registered GZ 664 for an unidentified Northern Ireland operator 1942.
DDV 662: War Office (GOV) (9/39?); W Makinson {Makinson's Purple Motor Coaches}, Manchester (LA) 5/45; rebodied Trans-United FC31F body c1947; withdrawn 1951; J Wilson, Airdrie (LK) at an unknown date; I Hutchison {Hutchison's Coaches}, Overtown (LK) 1956; D Smith, Wishaw (LK) 1959; Garner's Buses (Bridge of Weir) Ltd, Bridge of Weir (RW) 11 in 1961; last licensed 12/62.

Vehicles marked with an asterisk (*) acquired by Greenslades 11/39.

AG Bowerman   27, High Street, Taunton
AG Bowerman Ltd, 1/57   10/58 – 26, Bridge Street, Taunton
                                                                                                                                     Garage – Bathpool, Taunton

The business was acquired by JG Greenslade (son of Alderman GJ Greenslade) in 5/58. In 1/59 the business of AA Woodbury, Wellington was acquired, including an office at 50, High Street, Wellington and a garage at Longfield Road, Wellington.

Livery: Azure, green and cream

Reg	Chassis	Chassis No	Body	Body No	Seating	New	Acquired	Withdrawn
DCJ 691	Bedford WTB	111876	Willmott		C25F	–/38	6/46	10/47
DV 1994	Reo Sprinter	FAX6307	?		C20–	7/29	–/46	12/42
DV 6315	Reo Speed Wagon	FB1514	?		C20–	7/30	–/46	12/49
EF 6312	Bedford WTB	111061	Duple	8618	C25F	3/37	–/46	4/50
YD 3193	Bedford WLB	108107	Waveney		B20F	10/31	–/46	7/52
HYB 646	Bedford OB	41821	Duple	46708	C29F	1/47	1/47	3/52
HYB 984	Bedford OB	42347	Duple	44687	C29F	2/47	2/47	3/52
JYA 839	Bedford OB	60592	Duple	44688	C29F	10/47	10/47	9/58
HYN 420	Bedford OB	53454	Duple	44463	C29F	6/47	12/48	12/53
LYB 996	AEC Regal III	9621A788	Duple	45559	FC33F	1/50	1/50	11/63
LYD 134	AEC Regal III	9621A981	Duple	51446	FC33F	4/50	4/50	9/60
LYD 135	AEC Regal III	9621A982	Duple	51447	FC33F	5/50	5/50	5/57
MYD 985	AEC Regal III	9821E477	Harrington	926	C37C	8/51	8/51	12/61
GDM 169	Maudslay Marathon III	70585	Burlingham	4466	C35F	3/50	3/52	1/61
PYB 240	AEC Regal IV	9822S1453	Harrington	1208	C37C	7/53	7/53	1/62
XYD 700	Bedford SBG	49945	Duple	1074/31	C41F	6/57	6/57	4/64
EF 8132	Bedford OB	62378	Duple	44635	C29F	–/48	1/59	4/59
HYB 984	Bedford OB	42347	Duple	44687	C29F	2/47	1/59	2/59
JAU 804	Bedford OB	62688	Duple	43319	C29F	5/48	1/59	7/59
JAU 808	Bedford OB	61717	Duple	46976	C29F	5/48	1/59	1/60
JYA 630	Bedford OB	57071	Duple	48214	C29F	8/47	1/59	4/60
KUX 211	Bedford SBG	28122	Duple	1051/156	C36F	5/54	1/59	5/59
NVM 134	Bedford SB	15830	Harrington	1205	C36F	6/53	1/59	3/60
MLF 342	Leyland PSU1/15	504684	Bellhouse Hartwell		C35C	2/52	5/59	1/61
MLF 346	Leyland PSU1/15	504540	Bellhouse Hartwell		C35C	4/52	5/59	1/60
919 EYA	AEC Reliance	2MU3RV2569	Duple	1109/36	C41F	6/59	6/59	12/64
MLF 341	Leyland PSU1/15	504536	Bellhouse Hartwell	8213	C35C	2/52	7/59	1/60
107 GYC	Bedford SB3	75174	Duple	1120/206	C41F	3/60	3/60	12/64
108 GYC	Bedford SB3	75170	Duple	1120/207	C41F	3/60	3/60	10/64
109 GYC	Bedford SB3	74597	Duple	1120/187	C41F	4/60	4/60	12/64
LTA 624	AEC Regal III	9621A774	Duple	55177	C32F	5/50	9/60	3/64
LTA 627	AEC Regal III	9621A777	Duple	55180	C32F	5/50	10/60	6/64
LTA 623	AEC Regal III	9621A773	Duple	55181	C32F	5/50	1/61	10/64
312 KYC	Bedford SB1	87193	Duple	1133/349	C41F	3/61	3/61	12/64
500 NYD	Bedford SB5	89264	Harrington	2600	C41F	4/62	4/62	10/64
501 NYD	Bedford SB5	89479	Harrington	2601	C41F	4/62	4/62	9/64
NUO 690	AEC Regal IV	9822S1634	Willowbrook	53104	C41F	5/53	5/62	12/64
LFJ 876	Leyland PS2/3	496172	Yeates	239	C37F	7/51	11/63	12/64
LFJ 877	Leyland PS2/3	500449	Yeates	240	C37F	7/51	11/63	8/64
NUO 684	AEC Regal IV	9822S1628	Willowbrook	53098	C41F	5/53	3/64	12/64
NUO 686	AEC Regal IV	9822S1630	Willowbrook	53100	C41F	5/53	3/64	12/64

Previous History:

- **DV 1994:** New to FJ Blackmore {Greyhound Coaches}, Ilfracombe (DN); becoming FJ Blackmore and AV Rudd {Black and White Coaches}, Ilfracombe (DN) at an unknown date; FW Northcott, Taunton (SO) at an unknown date; from whom it was acquired.
- **DV 6315:** New to WH Gubb & Son {Lucky Violet Parlour Cars}, Ilfracombe (DN); FW Northcott, Taunton (SO) at an unknown date; from whom it was acquired.
- **EF 6312:** New to Wilson, Dunning & Barker {Bee Line Roadways Luxury Coaches}, Greatham (DM); FW Northcott, Taunton (SO) at an unknown date; from whom it was acquired.
- **EF 8132:** New to Alton Brothers (Trimdon) Ltd, Trimdon (DM); AA Woodbury, Wellington (SO) 11/48; from whom it was acquired.
- **YD 3193:** New to PG Hanks, Bishops Lydeard (SO), passing to Western National Omnibus Co Ltd, Exeter (DN) 3449 6/33; FW Northcott, Taunton (SO) at an unknown date; from whom it was acquired.
- **DCJ 691:** New to GT, GF, FL & HB Holland {Holland Bros), Oldbury (WO) registration unknown; War Department (GOV) at an unknown date; re-registered DCJ 691, probably by Praill (dealer), Hereford, for Bowerman in 6/46.
- **GDM 169:** New to WG Richardson & Sons, Buckley (CN); from whom it was acquired.
- **HYN 420:** New to Bradshaw's Super Coaches Ltd, London SE18 (LN); from whom it was acquired.
- **JAU 804:** New to A Skill, Nottingham (NG) 4; AA Woodbury, Wellington (SO) 10/49; licensed 1/50; from whom it was acquired.
- **JAU 808:** New to A Skill, Nottingham (NG) 8; AA Woodbury, Wellington (SO) 10/49; licensed 1/50; from whom it was acquired.
- **JYA 630:** New to AA Woodbury, Wellington (SO); from whom it was acquired.
- **KUX 211:** New to Corvedale Motor Co Ltd, Ludlow (SH) 31; AA Woodbury, Wellington (SO) 3/57; from whom it was acquired.
- **LFJ 876:** New to Greenslades Tours Ltd, Exeter (DN); from whom it was acquired.
- **LFJ 877:** New to Greenslades Tours Ltd, Exeter (DN); from whom it was acquired.
- **LTA 623:** New to Devon General Omnibus & Touring Co Ltd, Torquay (DN) TCR623; Greenslades Tours Ltd, Exeter (DN) 4/58; from whom it was acquired.
- **LTA 624:** New to Devon General Omnibus & Touring Co Ltd, Torquay (DN) TCR624; Greenslades Tours Ltd, Exeter (DN) 4/58; from whom it was acquired.
- **LTA 627:** New to Devon General Omnibus & Touring Co Ltd, Torquay (DN) TCR627; Greenslades Tours Ltd, Exeter (DN) 5/58; from whom it was acquired.
- **MLF 341:** New to Blue Cars (Continental) Ltd, London WC2 (LN); becoming Blue Cars Continental Coach Cruises Ltd, London WC2 (LN) 3/53; from whom it was acquired.
- **MLF 342:** New to Blue Cars (Continental) Ltd, London WC2 (LN); becoming Blue Cars Continental Coach Cruises Ltd, London WC2 (LN) in 3/53; from whom it was acquired.
- **MLF 346:** New to Blue Cars (Continental) Ltd, London WC2 (LN); becoming Blue Cars Continental Coach Cruises Ltd, London WC2 (LN) in 3/53; from whom it was acquired.
- **NUO 684:** New to Devon General Omnibus & Touring Co Ltd, Torquay (DN) TCR684; Greenslades Tours Ltd, Exeter (DN) 4/61; from whom it was acquired.
- **NUO 686:** New to Devon General Omnibus & Touring Co Ltd, Torquay (DN) TCR686; Greenslades Tours Ltd, Exeter (DN) 7/61; from whom it was acquired.
- **NUO 690:** New to Devon General Omnibus & Touring Co Ltd, Torquay (DN) TCR690; Greenslades Tours Ltd, Exeter (DN) 3/62; from whom it was acquired.
- **NVM 134:** New to Shearing Tours (Manchester) Ltd, Manchester (GM); withdrawn 10/53; Lancashire Motor Traders (dealer), Salford at an unknown date; AA Woodbury, Wellington (SO) 3/54; from whom it was acquired.

Disposals:

- **DV 1994:** Scrapped 9/46.
- **DV 6315:** Last licensed to Bowerman 12/49.
- **EF 6312:** CT, AJ & MH Parsons {Parsons Motors}, Greenham (SO) at an unknown date, not operated.
- **EF 8132:** AH Walker {AH Walker & Son / Wivey Coaches}, Wiveliscombe (SO) 4/59; withdrawn 5/64; AJ Pincombe, Rackenford (DN) 9/64; withdrawn 5/68.
- **YD 3193:** Unidentified owner, Guildford by 12/87; Homer, Quarry Bank for preservation 12/87; M Chivers, Shirley for preservation by 8/91.
- **DCJ 691:** Knight Brothers, Exeter (DN) 11/47; TW Halpin {Barking Coaches}, Barking (LN) 7/50; MR Posner and ER Atkinson {Gantshill Coaches}, Ilford (LN) 8/51; withdrawn 4/52; FVT Holland {Holland's Coaches}, London E6 (LN) 9/52; withdrawn 3/55; a photograph taken c1951 exists of this vehicle with 'Lindy's' in the destination glass. It is unclear whether this was an additional operator.
- **GDM 169:** TK O'Donoghue {The Aherlow}, Tipperary, Eire (EI) 1961; O'Malley, Newport (EI) by 1966; scrapped at the depot by 7/69.

HYB 646: AA Woodbury, Wellington (SO) 3/52; Corvedale Motor Co Ltd, Ludlow (SH) 3 3/57; AA & Mrs CM Higginbottom {Sargeant Bros}, Llanfaredd (RR) 1/58; withdrawn 9/63; scrapped.
HYB 984: AA Woodbury, Wellington (SO) 3/52; Bowerman's Tours Ltd (again) 1/59; withdrawn 2/59.
HYB 984: Not traced (second time)
HYN 420: Not traced.
JAU 804: FW Parker {Empress Coaches}, Ilminster (SO) 7/59; withdrawn 11/60; Woodcock Coaches Ltd, Corsham (WI) 6/61; withdrawn 8/63; Bleaken's Coaches Ltd, Hawkesbury Upton (GL) 1/64 withdrawn 5/65; Young Communists as a caravan 5/65.
JAU 808: EG & NEG Bryant and LM Clark, Monksilver (SO) 2/60; NEG Bryant and LM Clark, Williton (SO) at an unknown date; withdrawn 5/69.
JYA 630: Heard's Garages Ltd {Torrie Coaches}, Torrington (DN) 7/60.
JYA 839: Heard's Garages Ltd {Torrie Coaches}, Torrington (DN) 9/58.
KUX 211: GE Wright {Bow Belle}, Bow (DN) 5/59 withdrawn 2/65; CF Ware {Bell Luxury Coaches}, Hounslow (MX) 2/65; EG Wilmot, Southall (MX) 9/66; Carter and Blewitt Fruit Frams, Boxted (XEX) 8/68.
LFJ 876: Williams (contractor), Taunton (XSO) by 4/66.
LFJ 877: Staverton (contractor), Totnes (XDN) 194 4/65.
LTA 623: Unidentified showman 10/64.
LTA 624: Unidentified showman 3/64.
LTA 627: J Dyer & Sons (Weston-super-Mare) Ltd (contractor), Weston-super-Mare (XSO) 7/64; Penfold (dealer), Hewish for scrap 3/66.
LYB 996: J Dyer & Sons (Weston-super-Mare) Ltd (contractor), Weston-super-Mare (XSO) 11/63.
LYD 134: Darch and Willcox Ltd {Comfy-Lux}, Martock (SO) 9/60; withdrawn 4/64; re-seated to FC37F; GC Brown {CW Brown & Son / Witch Coaches}, Warboys (CM) 4/64; Fitzpatrick (contractor), London E3 (XLN) 10/65.
LYD 135: Wessex Coaches Ltd, Bristol (GL) 5/57; withdrawn 6/70; derelict at Seal Sands Power Station site, Hartlepool 8/71.
MLF 341: CW Banfield Ltd, London SE17 (LN) 5/60.
MLF 342: O'Brien Tours Ltd, Maryboro (EI) 1961.
MLF 346: CW Banfield Ltd, London SE17 (LN) 6/60.
MYD 985: V Bellamy {Victor's Coaches}, London E17 (LN) 5/62; Laceys (East Ham) Ltd, London E6 (LN) at an unknown date; withdrawn 7/63; Sherstonian Coaches Ltd, Sherston (WI) 8/63; Athelstan Coaches Ltd, Malmesbury (WI) 10/63; withdrawn 8/65; FA & JE Fanthom, Leigh Sinton (WO) 8/65; still owned 10/66.
NUO 684: Kingdom's Tours Ltd {Tivvy Coaches}, Tiverton (DN) 1/65; DP Gourd, Bishopsteignton (DN) 4/67; A, J & K Millman, Buckfastleigh (DN) 4/68 withdrawn 3/69; Ninestones Riding School, Liskeard (XCO) by 3/75; D Sayers, Halifax for preservation 7/79; sold for scrap 7/80; not collected by 10/80.
NUO 686: Kingdom's Tours Ltd {Tivvy Coaches}, Tiverton (DN) 1/65; withdrawn 2/66; M Ascough (dealer), Dublin 2/66; Richardson's Fertilizers Ltd, Belfast (XAM) 5/66.
NUO 690: Kingdom's Tours Ltd {Tivvy Coaches}, Tiverton (DN) 1/65; withdrawn 1/66; Dawlish Coaches Ltd {Tomlinson's}, Dawlish (DN) 1/66; DC Venner, Witheridge (DN) 3/66; LJ Hubber {Streamline Coaches}, Newquay (CO) 5/66; HG Brown and G Davies {Truronian Coaches}, Truro (CO) 5/68; withdrawn 6/70; Cornish Gliding and Flying Club, Perranporth as a clubhouse by 8/72.
NVM 134: AH Walker (AH Walker & Son/Wivey Coaches), Wiveliscombe (SO) 3/60; withdrawn 2/68.
PYB 240: BC & S Blackwell {S Blackwell & Son}, Earls Colne (EX) re-seated to C40C 1962; DR MacGregor {Hedingham and District}, Sible Hedingham (EX) L42 as C37C 10/65; Keenan, Bellurgan (EI) 3/68.
XYD 700: NEG Bryant & LM Clark, Williton (SO) at an unknown date.
919 EYA: PI Berry and JG Hemmings, Taunton (SO) 1/65.
107 GYC: PI Berry & JG Hemmings, Taunton (SO) 4/65; withdrawn 1/83; Wacton Trading/Coach Sales (dealer), Bromyard 1/83; Herefordshire Transport Collection for preservation 1/87; operated as psv by MJ Perry {Bromyard Omnibus}, Bromyard (HR) 2 between 7/90 and 9/90; AW Hall {Hamps Valley Coaches}, Winkill (ST) for preservation by operator; R Chambers, Bristol for preservation 8/05.
108 GYC: BJ Redwood {Redwood's Services}, Hemyock (DN) 10/64; retained as preserved vehicle from 10/80; becoming Redwoods Travel, Hemyock (DN) 5/08.
109 GYC: Osmond's Tours and Engineering Ltd {Curry Queen}, Curry Rivel (SO) 2/65.
312 KYC: Wake's Services (Sparkford) Ltd, Sparkford (SO) 12/64; withdrawn by 7/82; unidentified owner as a caravan by 8/83.
500 NYD: Darch & Willcox {Comfy-Lux}, Martock (SO) 10/64; withdrawn 2/66; CL Norman, Keynsham (SO) 3/66; IJ & K Evans {Vanguard Coaches}, Bulkington (WK) 5/69; withdrawn 2/78; M Shifley {395}, Coventry as a stock car transporter by 4/81.

2PH10/79

501 NYD: Margo's Luxury Coaches (Streatham) Ltd, London SW16 (LN) 4/65; ABC Taxis (J Lambley) Ltd, Guildford (SR) 8/65; licensed 3/66; withdrawn 10/70; HF Duncombe, Wendover (BK) at an unknown date.

| CG & L Burgoyne | Burgoyne Brothers/Grey Cars | Marine Garage, Esplanade, Sidmouth |
| CG Burgoyne | Grey Cars (from 1947) | |

Livery: Cream and red; blue and grey.

Business acquired by Greenslades 7/56.

T 7198	Sunbeam	16/5313/19	?		Car8	9/19	9/19	by -/29
DR 5066	Reo Sprinter	FAX10367	Mumford		C14-	5/29	5/29	9/37
UL 8878	?	?	?		Car6	-/29	-/29	7/50
DR 6993	Commer Invader 6TK	28075	Mumford		C20D	5/30	5/30	9/50
GC 2052	Le Salle Alluet	?	?		Car7	-/--	-/--	7/50
JY 2029	Commer Centurion	56003	Mumford		C20-	6/33	6/33	4/49
BOD 418	Commer PN3	46532	Mumford		C20-	7/36	7/36	4/49
EUO 250	Bedford WTB	112419	Tiverton		C20F	6/38	6/38	4/55
AGH 212	Austin		?		Car7	-/33	-/--	-/--
JTA 936	Bedford OWB	16023	Duple	33958	B32F	10/43	10/43	4/53
GUO 114	Bedford OB	25599	Willmott		C26F	9/46	9/46	5/55
NJ 5237	Bedford WLB	109950	Duple	4764	C20F	2/35	-/46	4/51
FPX 749	Bedford OWB	14445	Duple	32183	B29F	5/43	-/48	5/55
DUJ 253	Bedford OB	49817	Duple	43231	C29F	5/47	3/49	*
DUX 586	Bedford OB	60927	Duple	43233	C29F	10/47	4/49	*
LUO 359	Commer Avenger	23A0152	Harrington	666	C31F	12/49	12/49	*
HSP 144	Commer Avenger	23A0181	Harrington		C32F	-/49	5/55	*

Previous History:
T 7198 : New to Smith (private?), Bideford; from whom it was acquired.
GC 2052: Acquired from an unknown (probably private) owner.
NJ 5237: New to B French {French & Sons}, Seaford (ES); Osborne, Old Woking (SR) at an unknown date; from whom it was acquired.
UL 8878: Acquired from an unknown (probably private) owner.
AGH 212: Acquired from an unknown (probably private) owner.
DUJ 253: New to JT, FW & GE Whittle {JT Whittle & Sons}, Highley (SH); from whom it was acquired.
DUX 586: New to JT, FW & GE Whittle {JT Whittle & Sons}, Highley (SH); from whom it was acquired.
FPX 749: New to WV Roberts, Petworth (WS) as B32F; re-seated to B29F at an unknown date; from whom it was acquired.
GUO 114: The Willmott body was pre-war; acquired from an unknown source.
HSP 144: New to T Brown, Kelty (FE); A Ferguson and GB Murray {Comfort Coaches}, Dunfermline (FE) at an unknown date; H Collinson, Dewsbury (WY) 3/52; E & S Talbott {E Talbott & Son}, Gawthorpe (WY) 5/54; withdrawn 11/54; from whom it was acquired.
JTA 936: Re-seated to B26F and then to B24F at unknown dates.

Disposals:
T 7198: AA Woodbury, Wellington (SO) by 1929; Carpenter, Exeter for scrap at an unknown date.
DR 5066: No further operator.
DR 6993: No further operator.
GC 2052: Not traced.
JY 2029: AJ Smith (farmer), Elverway Forum, Branscombe (XDN) 4/49.
NJ 5237: LG Petherick, Chawleigh (DN) 4/51; E Osborne, East Worlington (DN) 7/52; withdrawn 7/55; DC Venner, Witheridge (DN) 11/55; withdrawn 6/56; scrapped.
UL 8878: Not traced.
AGH 212: Not traced.
BOD 418: AJ Smith (farmer), Elverway Forum, Branscombe (XDN) at an unknown date; withdrawn 12/60.
EUO 250: E Osborne, East Worlington (DN) 5/55; withdrawn 5/60; R Morgan (showman?), South Molton.
FPX 749: Mobile Shop, Black Cat, South Devon at an unknown date.
GUO 114: Mrs LF Lord {Astley Garage}, South Milton (DN) 5/55; RW & E Bloomfield {South Milton Bus Service}, South Milton (DN) 8/61; withdrawn 8/62; unidentified owner Thurlestone, Devon as a snack bar.

JTA 936: J, EM & AB Geddes {JM Geddes & Son/Burton Cars}, Brixham (DN) 9/53; withdrawn 8/60.

Vehicles marked with an asterisk (*) were transferred to Greenslades 7/56.

E Clatworthy	Supreme Motor Coaches	Fore Street, Tiverton
		Garage – on A396, Bampton Road
E Clatworthy Ltd 4/64	WJ Greenslade's Tiverton Coaches	15, Angel Hill, Tiverton

Business acquired by WJ Greenslade and the limited company (E Clatworthy Ltd) formed 4/64.
Livery: Cream with brown stripe.

Business sold to Cox Bros (Exeter) Ltd, Tiverton (DN) 6/71, then resold to Kingdom's Tours Ltd, Tiverton (CN) 9/71.

Reg	Chassis	Chassis No	Body	Body No	Seats	New	Acquired	Withdrawn
TA 5793	FIAT (15TER?)	53A6285	?		C14-	3/23	3/23	9/29
TA 2841	Garford 20 hp	25595	?		C18-	1/22	by2/24	6/28
FJ 2702	Lancia Z	?	?		C20-	9/23	-/28	9/31
DV 1183	Dodge D	D196339	?		C19-	5/29	5/29	10/36
DV 5632	Chevrolet U	66669	?		C14-	6/30	6/30	c-/38
OD 1855	Commer Centaur	46019	?		C20F	3/32	3/32	-/43
YV 3656	Albion PNA26	5055I	?		C26-	4/28	4/34	5/37
YD 2142	AJS Pilot	164	?		C26-	6/31	-/--	by 3/44
VV 10	Reo Pullman	GE155	Duple	1887	C20F	6/30	c-/36	-/40
UL 1846	Leyland PLC1	47810	?		C29-	3/29	5/37	1/42
EUO 508	Dodge SBF	777	?		C26R	7/38	7/38	by 9/43
HTA 938	Bedford OWB	10293	Duple	31798	B32F	1/43	5/43	9/56
HDV 754	Bedford OB	53419	Tiverton		C27F	3/48	11/47	12/56
UO 5792	Austin 6P	5119	?		T10	3/28	12/48	6/50
BWV 716	Bedford WTB	2690	Duple	5424/2	C25F	5/39	8/50	8/52
KYB 954	Bedford WTB	E1031	?		FC29F	1/49	12/50	8/56
JNP 888	Austin K4/--	143148	Kenex		FC32F	9/50	2/52	4/64
HTX 628	Commer Commando	17A1278	Harrington	444	C30F	12/48	6/52	8/61
CFB 190	Commer Avenger	23A0367	Churchill		C33C	11/50	8/56	2/63
SDR 249	Bedford SB3	78193	Duple	1120/282	C41F	4/60	4/64	4/66
SJY 61	Bedford SB3	73005	Duple	1120/85	C41F	4/60	4/64	2/69
SMU 447	Bedford SB	1084	Duple	56693	C33F	4/51	7/64	9/64
CTA 637C	Bedford J2SZ10	220380	Duple (Midland)	CFJ2/282	C19F	3/65	3/65	6/68
CDV 778C	Bedford SB5	95489	Duple	1183/6	C41F	4/65	4/65	6/71
GTA 688D	Bedford VAM14	6843478	Duple	1205/297	C45F	6/66	6/66	10/70
TFJ 440	Bedford SBG	46198	Duple	1060/447	C36F	6/56	7/67	11/67
UFJ 303	Bedford SBG	50749	Duple	1074/308	C41F	6/57	12/67	10/68
NTA 855F	Bedford VAS5	?T453769	Duple	1217/48	C29F	3/68	3/68	10/70
UGR 225	Bedford SB5	91053	Duple	1159/309	C41F	4/63	4/69	6/71

Previous History:

FJ 2702: New to F Tooze, Exeter (DN); from whom it was acquired.

TA 2841: New to WH Dalton, Paignton (DN) as C14-; from whom it was acquired.

UL 1846: New to AE Bradshaw {Bradshaw's Super Coaches}, London SE18 (LN) as C24D; from whom it was acquired.

UO 5792: New to Sidmouth Motor Co and Dagworthy Ltd, Sidmouth (DN); originally as a 6 seat taxi; operated as a psv from c1933; believed to have been rebodied as either a charabanc or a toastrack with 10 seats in 1936; SA Kingdom {Tivvy Coaches}, Tiverton (DN) at an unknown date; from whom it was acquired. This vehicle appears to have become confused with another similar vehicle registered GH 3281, which has a recorded last licensing date of 9/42.

VV 10: New to Allchin {Cream Cars}, Torquay (DN); from whom it was acquired.

YD 2142: New to E Ford, Alcombe (SO); HC Jennings & Son, Crowcombe (SO) at an unknown date; from whom it was acquired.

YV 3656: New to HJ Phillips & Sons Ltd {P & S Line Coaches}, London SW11 (LN); from whom it was acquired.

BWV 716: New to H, J & M Lampard {Lampard's Garages}, Pewsey (WI); C Bodman, Worton (WI) at an unknown date; becoming VG & RJ Bodman, Worton (WI) 5/46; from whom it was acquired.

CFB 190: New to Burrett and Wells Ltd, Melksham (WI) 28; from whom it was acquired.

HDV 754: Had a second-hand body transferred from an unidentified Western National Omnibus Co Ltd, Exeter (DN) vehicle and believed to have been rebuilt by Tiverton.

HTA 938: Re-seated B28F at an unknown date.
HTX 628: New to Pioneer Motors (Kenfig Hill), Ltd, Kenfig Hill (GG); from whom it was acquired.
JNP 888: This vehicle is believed to be based on an Austin K4 series goods chassis, converted to forward control. It has also been quoted as having a Mann Egerton body but this is thought to be incorrect. New to WD Smith {Fernhill Heath Motors}, Fernhill Heath (WO); withdrawn 3/51; from whom it was acquired.
KYB 954: The chassis was a rebuild of an unidentified pre-war vehicle, issued with a new chassis number and fitted with an unidentified second-hand body for E Tucker {Joyride Coaches}, Taunton (SO) in 1949; from whom it was acquired.
SDR 249: New to Embankment Motor Co (Plymouth) Ltd, Plymouth (DN); from whom it was acquired.
SJY 61: New to Embankment Motor Co (Plymouth) Ltd, Plymouth (DN); from whom it was acquired.
SMU 447: New to FR Harris, Grays (EX); becoming Frank Harris (Coaches) Ltd, Grays (EX) 4/60; Arlington Motor Co Ltd (dealer), Potters Bar 3/64; from whom it was acquired.
TFJ 440: New to Greenslades Tours Ltd, Exeter (DN); from whom it was acquired.
UFJ 303: New to Greenslades Tours Ltd, Exeter (DN); from whom it was acquired.
UGR 225: New to FW Stratton {Redby Coaches}, Sunderland (DM); Harrison {Arterial Motorways}, Derby (DE) 4/67; RA & ND Humphries, Bridgend (CC) 3/69; from whom it was acquired.

Disposals:
DV 1183: CE Heard, Burlescombe (DN) as C14- 10/36; SA Blake {Blake's Bus Services}, Delabole (CO) at an unknown date; last licensed 12/42.
DV 5632: Evans (farmer), Dunkeswell (GDN) as a lorry at an unknown date; last licensed 6/43.
FJ 2702: No further operator; scrapped.
OD 1855: W Maitland {Excelsior}, Bournemouth (DT) at an unknown date.
TA 2841: No further operator.
TA 5793: Not traced.
UL 1846: Unidentified owner as a lorry at an unknown date; last licensed 4/42.
UO 5792: Not traced.
VV 10: Greenslades Tours Ltd, Exeter (DN) 1940; F Baker {Bradninch Tours}, Bradninch (DN) 12/44; last licensed 6/46.
YD 2142: Maitland, Lymington (HA) at an unknown date.
YV 3656: Hansard, Merthyr Tydfil (GG) 5/37.
BWV 716: Not traced.
CFB 190: Derelict by 7/65.
EUO 508: Osmond's Tours and Engineering Co Ltd {Curry Queen}, Curry Rivel (SO) c1943; withdrawn 10/53.
HDV 754: Last licensed 12/56; derelict by 7/65.
HTA 938: Last licensed 9/56; derelict by 7/63.
HTX 628: Derelict by 7/65.
JNP 888: Not traced.
KYB 954: Not traced.
SDR 249: J Hoare & Sons Ltd {The Ivy}, Ivybridge (DN) 4/66; destroyed by fire 9/69.
SJY 61: GJ Way and J Collier {Way & Son}, Crediton (DN) 3/69; Pontesbury School, Pontesbury (XSH) by 5/76.
SMU 447: WA Hawkey & Sons Ltd, Wadebridge (CO) 9/64; HG Kinsman & Son Ltd, Bodmin (CO) 4/66; withdrawn 11/67; scrapped.
TFJ 440: C Pugsley {Imperial}, Yeo Vale (DN) 11/67; JW Pugsley, Swimbridge (DN) 11/73; withdrawn 3/76.
UFJ 303: C Pugsley {Imperial}, Yeo Vale (DN) 10/68; JW Pugsley, Swimbridge (DN) 11/73; withdrawn 9/74.
UGR 225: Cox Bros (Exeter) Ltd, Tiverton (DN) 6/71; Kingdom's Tours Ltd, Tiverton (DN) 9/71.
CDV 778C: Cox Bros (Exeter) Ltd, Tiverton (DN) 6/71; Kingdom's Tours Ltd, Tiverton (DN) 9/71.
CTA 637C: HT, D & WJD Oxenham {Mounts Bay Coaches}, Penzance (CO) 9/68; Mitchell's (Perranporth) Ltd, Perranporth (CO) 12/69; CG Cocks, Trewoon (CO) 11/70; WJ Yendell {Jack 'n Jill Coach Services}, Drayford (DN) 11/77; RJ Filer, Ilfracombe (DN) 3/78; RM Turner and Washington, Tiverton (DN) 1/80; MV & JM Edgcumbe {Sid Valley Coaches}, Sidmouth (DN) 1/81; Parsons, Aylesbeare (XDN) by 10/83.
GTA 688D: Osgood's Coaches Ltd, Totton (HA) 10/70; Kent's Coaches Ltd, Baughurst (HA) c2/71; C Cowdrey {Priory Coaches}, Gosport (HA) 8/79; St John's College, Southsea (XHA) 3/80; withdrawn by 4/84.
NTA 855F: Osgood's Coaches Ltd, Totton (HA) 10/70; Marchwood Motorways Ltd, Totton (HA) 10/72; WS Yeates Ltd (dealer), Loughborough 11/79; GE Nightingale, Budleigh Salterton 6/80; unknown owner as a mobile home by 7/84.

WA Dagworthy

Western Garage, Sidmouth

Sidmouth Motor Co and Dagworthy Ltd, Sidmouth formed 11/27 (For subsequent information see p86).

WA Dagworthy had acquired the business of the Sidmouth Motor Company Ltd at the end of the 1921 season (see p85).

T 2125	Daimler 18hp	?	?	W---	8/11	8/11	-/--
LF 90--	Commer	?	?	Ch14	2/13	2/13	by-/20
T 3152	Commer 25hp	?	?	Ch--	5/13	5/13	3/14
LC 3-39	Commer	?	?	Ch18	-/13	-/13	by-/20
T 5926	FIAT 25hp	66265Y	?	Ch14	9/16	9/16	by11/27
T 3630	FIAT 30hp	8163	?	Ch14	-/11	6/19	7/26?
T 7014	Dennis Subsidy 4 ton	12566	?	Ch23	6/19	6/19	*
T 6140	FIAT 15hp	?	?	Ch14	4/17	11/19	12/20
T 8226	Napier 25/30hp	3173N	?	Ch14-	3/20	3/20	*
T 9360	FIAT 25hp	203607	?	Ch14	7/20	7/20	c-/24
TA 771	FIAT (15TER?)	173355	?	Ch14-	3/21	3/21	5/22
TA 998	FIAT (15TER?)	173090	?	Ch14	4/21	4/21	2/25
TA 1763	FIAT	2200142	?	Ch14-	7/21	7/21	10/21
TA 1814	FIAT (15TER?)	173480	?	C14-	7/21	7/21	by11/27
TA 2514	FIAT (15TER?)	173490	?	Ch14	11/21	11/21	*
HP 1277	Daimler CK	3407	?	Ch20	c-/19	9/22	*
TA 6369	Dennis Chara	25068	?	Ch20	5/23	5/23	*
TA 6649	Dennis Chara	25063	?	B20	6/23	6/23	*
TT 758	Guy BA	BA2155	?	Ch20	7/24	7/24	*
TT 1043	Lancia Tetraiota	545	?	Ch20	8/24	8/24	*
T 7876	Guy (B?)	(B?)579	Dowell	Ch20	1/20 by 9/26		*
UO 3396	Leyland PLC1	45881	Leyland	C24-	7/27	7/27	*

Previous History:

T 3630: New as a landaulette with a private owner; fitted with the Ch14 body on acquisition.
T 6140: New as an ambulance; rebodied as a charabanc in 1919.
T 7876: New to Dean, Sidmouth (DN); from whom it was acquired.
HP 1277: New as a Daimler demonstrator; Shepherd and Blackburne, Budleigh Salterton (DN) at an unknown date; from whom it was acquired.

Notes:

T 7014: Rebodied by an unknown manufacturer as B23- c1922.
HP 1277: Converted to B--- at an unknown date, possibly having been fitted with another body from an unknown source.

Disposals:

T 2125: Not traced.
T 3152: R trevett, Seaton (DN) 3/14; withdrawn 1/15.
T 3630: F Tooze & Son, Exeter (DN) 7/26; Kitcher & Dunham Ltd {Greybird}, Bridport (DT) at an unknown date; National Omnibus & Transport Co, London SW3 (LN) (12/27?); no further operator.
T 5926: TE Herring, Burnham-on-Sea (SO) at an unknown date; last licensed 12/30.
T 6140: R Summers, Ottery St Mary (DN) 12/20; destroyed by fire 5/22 and replaced by a Crossley to which this registration was transferred.
T 9360: H Busby, Weare Giffard (DN) c1924; last licensed 9/31.
LC 3-39: Not traced.
LF 90--: Not traced.
TA 771: C Wakeham {Blue Motors}, Lynmouth (DN) at an unknown date; last licensed 9/34.
TA 998: DG Kendrick, Great Yarmouth (NK) at an unknown date; last licensed 9/30.
TA 1763: Hayball, Bridport (XDT) 10/21; Barker, Langley (GBK); last licensed 12/32.
TA 1814: Crabb, Upottery (GDN) as a van at an unknown date; last licensed 8/28.

Vehicles marked with an asterisk (*) were transferred to Sidmouth Motor Co and Dagworthy Ltd, Sidmouth (DN) 11/27 (qv).

HL Gunn Gunn's Tours   The Garage and Post Office, Rackenford, Tiverton

Business acquired by Greenslades 11/38

DV 340	Chevrolet LQ	51249	Gunn	B18F	4/29	4/29	-/--
DV 4280	GMC T30	303230	Gunn	C20F	3/30	3/30	*
UO 7597	Chevrolet LO	42023	?	-14-	7/28	c-/30	c-/36
OD 2686	Reo	ML241	Gunn	C20F	6/32	6/32	*
VF 6229	Reo Pullman	GE84	Taylor (Eaton)	C26F	6/29	6/35	*
AG 5348	Reo Pullman	GE177	Taylor (Eaton)	C20F	3/30	5/36	*
RX 7787	Reo	FD4335	?	C26-	12/30	1/38	*

Previous History:
   AG 5348: New to D Blane {Blane's Pullman Services}, Kilmarnock (AR) as B26F; Scottish General Transport Co Ltd, Kilmarnock (AR) 48 9/31; Western SMT Co Ltd, Kilmarnock (AR) 9/31; Gilford Motor Co Ltd (as dealer), London NW1 1/32; FH Nugus, Herongate (EX) 1932; City Coach Co Ltd, Brentwood (EX) 5/36; not operated; from whom it was acquired.
   RX 7787: New to Elliotts of Newbury Ltd, Newbury (GBE) as a van; JW Barnard {B & B Services}, Potten End (HT) and rebodied by an unknown manufacturer 7/37; from whom it was acquired.
   UO 7597: New to Witheridge Motor Transport Co, Witheridge (DN); from whom it was acquired.
   VF 6229: New to WJ Crisp, Northwold (NK); from whom it was acquired.

Disposals:
   DV 340: T Pritchard, Aberdare (GG) at an unknown date; last licensed 9/33.
   UO 7597: Le Paturel, Saltash (GCO) as a lorry; last licensed 3/38.

Vehicles marked with an asterisk (*) passed to Greenslades 11/38.

AJ Heywood
Mrs EJ Heywood (from 1932)
Mrs EJ Heywood & Samuel E Greenslade (from 1936)   Half Moon Inn, Cheriton Fitzpayne

Business acquired by Greenslades 11/45.

T 9436	Ford 22.4hp	?	?	-14-	-/20	8/20	5/21
T 8848	Packard	E107605	?	-20-	-/18	2/21	-/23
TA 808	GMC 25 hp	C24	?	Ch20	-/19	-/23	9/28
UO 6306	International SFR	46503D	?	C20-	4/28	4/28	by 3/37
UO 7609	Chevrolet LO	42787	?	C14-	7/28	7/28	5/33
YC 9718	Morris Viceroy	067Y	Dunn	C20-	6/30	c-/34	6/36
FH 5515	Dennis G	70150	?	C20F	5/28	6/36	*
BFJ 938	Bedford WTB	110644	Tiverton	C26F	6/36	6/36	*

Previous History:
   T 8848: New to L Lind, Exeter (GDN) probably as a van; fitted with the body listed before entering service.
   FH 5515: New to Davis & Sons {Westgate}, Gloucester (GL); PA Grindle {Forest Greyhound}, Cinderford (GL) c1930; from whom it was acquired.
   TA 808: Chassis new to Langridge {Comfy Cars}, Paignton (DN); re-registered on acquisition; original registration not known.
   YC 9718: New to EJ Dunn, Taunton (SO); Hart, Budleigh Salterton (DN) 7/32; from whom it was acquired.

Notes:
   UO 7609: Licensed as goods/hackney with 6 seats immediately prior to withdrawal date.

Disposals:
   T 8848: Turner, Cheriton Fitzpaine (GDN) as agricultural goods 1923; last licensed 12/30.
   T 9436: Not traced.
   TA 808: Not traced.
   UO 6306: JE Greenslade, Cheriton Fitzpaine (GDN) as a lorry at an unknown date; last licensed 3/37.
   UO 7609: No further operator.
   YC 9718: Scrapped.

An asterisk (*) denotes a vehicle which passed to Greenslades 11/45.

2PH10/84

RC & AC Hopkins   Hopkins & Sons   15 Piermont Place, Dawlish
                           Blue Moorland Coaches (from 1934)
                           Blue Mercury Coaches (GN 7321/3)

Livery: Light and dark blue

Business acquired by Greenslades 10/57.

Reg	Chassis	Chassis No	Body	Body No	Body Type	New	Acq	Disp
TA 2018	FIAT 30hp	85043	?		Ch14	-/17	8/21	-/23
TA 5745	Lancia Tetraiota	123	Burlingham		C20-	3/23	3/23	-/31
TA 7461	Lancia	215	?		C20-	8/23	8/23	5/36
TT 7464	Austin 5P	1224	?		Ch10	3/26	3/26	9/36
DV 9464	Morris Viceroy	155Y	RSJ?		C20-	6/31	6/31	9/45
OD 2224	Morris Director	049RP	Duple	2872	C14F	4/32	4/32	-/40
DV 7121	Chevrolet U	68283	?		C14F	10/30	6/34	-/40
DV 9147	Morris Viceroy	149Y	RSJ	1307	C24-	5/31	6/34	by -/43
DV 9350	Morris Viceroy	150Y	RSJ	1308	C24-	6/31	6/34	9/48
TT 4425	Buick	1347608	?		Car8	6/25	6/34	6/34
GN 7321	AEC Mercury	640072	Harrington		C20R	3/31	5/36	12/49
GN 7323	AEC Mercury	640128	Harrington		C20R	3/31	5/36	5/49
FDV 8	Bedford OB	47141	Duple	46954	C29F	4/47	4/47	10/57
DRM 36	Bedford WTB	11800	Duple	6082/2	C26F	2/39	3/48	2/52
KDV 226	Austin K4/VB	135633	Mann Egerton		C29F	3/49	3/49	10/57
MMP 809	Bedford OB	37276	Duple	43159	C29F	11/46	4/49	2/56
LTT 138	Bedford OB	117736	Duple	46955	C29F	9/49	10/49	10/57
MOD 737	Bedford SB	1749	Duple	57025	C33F	7/51	7/51	*
NTT 578	Bedford SB	6686	Duple	1013/15	C33F	1/52	1/52	*
UTT 985	Bedford SBG	42981	Duple	1060/283	C41F	2/56	2/56	*
VOD 549	Bedford SBG	50779	Duple	1074/204	C41F	2/57	2/57	*

Previous History:
  DV 7121: New to W Parker, Chulmleigh (DN); Coombes, Starcross (DN) at an unknown date; LJ Shapter
         {Blue Moorland Cars}, Dawlish (DN) at an unknown date; from whom it was acquired.
  DV 9147: New to LJ Shapter {Blue Moorland Cars}, Dawlish (DN); re-seated to C22-, then to C25- at
         unknown dates; from whom it was acquired.
  DV 9350: New to LJ Shapter {Blue Moorland Cars}, Dawlish (DN); re-seated to C20- at an unknown date;
         from whom it was acquired.
  DV 9464: Re-seated to C25- at an unknown date.
  GN 7321: New to A Timpson & Sons Ltd {Grey Cars}, London SE6 (LN) 321; Grey Cars Ltd, Torquay (DN)
         16 7/32; Devon General Omnibus & Touring Co Ltd, Torquay (DN) 316 11/33; re-seated to
         C21R at an unknown date; from whom it was acquired.
  GN 7323: New to A Timpson & Sons Ltd {Grey Cars}, London SE6 (LN) 323; Grey Cars Ltd, Torquay (DN)
         18 7/32; Devon General Omnibus & Touring Co Ltd, Torquay (DN) 318 11/33; re-seated to
         C21R at an unknown date; from whom it was acquired.
  TA 2018: Chassis new to War Office (GOV); from whom it was acquired; re-registered and rebodied by an
         unknown manufacturer.
  TT 4425: New to LJ Shapter {Blue Moorland Cars}, Dawlish (DN); from whom it was acquired.
  DRM 36: New to E Hartness {Hartness Bus and Coach Service}, Penrith (CU); from whom it was acquired.
  MMP 809: New to Oliver Taylor (Coaches) Ltd, Caterham (SR) 16; from whom it was acquired.

Notes:
  TT 7464: First registered to "Hopkins & Sons"; re-seated to Ch7 at an unknown date.

Disposals:
  DV 7121: WJ Bishop, Trull, Taunton (SO) at an unknown date; withdrawn 12/44; FJ Hartland, Taunton
         (GSO) as goods at an unknown date.
  DV 9147: CW & WHM Terraneau, South Molton (DN) at an unknown date; withdrawn 10/48; JE Lee,
         Meddon (DN) 9/49; last licensed 6/51.
  DV 9350: Last licensed to Hopkins 9/48; scrapped.
  DV 9464: Bell & West, West Pennard (SO) 12/50; last licensed as private to AR Kelly, Nympsfield, Gloucs
         7/54.
  GN 7321: EE Down, Newton Abbot (GDN) as a lorry 12/49.
  GN 7323: United Steel Co, Colsterworth (XKN) 5/49; scrapped 1/55.
  OD 2224: CA Gayton, Ashburton (DN) at an unknown date; withdrawn 4/49; scrapped.

TA 2018: Margrett & Gloyne, Yelverton (GDN) at an unknown date; last licensed 3/29.
TA 5745: LH Babbage, Chulmleigh (GDN) as a lorry 1931; last licensed 6/34.
TA 7461: Egerton (showman), Bristol at an unknown date; last licensed 11/36.
TT 4425: No further operator.
TT 7464: Goodrich Bros (dealer), Salisbury for scrap at an unknown date.
DRM 36: Couch and Stoneman Ltd, Dartmouth (DN) 5/52; withdrawn 3/58, DK Evans, Dartmouth (GDN) as a moble shop at an unknown date; last licensed 11/60.
FDV 8: EF Eggleton, Canterbury (KT) 3/58; JC Bailey, Faversham (KT) 7/61; DE Wren {Drew's Coaches}, Canterbury (KT) 3/62; withdrawn 5/64; Higgins, Folkestone as a caravan 3/65; last licensed 10/66.
KDV 226: T Budgen & Sons Ltd, Wincanton (SO) 12/57; withdrawn 8/65.
LTT 138: J Heathcoat and Co Ltd (contractor), Tiverton (XDN) by 9/59; A & AR Turner, Chulmleigh (DN) 1/70.
MMP 809: PA Newton, Chulmleigh (DN) 2/56; DC Venner, Witheridge (DN) 9/61; AFC & WH Greenslade {F Greenslade & Sons}, Dulverton (H) 10/62.

Vehicles marked with an asterisk (*) passed to Greenslades 10/57.

HA Knight   **Knight Brothers**   **Haven Road Garage, Exeter**
Knight's Tours (Exeter) Ltd (1/51)

Livery: Light and dark blue.

Business acquired by Greenslades 7/54.

GFJ 867	Bedford OB	34543	Duple	43087	C29F	12/46	12/46	*
DCJ 691	Bedford WTB	111876	Willmott		C25F	-/38	11/47	7/50
EVJ 439	Bedford OB	56990	Duple	46453	C29F	8/47	7/50	*
EFR 226	Bedford OB	134738	Duple	56105	C29F	4/50	3/53	*

Previous History:
DCJ 691: New to GT, GF, FL & HB Holland {Holland Bros}, Oldbury (WO) registration unknown; War Department (GOV) at an unknown date; re-registered, probably by Praill (dealer), Hereford, for Bowerman's Tours Ltd, Taunton (SO) 6/46; from whom it was acquired.
EVJ 439: New to WE Morgan {Wye Valley Motors}, Hereford (HR); from whom it was acquired.
EFR 226: New to A Whiteside Ltd, Blackpool (LA); from whom it was acquired.

Disposals:
DCJ 691: TW Halpin {Barking Coaches}, Barking (EX) 7/50; MR Posner and ER Atkinson {Gantshill Coaches}, Ilford (EX) 8/51 withdrawn 4/52; FVT Holland {Holland's Coaches}, East Ham (EX) 9/52; withdrawn 3/55.

Vehicles marked with an asterisk (*) passed to Greenslades 7/54.

Sidmouth Motor Company Ltd   **Fore Street, Sidmouth**

Business acquired by WA Dagworthy 1921.

T 8828	Leyland 36hp	8142	?		Ch26	-/18	-/18	-/21?
T 9614	Garford	WUT584A	?		Ch14	9/20	9/20	-/21
TA 1961	Vim	63198	?		Ch11	8/21	8/21	by-/25

Disposals:
T 8828: Chaplin & Rogers, Chard (SO) by 1/24; Stallabrass, London SE16 (GLN) as a lorry at an unknown date; last licensed 12/31.
T 9614: W Dagworthy, Sidmouth (DN) 1921; Sidmouth Motor Co & Dagworthy Ltd, Sidmouth (GDN) as a van; last licensed 12/31.
TA 1961: Abbot & Searle, Exmouth (DN) at an unknown date; AE Ford, (Exmouth?) (GDN) as a lorry; last licensed 3/27.

Sidmouth Motor Co & Dagworthy Ltd — Western Garage, Sidmouth

The company was formed in 11/27 to acquire the business of WA Dagworthy.

Livery: Originally maroon and putty, later cream and blue; toastracks were blue and cream.

Business acquired by Greenslades 6/56

Reg	Chassis	Chassis No	Body builder	Body No	Body	New	Acq	Disp
T 7014	Dennis Subsidy 4 ton	12566	?		B26-	6/19	11/27	9/31
T 7876	Guy (B?)	(B?)579	Dowell		Ch20	-/20	11/27	9/32
T 8226	Napier 19.6hp	3173N	?		Ch14	3/20	11/27	9/39
HP 1277	Daimler CK	3407	?		Ch20	c-/21	11/27	3/33
TA 2514	FIAT (15TER?)	173490	?		Ch14	11/21	11/27	11/28
TA 6369	Dennis Chara	25068	?		Ch20	5/23	11/27	9/33
TA 6649	Dennis Chara	25063	?		Ch20	6/23	11/27	9/33
TT 758	Guy BA	BA2155	?		Ch20	7/24	11/27	9/30
TT 1043	Lancia Tetraiota	545	?		Ch20	8/24	11/27	9/32
UO 3396	Leyland PLC1	45881	Leyland		C24-	6/27	11/27	-/30?
DV 3539	Vulcan Duchess	D39	?		C20-	1/30	1/30	3/39
Y 7422	Napier 25/30hp	?	?		T17	7/20	by-/31	8/39
UO 2331	Austin 5PL	4697	Tiverton?		B13-?	5/27	c-/33?	3/54
UO 5792	Austin 6PL	5119	?		T10?	3/28	c-/33?	-/--
ATA 507	Commer Centurion B50	56048	Mumford		C20F	8/34	8/34	6/49
HT 6792	Daimler		?		Car8	-/23	9/36	12/41
TT 5132	Austin 5PL	3345	Caseley		T10	7/25	c-/36	6/54
YH 2061	Austin		?		Car7	-/27	-/38	-/39?
EDV 433	Bedford WTB	14309	Duple	6027/2	C20F	3/39	3/39	*
EDV 975	Bedford WTB	14379	Duple	6028/2	C26F	5/39	5/39	-/41
UO 1477	Austin 5PL	4593	Dowell		T13	3/27	7/46	9/55
FFJ 968	Bedford OWB	13030	Duple	32068	B30F	3/43	7/46	*
FFJ 971	Bedford OWB	13475	Duple	32102	B31F	4/43	7/46	*
JUO 324	Bedford OB	43981	Duple	46524	C29F	2/47	2/47	*
YC 9715	Guy ONDL	ONDL9604	Guy		B20F	5/30	3/47	n/a
GDV 802	Guy Vixen	LV29603	Guy		FB18F	7/47	7/47	*
UO 7095	Austin (6PL?)	6278	Caseley		T13	6/28	c-/47	3/56
HOD 471	Guy Vixen	LV38778	?		FB24F	3/48	3/48	*
KOD 276	Guy Vixen	LLV40907P	Duple		FC27F	5/49	5/49	*
KOD 363	Guy Vixen	LLV40344P	Wadham		FC27F	6/49	6/49	*
KOD 364	Guy Vixen	LV38950	Devon Coachbuilders		FC23F	6/49	6/49	*
KOD 983	Guy Vixen	LV40440	Devon Coachbuilders		FC23F	7/49	7/49	*
CDV 772	Austin 16	E/RZ53790			Car6	11/38	1/51	1/53
DDD 166	Wolseley 25hp	325-3539	?		Car6	9/38	1/51	1/54
GHU 105	Austin 16	?	?		Car6	7/39	1/51	9/55
NUO 651	Bedford SB	7694	Duple	1009/144	C33F	3/52	3/52	*
EYE 144	Austin	?	?		Car6	-/38	12/53	11/55

Previous history:

T 7014: New to WA Dagworthy, Sidmouth (DN); from whom it was acquired.
T 7876: New to Dean, Sidmouth (DN); WA Dagworthy, Sidmouth (DN) by 9/26; from whom it was acquired.
T 8226: New to WA Dagworthy, Sidmouth (DN); from whom it was acquired.
T 8828: New to an unknown operator; Sidmouth Motor Touring Co, Sidmouth (DN) 3/21; from whom it was acquired.
T 9614: New to an unknown operator; Sidmouth Motor Touring Co, Sidmouth (DN) 3/21; from whom it was acquired.
Y 7422: New to Marshalsea Brothers, Taunton (SO) with an unidentified Ch20 body; from whom it was acquired.
HP 1277: New as a Daimler demonstrator; Shepherd & Blackbourne, Budleigh Salterton (DN) at an unknown date; WA Dagworthy, Sidmouth (DN) 6/26; from whom it was acquired.
HT 6792: New to an unknown (probably private) owner.
TA 2514: New to WA Dagworthy, Sidmouth (DN); from whom it was acquired.
TA 6369: New to WA Dagworthy, Sidmouth (DN); from whom it was acquired.
TA 6649: New to WA Dagworthy, Sidmouth (DN); from whom it was acquired.
TT 758: New to WA Dagworthy, Sidmouth (DN); from whom it was acquired.
TT 1043: New to WA Dagworthy, Sidmouth (DN); from whom it was acquired.
TT 5132: New to WA Dagworthy, Sidmouth (DN); from whom it was acquired.

UO 1477: New to WA Dagworthy, Sidmouth (DN); from whom it was acquired.
UO 2331: New to WA Dagworthy, Sidmouth (DN); from whom it was acquired.
UO 3396: New to WA Dagworthy, Sidmouth (DN); from whom it was acquired.
UO 5792: New to Sidmouth Motor Co & Dagworthy Ltd, Sidmouth (DN) as a taxi.
UO 7095: New to Sidmouth Motor Co & Dagworthy Ltd, Sidmouth (DN) as a taxi.
YC 9715: New to Burnell's Motors {Lorna Doone Coaches}, Weston-Super-Mare (SO), as B19F; passing to Bristol Tramways and Carriage Co Ltd, Bristol (GL) X160 8/33; re-seated to B20F 7/34; renumbered 127 1/37; Cole (dealer), Corsham 2/47; from whom it was acquired.
YH 2061: Acquired from an unknown (probably private) owner.
CDV 772: Previous history not known.
DDD 166: Acquired from an unknown (probably private) owner.
EYE 144: Acquired from an unknown (probably private) owner.
FFJ 968: New to Exeter Corporation (DN) 72 as B32F; Greenslades (qv) in 5/46; from whom it was acquired.
FFJ 971: New to Exeter Corporation (DN) 75 as B32F; Greenslades (qv) in 5/46; from whom it was acquired.
GHU 105: Acquired from an unknown (probably private) owner.

Notes:

T 8226: Converted to toastrack configuration prior to commencement of Peak Hill and Salcome Hill services in 1933; believed to have been T20 originally, subsequently re-seated to T17.
Y 7422: Rebodied as listed on acquisition.
TA 2514: Re-seated to Ch10 at an unknown date.
TA 6369: Rebuilt or rebodied as C20D at an unknown date.
TA 6649: Rebuilt or rebodied as C20D at an unknown date.
TT 5132: Originally a taxi; rebodied Caseley T10 5/36.
UO 1477: Rebodied Dowell T13 body 7/46.
UO 2331: Originally a 6 seat taxi; operated as a psv from c1933; believed to have been rebodied, or possibly fitted with an older, rebuilt, body by Tiverton B13- 8/40; though it is suggested this may have taken place in 1946.
UO 5792: Originally a 6 seat taxi; operated as a psv from c1933; believed to have been rebodied as either a charabanc or a toastrack with 10 seats in 1936.
UO 7095: Originally a 6 seat taxi; rebodied Caseley T13 9/47.
YC 9715: Not operated; body rebuilt and transferred to new Guy Vixen GDV 802 8/47.
GDV 802: Body new 1930 transferred from Guy ONDL YC 9715; having been rebuilt without side windows and fitted behind a lorry cab with full front.
HOD 471: Had a pre-war coach body with folding canvas roof, possibly transferred from Commer Centurion B50 ATA 507; rebuilt to full-front configuration with bus seats and without side windows, possibly by Tiverton, for fitting to the new chassis.
KOD 983: A photograph exists showing this vehicle carrying the incorrect registration KOD 987.

Disposals:

T 7014: No further operator; last licensed 9/31.
T 7876: No further operator; last licensed 9/32.
T 8226: Last licensed 9/39.
Y 7422: No further operator; last licensed 8/39.
DV 3539: Home Office, London SW1 (GOV) for use as a fire tender; last licensed 3/39.
HP 1277: No further operator.
HT 6792: Not traced.
TA 2514: No further operator; last licensed 11/28.
TA 6369: No further operator; last licensed 9/33.
TA 6649: No further operator; last licensed 5/34.
TT 758: No further operator; last licensed 9/30.
TT 1043: No further operator; last licensed 9/32.
TT 5132: West of England Transport Collection, Winkleigh for preservation late 1963; Clinton Devon Estates, Bicton (XDN) for spares (11/66?); body transferred to a Sunbeam Talbot car chassis, then transferred to a 1936 Austin 20 CLJ 566; chassis presumed scrapped; CLJ 566 subsequently to C Shears, Winkleigh for preservation 2/91; A Jones, Lyme Regis for preservation 1994; R Austin, Raunds for preservation 3/00; deceased by 6/07; not traced further.
TT 7154: No further operator; last licensed 9/34.
UO 1477: C Shears, Winkleigh for preservation 3/56; DJR Stewart, Guildford for preservation 11/56; SB Lacy, Milford for preservation at an unknown date; D Bygrave, Baldock for preservation by 5/68.

R Rye, Buntingford for preservation by 4/00; R & S Eley & T Griffiths, Sidmouth for preservation 12/03; restored in a white livery; Tom Griffiths is the grandson of W Dagworthy.

UO 2331: B Thompson, Weymouth for preservation 1954; fitted with the fleet number plate 2854 which had been removed from Western National (DN) DR 5163; C Shears, West of England Transport Collection, Winkleigh for preservation 5/59; D Shears, West of England Transport Collection, Winkleigh for preservation by 10/91.

UO 3396: John's Transport, Slough (BK) at an unknown date; last licensed 12/42.

UO 5792: SA Kingdom {Tivvy Coaches}, Tiverton (DN) at an unknown date; E Clatworthy, Tiverton (DN) 12/48; last licensed 6/50. This vehicle appears to have become confused with another similar vehicle registered GH 3281, which has a recorded last licensing date of 9/42.

UO 7095: C Shears, Winkleigh for preservation late 1963; Clinton Devon Estates, Bicton (XDN) 11/66; on loan to Devon Bus Preservation Group, Exeter c9/81; returned to Clinton Devon Estates by 10/84; West of England Transport Collection, Winkleigh for preservation 2/91; A Blackman, Kent for preservation 12/93; body removed (owner uncertain, possibly still Blackman) 1996; body sold to P Budgen, Scarisbrick and fitted to Morris T chassis CP 3828 for preservation by 9/99, chassis retained by Blackman and to be given a car body; CP 3828 G Taylor, Witney for preservation; emigrated to New Zealand 9/05; subsequently re-registered MC.1925 for use in New Zealand.

YC 9715: Chassis scrapped 1948; body transferred to GDV 802 (see above).

YH 2061: Not traced.

ATA 507: Body probably rebuilt and transferred to new Guy Vixen HOD 471 (see above); chassis believed fitted with goods body for own use; last licensed by Sidmouth Motor Co & Dagworthy Ltd (GDN) as a lorry 6/52.

CDV 772: Not trsced.

DDD 166: WH Newcombe, Exeter (private?).

EDV 975: RE Wake {Wake's Services}, Sparkford (SO) 14 -/41; E Toomer, Moor Crichel (DT) 1/50 withdrawn 8/57; Wood Brothers Ltd, Mansfield (NG) 12/60; scrapped.

EYE 144: Not traced.

GHU 105: Not traced.

Vehicles marked with an asterisk (*) acquired by Greenslades 6/56

WJ Taylor
Taylor's Central Garages (Exeter) Ltd (5/30)

6 Bridge Street, Exeter

Livery: Ivory and blue.

Business acquired by Greenslades from HJ & FM Beal, a motor dealer of Exeter 1/54. HF & FM Beal having acquired an interest in the company in 1948.

Reg	Make	Chassis				Body	In	Acq	Out
FJ 1331	FIAT (15TER?)	?	?			Ch12	6/20	6/20	-/29
FJ 1751	FIAT 15TER	173504	?			Ch14	6/21	6/21	-/28
FJ 1920	FIAT 15TER	174151	?			Ch20	1/22	1/22	by9/27
FJ 2151	FIAT 15TER	?	?			Ch14	6/22	6/22	9/34
FJ 2164	FIAT 15TER	?	?			Ch14	7/22	7/22	9/30
FJ 2553	FIAT 15TER	174664	?			Ch14	5/23	5/23	9/32
FJ 2615	FIAT (15TER?)	205107	?			Ch14	6/23	6/23	9/31
FJ 3103	FIAT (15TER?)	205274	?			Ch14	6/24	6/24	11/35
FJ 3687	FIAT (15TER?)	?	?			Ch14	5/25	5/25	11/35
FJ 3840	Minerva	12020	?			Ch20	8/25	8/25	9/35
FJ 4367	Thornycroft A1	12745	?			C14F	6/26	6/26	10/38
FJ 4368	Thornycroft A1	12753	?			C14F	6/26	6/26	10/38
NK 5752	FIAT (15TER?)	205186	?			C14F	6/23	10/26	-/--
NK 5070	FIAT (15TER?)	205056	?			C14F	1/23	12/26	-/38
FJ 4950	Minerva MBR	26049	?			C26F	5/27	5/27	7/48
FJ 4951	Minerva MBR	26048	?			C26F	5/27	5/27	12/48
FJ 5776	Minerva MBR	28014	C20-	4695		C20-	7/28	7/28	9/37
FJ 5777	Minerva MBR	28012	Beadle	4696		C20-	7/28	7/28	9/37
FJ 6431	Minerva MBR	28070	Beadle	4957		C26-	7/29	7/29	6/34
TO 7451	Minerva HTM	26064	?			C32-	3/28	-/30	9/34
PT 8628	Minerva MBR	26560	?			C26-	10/26	3/31	9/37
PT 9511	Minerva MBR	26563	?			C26-	6/27	3/31	12/37
UP 212	Minerva MBR	26570	?			C26-	9/27	3/31	-/46
GU 8133	Thornycroft BC	18428	--			?	5/29	2/33	7/34

Reg	Chassis	Chassis No	Body		Body	Seats	New	Acq	Wdn
LA 5730	Lancia	?	?		C11-		-/11	-/33	7/34
UV 4079	Thornycroft BC	18815	Vickers		B30R		7/29	-/34	6/49
FM 4502	Daimler CF6	7242S	Brush		B30F		7/27	5/35	2/49
UN 190	Daimler CF6	7232S	Brush		B26F		7/27	5/35	9/37
YP 9979	Daimler		?		Car7		-/--	-/--	-/--
SX 2945	Daimler CF6	7158S	Hoyal		B32D		-/29	c-/37	by8/40
DFJ 935	Bedford WTB	111967	Heaver		C25F		4/38	4/38	3/51
DFJ 936	Bedford WTB	112013	Heaver		C25F		4/38	4/38	3/51
DFJ 937	Bedford WTB	112121	Heaver		C25F		4/38	4/38	3/51
EFJ 90	Commer PN3	46H715	Heaver		C14F		6/38	6/38	8/52
EFJ 91	Commer PN3	46H716	Heaver		C14F		6/38	6/38	7/52
EFJ 92	Bedford WTB	112122	Heaver		C25F		6/38	6/38	2/52
UV 4082	Thornycroft BC	18822	Vickers		B30R		7/29	7/38	7/50
DLX 916	AEC Regal	6622125	Strachan		C31F		4/37	-/38	9/39
DLX 918	AEC Regal	6622127	Strachan		C31F		4/37	-/38	9/39
FFJ 112	Commer PN3	46H726	Heaver		C14F		5/39	5/39	11/51
TW 8935	Leyland PLC1	45714	Mumford		C26R		4/27	4/46	7/46
UL 2655	Leyland PLC1	45327	Mumford		C20R		3/29	4/46	7/46
HFJ 117	Daimler CVD6	13337	Heaver		C33F		2/47	2/47	*
HFJ 300	Daimler CVD6	13336	Heaver		C35F		5/47	5/47	*
HFJ 390	Daimler CVD6	13866	Heaver		C35F		6/47	6/47	*
HTA 472	Bedford OWB	8776	Duple	31704	DP30F		8/42	2/48	1/52
JFJ 198	Bedford OB	67396	Heaver		C25F		6/48	6/48	*
FW 7106	AEC Regal	6621788	Willowbrook	2852	C32F		2/36	8/48	1/54
FW 7108	AEC Regal	6621790	Willowbrook	2854	C32F		2/36	8/48	6/51
JFJ 346	Bedford OB	70107	Heaver		C25F		8/48	8/48	*
EBU 223	Bedford OB	65698	Pearson		C25F		2/48	3/49	*
FPT 219	Bedford OWB	13121	SMT		DP28F		4/43	3/49	5/49
EBU 13	Bedford OB	34093	Pearson		C26F		7/47	5/49	*
JEH 407	Bedford OWB	12686	Mulliner		DP28F		3/43	5/49	2/52
GTD 460	AEC Regal	06624695	Santus		C32F		10/46	7/49	*
LPC 187	Foden PVSC5	23004	Whitson		C35F		3/47	7/49	*
GRL 70	Bedford OWB	17138	Duple	38570	DP28F		12/43	7/50	9/50
GCV 806	Bedford OWB	15986	Duple	33955	DP30F		10/43	8/50	1/51
LDH 712	Daimler CVD6	15943	Plaxton	149	C33F		10/48	5/51	*
LFJ 931	Daimler CVD6	17661	Duple	50209	C37F		7/51	7/51	*
MMT 880	Bedford OB	37258	Duple	43162	C29F		11/46	7/51	*
DVH 531	Bedford OB	76861	Duple	50419	C29F		6/48	1/52	*
DVH 837	Bedford OB	83793	Duple	50420	C29F		8/48	1/52	*
ECX 566	Bedford OB	108291	Duple	54362	C29F		6/49	1/52	*

Previous History:
Many of the early vehicles had bodies built in Exeter by unidentified manufacturers.

- FM 4502: New to Western Transport, Wrexham (DH), as B32F; Crosville Motor Services Ltd, Chester (CH) 828 in 5/33; from whom it was acquired.
- FW 7106: New to Enterprise and Silver Dawn Motors Ltd, Scunthorpe (LI) 12; Enterprise (Scunthorpe) Passenger Services Ltd, Scunthorpe (LI) 12 in 5/47; from whom it was acquired.
- FW 7108: New to Enterprise and Silver Dawn Motors Ltd, Scunthorpe (LI) 15; Enterprise (Scunthorpe) Passenger Services Ltd, Scunthorpe (LI) 15 in 5/47; from whom it was acquired.
- GU 8133: New to London & North Eastern Railway Co (Northern Scottish Area), Aberdeen (AD) 40; Scottish General Omnibus Co (Northern) Ltd, Elgin (MR) 53 9/30; W Alexander & Sons Ltd, Falkirk (SN) 53 11/31; from whom the chassis was acquired.
- LA 5730: Acquired from Teign Cars Ltd, Teignmouth by whom it had been acquired by 3/25; previous history not known.
- NK 5070: New to CW Dunford {Barnet Motor Services}, Barnet (HT); B Ringrose {Waltham Motor Services}, Waltham Cross (HT) 3/26; from whom it was acquired.
- NK 5752: New to CW Dunford {Barnet Motor Services}, Barnet (HT); B Ringrose {Waltham Motor Services}, Waltham Cross (HT) 3/26; from whom it was acquired.
- PT 8628: New to Blaydon 'A' Omnibuses Ltd (owning member J Robinson, Greenside (DM)); United Automobile Services Ltd, York (YK) B49 3/30; Hurlock (dealer), London SW2 5/30; from whom it was acquired.

PT 9511: New to Blaydon 'A' Omnibuses Ltd (owning member J Robinson, Greenside (DM)); United Automobile Services Ltd, York (YK) B46 3/30; Hurlock (dealer), London SW2 5/30; from whom it was acquired.
SX 2945: New to Thom {West Lothian Motor Services}, Edinburgh (MN); Scottish Motor Traction Co Ltd, Edinburgh (MN) 737 9/29; renumbered D10 1931; Leyland Motors Ltd (as dealer) 3/33; Henry Russett & Son Ltd {Royal Blue}, Bristol (GL) 4/33; from whom it was acquired.
TO 7451: New to Timmins, Nottingham (NG); W, AW, L, E, F & S Dutton {Unity Bus Services}, Nottingham (NG) 1929; from whom it was acquired.
TW 8935: New to National Omnibus and Transport Co Ltd, London SW3 (LN) 2332; Western National Omnibus Co Ltd, Exeter (DN) 2332 1930; from whom it was acquired. It originally had a Strachan and Brown B26R body and was rebodied when with Western National 6/36.
UL 2655: New to Leyland Motors as a demonstrator; JE Bower, Holmbridge (WR) for whom it was first registered WW 1661 6/27; Joseph Hanson & Sons Ltd, Huddersfield (WR) 1/29; Alldays Commercial Motors Ltd (dealer), London SW1 1/29; rebuilt and re-registered UL 2655 for Thomas Motors Ltd, Taunton (SO) 6/29; Western National Omnibus Co Ltd, Exeter (DN) 3414 in 4/33; from whom it was acquired. Rebodied when with Western National 6/35, original body not known.
UN 190: New to Western Transport, Wrexham (DH) as B32F; Crosville Motor Services Ltd, Chester (CH) 821 5/33; from whom it was acquired.
UP 212: New to Blaydon 'A' Omnibuses Ltd (owning member J Robinson, Greenside (DM)); United Automobile Services Ltd, York (YK) B45 3/30; Hurlock (dealer), London SW2 5/30; from whom it was acquired.
UV 4079: New to Great Western Railway Co Ltd, London W2 (LN) 1605 as B26R; Wrexham and District Transport Co Ltd, Wrexham (DH) 5/30; Western Transport Co Ltd, Wrexham (DH) 1/31; Crosville Motor Services Ltd, Chester (CH) 903 in 5/33; renumbered 894 in 1934; from whom it was acquired.
UV 4082: New to Great Western Railway Co Ltd, London W2 (LN) 1608 as B26R; Wrexham and District Transport Co Ltd, Wrexham (DH) 5/30; Western Transport Co Ltd, Wrexham (DH) 1/31; Crosville Motor Services Ltd, Chester (CH) 904 in 5/33; renumbered 895 in 1934; from whom it was acquired.
YP 9979: Acquired from an unknown (probably private) owner.
DLX 916: New to Pullman and European Motorways Ltd, London W1 (LN); from whom it was acquired.
DLX 918: New to Pullman and European Motorways Ltd, London W1 (LN); from whom it was acquired..
DVH 531: New to Hansons Buses Ltd, Huddersfield (WY) 263; from whom it was acquired.
DVH 837: New to Hansons Buses Ltd, Huddersfield (WY) 264; from whom it was acquired.
EBU 13: New to Shearing's Tours (Oldham) Ltd, Oldham (LA); withdrawn 8/48; from whom it was acquired.
EBU 223: New to H Harrison, Oldham (LA); Shearing's Tours (Oldham) Ltd (LA) 3/48; from whom it was acquired.
ECX 566: New to Hansons Buses Ltd, Huddersfield (WY) 272; from whom it was acquired.
FPT 219: New to G Pennington {Meadowfield Motor Co/Cosy Coaches}, Meadowfield (DM), as B32F; from whom it was acquired.
GCV 806: New to TW Mundy & Sons {Silver Queen}, Camborne (CO), as B32F; from whom it was acquired.
GRL 70: New to Newquay Motor Co {Red & White Tours}, Newquay (CO) as B32F; TW Mundy & Sons {Silver Queen}, Camborne (CO) 1/47; from whom it was acquired.
GTD 460: New to Mitton's Motors Ltd, Colne (LA) as C32F; from whom it was acquired..
HTA 472: New to CA Gayton {Gayton's Coaches}, Ashburton (DN); from whom it was acquired.
JEH 407: New to Thomas Tilstone & Sons Ltd, Tunstall (ST) 28 as B32F; from whom it was acquired.
LDH 712: New to JN & FN Boult {Boult's Tours}, Walsall (WM) 42; from whom it was acquired.
LPC 187: New to WS Hunt, Ottershaw (SR) F1; from whom it was acquired.
MMT 880: New to WJ Ray {Ray Coaches}, Edgware (LN); becoming Ray Coaches (Edgware) Ltd, Edgware (LN); from whom it was acquired..

Notes:
GU 8133: Believed to have been fitted with a body for use by Taylor, but not details known.
NK 5070: Rebodied Beadle C14F (4944) 1929.
NK 5752: Rebodied Beadle C14F (4945) 1929.
DFJ 937: Re-seated to C20F at an unknown date.
EFJ 92: Re-seated to C17F at an unknown date (possibly only temporarily).

Disposals:
FJ 1331: F Baker, Bradninch (DN) 1929; last licensed 6/30.

FJ 1751: JC Screech, Appledore (DN) 1928; withdrawn 9/29; Seaward & Warmington, Bideford (DN) at an unknown date.
FJ 1920: S Harris, Manchester (GM) at an unknown date; withdrawn 9/27; last licensed 9/27.
FJ 2151: No further operator; last licensed by Taylor 9/34.
FJ 2164: No further operator; last licensed by Taylor 9/30; scrapped.
FJ 2553: No further operator; last licensed by Taylor 9/32.
FJ 2615: No further operator; last licensed by Taylor 9/31.
FJ 3103: No further operator.
FJ 3687: Lorry of Taylor's; last licensed 12/38.
FJ 3840: No further operator; last licensed by Taylor 9/35.
FJ 4367: No further operator; last licensed by Taylor 10/38.
FJ 4368: National Fire Service vehicle, Dorset at an unknown date; scrapped 3/44.
FJ 4950: ME Williams {Seatax}, Paignton (DN) 7/48; RC Holmes, Greenbank, Plymouth as a mobile snack bar "Bob's Snack Bar" at an unknown date; withdrawn 9/52; last licensed 9/52.
FJ 4951: Rifle club, Winterbourne Strickland at an unknown date, used as a hut; last licenced 12/44 and scrapped.
FJ 5776: No further operator.
FJ 5777: No further operator.
FJ 6431: Teign Cars Ltd, Teignmouth (DN) 6/34; 120th Field Regiment, Royal Artillery, Budleigh Salterton (XDN) 9/39 – moved to Moreton Morrell (XWK) 2/40; last licensed 12/40.
FM 4502: W Bennetto {Majestic Motors}, Fraddon (CO) 6/49 withdrawn 3/51; Stevenson (showman), London at an unknown date, and to an unidentified showman, Cardiff 10/51.
FW 7106: Greenslades Tours Ltd, Exeter (DN) 1/54.
FW 7108: DC Venner, Witheridge (DN) 6/51; withdrawn 7/53 and to an unidentified showman, Exeter by 4/63.
GU 8133: Destroyed by fire 7/34.
LA 5730: Not traced.
NK 5070: Not traced.
NK 5752: Not traced.
PT 8628: No further operator; last licensed 9/37, by Taylor's.
PT 9511: No further operator; last licensed 12/37, by Taylor's.
SX 2945: No further operator. Last owner was Taylor's. Registration number void 8/40.
TO 7451: No further operator; last licensed 9/34, by Taylor's.
TW 8935: Last licensed by Taylor 7/46; United Nations Relief and Rehabilitation Administration, London W1 (XLN) at an unknown date, and exported to an unknown country.
UL 2655: Last licensed by Taylor 7/46; United Nations Relief and Rehabilitation Administration, London W1 (XLN) at an unknown date, and exported to an unknown country.
UN 190: No further operator; last licensed 9/37.
UP 212: JH Clark {Tally Ho!}, East Allington (DN) -/46; withdrawn 4/49, and scrapped; last licensed 12/49.
UV 4079: Sold for use as a caravan.
UV 4082: Sold for use as a caravan.
YP 9979: Not traced.
DFJ 935: Arlington Motor Co Ltd (dealer), London SW1 3/51 and exported to Egypt 2/52.
DFJ 936: Arlington Motor Co Ltd (dealer), London SW1 3/51 and exported to Egypt 2/52.
DFJ 937: Last licensed 12/53; HF & FM Beal (dealer), Exeter by 12/55.
DLX 916: Admiralty (Royal Navy) (GOV) 9/39; R Blackhurst (Blackpool) Ltd, Blackpool (LA) 7/45, rebodied Samlesbury C33F; JF Elsworth & Sons Ltd, Blackpool (LA) 10/50; R Coupland and AH Hay {C&H Coaches}, Fleetwood (LA) 5/54; withdrawn -/61.
DLX 918: Admiralty (Royal Navy) (GOV) 9/39; loaned to Belfast Corporation (AM) A161 in 1943; Matthais Luxury Coaches Ltd, Morriston (GG) at an unknown date; last licensed 3/54.
EFJ 90: CW & WHM Terraneau, South Molton (DN) 9/52; Passenger Vehicle Disposals Ltd (dealer), Dunchurch 9/55.
EFJ 91: Williamsons of Billingshurst Ltd {Billingshurst Coaches}, Billingshurst (WS) as C18F 7/52 withdrawn 2/54; JHW Moore, Stone as a mobile shop at an unknown date; last licensed 8/61.
EFJ 92: Trenwith and Perry, St Marys, Isles of Scilly (IS) 2/52; Provincial 35 Group, Enfield for preservation 10/71; Dunlop, Rochdale for preservation by 4/85; Museum of Transport, Manchester for preservation 4/85; West Country Historic Omnibus and Transport Trust for preservation 1/09; undergoing restoration 9/12
FFJ 112: E Joblin, Paignton (DN) 11/51; withdrawn 6/52; WN Moss, Yeovil (GSO) as a goods vehicle at an unknown date; last licensed 12/54.
FPT 219: Arlington Motor Co Ltd (dealer), London SW1 at an unknown date; EJ Hazell, Senghenydd (GG) 10/50; last licensed 3/53.
GCV 806: DC Venner, Witheridge (DN) 2/51; MWJ Burrows, Lapford (DN) 5/51; withdrawn 5/56.
GRL 70: RC Hatton {Blue Venture Coaches}, Culmstock (DN) 9/50; withdrawn 10/59 and derelict by 10/60.

HTA 472: Arlington Motor Co Ltd (dealer), London SW1 at an unknown date; CW Banfield Ltd, London SE17 (LN) 3/52 withdrawn 11/54; Henderson, Dummington as a goods vehicle at an unknown date; last licensed 6/58, and scrapped.

JEH 407: Arlington Motor Co Ltd (dealer), London SW1 at an unknown date; AE Connorton Ltd (dealer), London SW9 at an unknown date; last licensed 12/54; recorded with Scammell Lorries, Watford (as a staff bus?), no other details or date known.

Vehicles marked with an asterisk (*) acquired by Greenslades 1/54.

Teign Cars Ltd
2 Regent Street, Teignmouth

Livery: Cream and silver-blue

Business acquired by Greenslades from HJ & FM Beal, a motor dealer of Exeter 1/54. HF & FM Beal having acquired an interest in the company in 1948.

Reg	Chassis	Chassis No	Body	Body No	Seating	New	Acquired	Withdrawn
FX 5474	Thornycroft J	?	?		Ch32	3/20	5/20	-/--
T 8718	Thornycroft J	8436	?		Ch32	6/20	6/20	-/--
TA 1921	Republic 30hp	12438	?		Ch19	-/20	7/21	by6/34
TA 5686	Lancia Tetraiota	120	Torquay Carriage		Ch19	3/23	3/23	9/34
TA 5687	Lancia Tetraiota	119	Torquay Carriage		Ch19	3/23	3/23	9/33
TA 6081	Lancia Tetraiota	149	Torquay Carriage		Ch19	4/23	4/23	9/35
TT 78	Lancia Tetraiota	232	?		Ch19	5/24	5/24	9/37
TT 79	Lancia Tetraiota	231	?		Ch19	5/24	5/24	9/37
LA 5730	Lancia	?	?		Ch11	-/10	by3/25	2/33
TT 8511	Lancia Pentaiota	1051	?		C26-	6/26	6/26	9/38
L 5970	Lancia	?	?		Ch10	-/--	by5/28	-/35
TA 9218	Lancia Tetraiota	306	Torquay Carriage		Ch19	3/24	5/28	9/37
OD 3157	Morris Viceroy	262Y	?		C20-	7/32	7/32	5/48
UY 3367	Lancia Pentaiota	1996	?		C20-	5/28	-/33	5/36
FJ 6431	Minerva MBR	28070	Beadle	4957	C26-	7/29	6/34	9/39
AOD 103	Bedford WTB	110341	Heaver		C25F	4/36	4/36	4/51
AOD 773	Bedford WTB	110399	Heaver		C25F	5/36	5/36	12/50
YF 4170	Daimler		?		Car 7	-/28	-/37	-/37
EUO 122	Bedford WTB	112206	Heaver		C20F	5/38	5/38	*
EUO 123	Bedford WTB	112202	Heaver		C20F	5/38	5/38	*
GDV 885	Daimler CVD6	13867	Heaver		C33F	7/47	7/47	*
HDV 357	Daimler CVD6	14339	Heaver		C33F	8/47	8/47	*
RD 4748	Bedford WLB	109206	Duple	3723	C20F	9/33	9/47	4/49
ACN 682	Daimler CVD6	15557	ACB		C33F	1/48	5/48	*
JOD 354	Bedford OB	68371	Heaver		C29F	5/48	5/48	*
FW 7105	AEC Regal	6621787	Willowbrook	2851	C32F	2/36	9/48	1/53
FW 7107	AEC Regal	6621789	Willowbrook	2853	C32F	2/36	9/48	*
EBU 771	Bedford OB	72999	Pearson		C25F	7/48	4/49	*
JNC 214	Daimler CVD6	13888	KW Bodies		C33F	4/48	5/51	*
MMT 879	Bedford OB	37115	Duple	43163	C29F	11/46	7/51	*
MOD 533	Daimler CVD6	17637	Duple	50210	C37F	7/51	7/51	*
DVH 434	Bedford OB	74943	Duple	50407	C29F	5/48	1/52	*
ECX 412	Bedford OB	103155	Duple	50412	C29F	4/49	2/52	*
ECX 413	Bedford OB	104100	Duple	50413	C29F	4/49	2/52	*

Previous History:

FJ 6431: New to Taylor's Central Garages Ltd, Exeter (DN); from whom it was acquired.

FW 7105: New to Enterprise and Silver Dawn Motors Ltd, Scunthorpe (LI) 11; becoming Enterprise (Scunthorpe) Passenger Services Ltd, Scunthorpe (LI) 11 in 5/47; from whom it was acquired.

FW 7107: New to Enterprise and Silver Dawn Motors Ltd, Scunthorpe (LI) 14; becoming Enterprise (Scunthorpe) Passenger Services Ltd, Scunthorpe (LI) 14 in 5/47; from whom it was acquired.

FX 5474: New to Robins, Shaftesbury (DT); from whom it was acquired.

RD 4748: New to AC Cox, Reading (BE); HC Wilkins {Creamline Motor Services}, Bordon (HA) by 7/45; from whom it was acquired.

TA 1921: Chassis new to War Department (GOV); original identity not known; fitted with the body listed on acquisition.

TA 9218: New to Mortimore and Milne, Torquay (DN); from whom it was acquired.

UY 3367: New to GE Rouse, Blockley (WO); AE Marsh {Black and White Garages}, Harvington (WO) 1928; from whom it was acquired.
YF 4170: Acquired from an unknown (probably private) owner.
ACN 682: First registered by Walton (dealer), Gateshead and used as a demonstrator for Associated Coachbuilders, Sunderland; from whom it was acquired.
DVH 434: New to Hanson's Buses Ltd, Huddersfield (WR) 262; Taylor's Central Garages Ltd, Exeter (DN) 1/52; not operated; from whom it was acquired.
EBU 771: New to Hilditch Tours Ltd, Oldham (LA); withdrawn 10/48; from whom it was acquired.
ECX 412: New to Hanson's Buses Ltd, Huddersfield (WR) 270; from whom it was acquired.
ECX 413: New to Hanson's Buses Ltd, Huddersfield (WR) 271; from whom it was acquired.
JNC 214: New to Sharp's Motor Services (Manchester) Ltd, Manchester (GM); withdrawn 8/48; TW Mundy & Sons {Silver Queen}, Camborne (CO) 6/49; from whom it was acquired.
MMT 879: New to WJ Ray {Ray Coaches}, Edgware (LN) as C27F; Ray Coaches (Edgware) Ltd, Edgware (MX) at an unknown date; from whom it was acquired.

Notes:

FW 7107: Fitted with a pre-war full fronted coach body believed to be a Duple body (probably from a Ribble Motor Services Leyland TS7) rebuilt by Heaver.
TT 8511: Re-seated to C19- at an unknown date.
JNC 214: This vehicle has been quoted as being rebodied by Heaver as FC33F prior to operation by Teign Cars in 5/51, but it is believed that it was only rebuilt with a full-front (by Heaver) at that date.

Disposals:

T 8718: Peck, Rushden (GNO) as a van at an unknown date; last licensed 6/33.
FJ 6431: 120th Field Regiment, Royal Artillery, Budleigh Salterton (XDN) 9/39 – moved to Moreton Morrell (XWK) 2/40; last licensed 12/40.
FW 7105: Marston Coaches Ltd, Oxford (OX) 1/53; last licensed 9/57; no further operator.
FX 5474: Turner and Knight, Brentford (N?) at an unknown date.
OD 3157: SK Hill, Stibb Cross (DN) at an unknown date; last licensed 9/52.
RD 4748: Scrapped.
TA 1921: AV Harris, Paignton as a goods vehicle by 6/34; last licensed 6/34; scrapped 7/34.
TA 5686: No further operator; last licensed 6/34, by Teign Cars.
TA 5687: No further operator; last licensed 6/33, by Teign Cars.
TA 5790: Ajax Builders' Supplies, Mitcham (XLN) at an unknown date; last licensed 6/33.
TA 6081: Sold for scrap; last licensed by Teign Cars 9/35.
TA 9218: No further operator; last licensed by Teign Cars 9/37.
TT 78: No further operator; last licensed by Teign Cars 9/37.
TT 79: No further operator; last licensed by Teign Cars 9/37.
TT 8511: No further operator; last licensed by Teign Cars 9/38.
UY 3367: Not traced.
YF 3367: Not traced.
AOD 103: HJ Lyne, Puddington (DN) 4/51; withdrawn 7/57; Blair and Salmon (dealer), Manchester for scrap at an unknown date.
AOD 773: Unidentified operator or dealer, Middlesex; exported to Egypt 2/52.

Vehicles marked with an asterisk (*) acquired by Greenslades 1/54.

AE & LC Thomas — Thomas Brothers — Trafalgar Square, Tiverton

Business acquired by Witheridge Motor Transport Co 3/20 (see page 94)

T 4494	Scout 25hp	?	Tiverton	B---	9/14	9/14	3/20
T 6872	Dennis Subsidy 4 ton	12014	?	B---	5/19	5/19	3/20

Disposals:

T 4494: Witheridge Motor Transport Co (DN) 3/20.
T 6872: Witheridge Motor Transport Co (DN) 3/20.

FJ & WT Tidball — Tidball Brothers — Witheridge

Business acquired by Witheridge Motor Transport Co 3/20 (see page 94)

T 4442	Overland 30hp	?		Brake	8/14	8/14	-/19

T 6396	Willys 25/30hp	2049C		(see note)	-/15	8/18	1/19
T 6746	Leyland 36/40hp	WD9044		Van	4/19	4/19	3/20

Previous History:
    T 6396: Chassis acquired from the War Department (GOV); fitted with a carrier's van body on acquisition.

Notes:
    T 6746: Had a carrier's van body.

Disposals:
    T 4442: Not traced.
    T 6396: Bridgwater Motor Co (dealer), Bridgwater 1/19; AH Cowan, Taunton (GSO) 4/19 as goods; Taunton & District Express Delivery Ltd, Taunton (GSO) 12/20 as goods; W Milton, Crediton (DN) by 9/27; last licensed 9/27.
    T 6746: Witheridge Motor Transport Co (DN) 10/20.

RW Weller
TW & RT Weller   Sellers and Co   Arcadia Coaches   Exmouth

Business acquired by Greenslades 3/38.

TA 5772	Lancia Tetraiota	139	?		Ch20	4/23	4/23	by6/31
TA 6392	FIAT	174508	?		Ch20	5/23	5/23	c-/29
UO 3287	Reo Sprinter Type F	142813	?		Ch14	7/27	7/27	-/34
DV 833	Thornycroft A6	18277	Mumford		C20F	5/29	5/29	*
DV 5422	Chevrolet U	65393	?		C14F	5/30	5/30	3/38
DV 9046	Thornycroft A12	20916	?		C20-	5/31	5/31	*
OD 9843	Dodge KB	KB171	Thurgood	522	C20R	6/34	6/34	*

In addition, an unidentified Buick 8 seater charabanc was operated by 1928.

Previous History:
    DV 833: Originally intended for Worthen, Elvanton.

Disposals:
    DV 5422: CW & WHM Terraneau, South Molton (DN) as goods/coach 3/38; becoming goods only at an unknown date; last licensed 9/44.
    TA 5772: EWF Alpin, Wennington as a lorry at an unknown date; last licensed 6/32.
    TA 6392: Seatherton, North Tawton (GDN) at an unknown date; last licensed 9/30.
    UO 3287: Stuart, Edinburgh (GMN) as a lorry at an unknown date; last licensed 3/30.

Vehicles marked with an asterisk (*) acquired by Greenslades 3/38.

Witheridge Motor Transport Co
Witheridge Motor Transport Co Ltd, 7/3/30   Witheridge

Livery: Red.

The coach and haulage business of the Witheridge Motor Transport Co Ltd was acquired 5/33. From that date the goods fleet at Witheridge was licensed to Miltons Services (Crediton) Ltd though still trading under the name of Witheridge Motor Transport, with the Witheridge Motor Transport Co Ltd being renamed Greenslades Tours Ltd 9/5/33. The haulage business was sold to Whittons Haulage Co, Cullompton in 1946.

T 7312	Dennis 30hp (4 ton?)	12843	Tiverton	B32-	1/20	1/20	-/--
T 4494	Scout 25hp	?	?	B---	9/14	3/20	10/20
T 6746	Leyland 36/40hp	WD9044	?	Van	4/19	3/20	-/--
T 6872	Dennis Subsidy 4 ton	12014	?	B---	5/19	3/20	-/--
T 8640	Ford T	3644232	?	B14F	5/20	5/20	c-/23
T 9795	Burford 20hp	B155	Tiverton	B20-	11/20	11/20	-/29
TA 3714	Dennis (25/30 cwt)	?	Tiverton?	-20-	6/22	6/22	by9/32
TA 340	Ford TT	4116291	?	Ch14	-/20	9/23	9/27
T 8932	Dennis Subsidy 4 ton	12871	?	Ch32	6/20	4/25	6/31
T 7180	Guy 45hp	2829	Dowell	C18-	9/19	2/26	c-/30
TT 9217	Reo Speed Wagon F	129764	?	-20-	7/26	7/26	c-/32

Reg	Make	Chassis	Body	Seat	New	Acquired	Disposed
TT 9819	Chevrolet X	10637	?	C14F	10/26	10/26	*
FJ 1691	Guy (30 cwt?)	1135	Dowell	Ch20	5/21	-/--	6/30
FJ 1679	Dennis Chara	25001	Tiverton	Ch20	5/21	11/27	9/32
UO 7110	Reo Sprinter	FAX5798	?	C20-	6/28	6/28	*
UO 7597	Chevrolet LO	42023	?	-14-	7/28	7/28	c-/30
DV 1370	Chevrolet LQ	51951	?	C18-	6/29	6/29	*
DV 5712	Reo FB	FB1421	?	C20-	6/30	6/30	*
FJ 2932	Dennis 2½ ton	30632	?	Ch20	5/24	-/31	*
FJ 6308	GMC T30C	301356	Duple	1572 C20F	5/29	-/33	*

Previous History:
  T 4494: New to Thomas Brothers, Witheridge (DN); from whom it was acquired.
  T 6746: New to Tidball Brothers, Witheridge (DN); from whom it was acquired.
  T 6872: New to Thomas Brothers, Witheridge (DN); from whom it was acquired.
  T 8932: New to AC Bulpin, Newton Abbot (DN); from whom it was acquired.
  FJ 1679: New to Greenslades, Exeter (DN); from whom it was acquired.
  FJ 1691: New to Dowell, Exeter (DN); from whom it was acquired.
  FJ 2932: New to Greenslades, Exeter (DN); from whom it was acquired.
  FJ 6308: New to Greenslades, Exeter (DN); from whom it was acquired.
  TA 340: New to Edmonds {Vowler's Garage}, Torquay (DN); from whom it was acquired.

Notes:
  T 4494: Not operated by Witheridge Motor Transport.
  T 6746: Originally had a carrier's van body; fitted with a (new?) coach body possibly 32 seat (3/21?).
  T 7312: Official documentation quotes the engine number as 12843 and chassis number as 18378, which would appear to be transposed.; re-seated to B28- 1922.
  TA 3714: Official documentation quotes the chassis number as being 18378 with the engine number '14802', but a 'chassis' number 77 has also been quoted.

Disposals:
  T 4494: Last licensed 10/20.
  T 6746: Knee Brothers, Bristol (GGL) as a lorry at an unknown date; last licensed 12/31.
  T 6872: Used as a lorry.
  T 7312: Bentley, Guildford as a lorry at an unknown date; last licensed 3/36.
  T 8640: RJ Perry, Stogursey (SO) at an unknown date; last licensed 11/29.
  T 8932: Not traced.; last licensed 6/30, by Witheridge.
  T 9795: Parslow, Birmingham as an open lorry at an unknown date; last licensed 3/29.
  FJ 1691: Not traced; last licensed 6/30, by Witheridge.
  TA 340: Scrapped at an unknown date.
  TA 3714: Unidentified owner (possibly still Witheridge Transport) as a lorry at an unknown date; last licensed 9/32.
  TT 9217: Moor & Son, South Molton (GDN) as a lorry at an unknown date; last licensed 12/34.
  UO 7597: EL Gunn, Rackenford (DN) c1930; Le Paturel, Saltash (GCO) as a lorry at an unknown date; last licensed 3/38.

Vehicles marked with an asterisk (*) acquired by Greenslades 6/33.

ANCILLARY VEHICLES

	Reg	Make/Model	Chassis				
	RX 7787	Reo FD	FD4335	Van	-/30	9/39	9/41
	VFJ 261	Commer Cob		Van	11/57	11/57	-/64
	BFJ 951B	Morris JO2VM16		Van	-/64	-/64	-/72
VG1	XFJ 810K	Austin A60		Van	-/72	-/72	-/74
RV1	HFJ 930E	Ford D---		Recovery	-/67	-/74	5/81
VG2	BTT 767L	Austin Marina		Van	-/73	-/74	-/78
RV2	YDG 619S	Bedford CF250		Dropside	-/78	-/78	5/81
	VMJ 663K	Foden HAXB6/32		Recovery	-/72	-/80	4/81

Notes:

Recovery vehicles were provided by Devon General Omnibus & Touring Co Ltd, Torquay (DN) and Western National Omnibus Co Ltd, Exeter (DN) from 1954 until 1974. In addition, specific coaches, fitted with towing hooks, were also used, including LTA 629.

RX 7787: Transferred from the coach fleet and converted to van.
HFJ 930E: Acquired from Dawlish Coaches, Dawlish (XDN).
VMJ 663K: Acquired from an unknown owner.
BTT 767L: New to Western National Omnibus Co Ltd {Royal Blue}, Exeter (XDN) V12; from whom it was acquired. It is believed that this vehicle was initially allocated fleet number V11.

Disposals:

RX 7787: Not traced.
VFJ 261: Not traced.
BFJ 951B: Bolt, Exeter at an unknown date.
HFJ 930E: Western National Omnibus Co Ltd, Exeter (XDN) 9912 5/81.
VMJ 663K: National Travel (West) Ltd, Cheltenham (XGL) 4/81.
XFJ 810K: Not traced.
BTT 767L: Not traced.
YDG 619S: Western National Omnibus Co Ltd, Exeter (XDN) 9416 5/81.

REGISTRATION TO CHASSIS NUMBER CROSS REFERENCE
(UK & Irish Civilian Registrations Only)

Reg	Chassis	Reg	Chassis	Reg	Chassis	Reg	Chassis	Reg	Chassis
K 7866	69	DV 1293	71	FJ 3687	88	GN 7321	84	TA 2514	82
L 5970	92	DV 1370	11	FJ 3840	88	GN 7323	84	TA 2514	86
N 7939	69	DV 1370	95	FJ 4163	9	GU 2928	14	TA 2841	80
T 528	8	DV 1698	72	FJ 4367	88	GU 2929	14	TA 3714	94
T 1246	8	DV 1939	71	FJ 4368	88	GU 2931	14	TA 5686	92
T 2125	82	DV 1994	76	FJ 4950	88	GU 8133	88	TA 5687	92
T 3152	82	DV 3145	69	FJ 4951	88	GU 9528	13	TA 5745	84
T 3630	82	DV 3371	13	FJ 4986	9	GZ 664	76	TA 5772	94
T 3928	71	DV 3539	86	FJ 4987	9	HP 1277	82	TA 5793	80
T 4442	93	DV 4280	17	FJ 5123	20	HP 1277	86	TA 6081	92
T 4494	93	DV 4280	83	FJ 5607	10	HT 6792	86	TA 6356	69
T 4494	94	DV 4498	75	FJ 5607	72	JU 2029	79	TA 6369	82
T 5926	82	DV 5419	69	FJ 5623	9	JX 501	18	TA 6369	86
T 6140	82	DV 5422	94	FJ 5688	9	JX 501	75	TA 6392	94
T 6396	72	DV 5632	80	FJ 5689	9	JY 454	19	TA 6422	71
T 6396	94	DV 5649	71	FJ 5731	9	JY 454	73	TA 6649	82
T 6744	8	DV 5712	11	FJ 5776	88	LA 5730	89	TA 6649	86
T 6746	94	DV 5712	95	FJ 5777	88	LA 5730	92	TA 7461	84
T 6872	93	DV 6315	76	FJ 6172	9	LX 6167	69	TA 9218	92
T 6872	94	DV 7121	84	FJ 6308	9	NJ 5237	79	TK 5760	69
T 7014	82	DV 8410	73	FJ 6308	11	NK 5070	88	TO 7451	88
T 7014	86	DV 8411	69	FJ 6308	95	NK 5752	88	TR 2129	13
T 7180	71	DV 9046	16	FJ 6320	10	OB 5297	69	TT 78	92
T 7180	94	DV 9046	94	FJ 6431	88	OD 1855	80	TT 79	92
T 7198	79	DV 9147	84	FJ 6431	92	OD 2224	84	TT 414	71
T 7312	94	DV 9216	17	FJ 7010	10	OD 2488	18	TT 758	82
T 7876	82	DV 9218	17	FJ 7011	10	OD 2488	69	TT 758	86
T 7876	86	DV 9220	17	FJ 7012	10	OD 2686	17	TT 1043	82
T 8226	82	DV 9335	17	FJ 7042	10	OD 2686	83	TT 1043	86
T 8226	86	DV 9336	17	FJ 7411	16	OD 3157	92	TT 4425	84
T 8640	94	DV 9337	17	FJ 7412	16	OD 6003	71	TT 5132	86
T 8718	92	DV 9350	84	FJ 7414	16	OD 6025	71	TT 5882	75
T 8754	71	DV 9464	84	FJ 7716	10	OD 6288	14	TT 7391	75
T 8828	85	DV 9548	14	FJ 7820	16	OD 6288	73	TT 7464	84
T 8848	83	DV 9548	69	FJ 7825	16	OD 9497	75	TT 7987	73
T 8932	94	EF 6312	76	FJ 8005	14	OD 9617	71	TT 8232	69
T 9360	82	EF 8132	76	FJ 8005	72	OD 9843	16	TT 8371	71
T 9436	83	FH 4762	13	FJ 8278	10	OD 9843	94	TT 8511	92
T 9614	85	FH 4762	72	FJ 8350	72	OE 3645	69	TT 8819	73
T 9743	72	FH 5515	20	FJ 8351	10	PR 2802	75	TT 9217	94
T 9795	94	FH 5515	83	FJ 8351	69	PT 8628	88	TT 9819	11
Y 1035	72	FJ 1331	88	FJ 9060	11	PT 9511	88	TT 9819	95
Y 7422	86	FJ 1679	8	FJ 9060	72	RD 4748	92	TW 8935	89
AF 2589	9	FJ 1679	11	FJ 9061	11	RL 3361	12	TW 9856	21
AG 5348	17	FJ 1679	95	FJ 9066	11	RL 7545	14	TX 1506	75
AG 5348	83	FJ 1691	95	FJ 9581	72	RL 8061	14	UL 1846	80
BX 7340	15	FJ 1751	88	FM 4502	89	RU 4802	75	UL 2655	89
CN 3967	75	FJ 1920	88	FR 4666	69	RX 7787	17	UL 8878	79
DB 5134	71	FJ 2074	8	FW 7105	92	RX 7787	83	UN 190	89
DL 5576	75	FJ 2074	72	FW 7106	26	SX 2945	89	UO 1276	72
DR 3421	12	FJ 2151	88	FW 7106	89	TA 340	94	UO 1477	86
DR 5066	79	FJ 2164	88	FW 7107	27	TA 771	82	UO 1895	11
DR 6993	79	FJ 2553	88	FW 7107	92	TA 804	71	UO 1973	75
DV 340	83	FJ 2615	88	FW 7108	89	TA 808	83	UO 2039	71
DV 833	16	FJ 2702	88	FX 5474	92	TA 998	82	UO 2040	71
DV 833	94	FJ 2852	8	FX 7174	73	TA 1763	82	UO 2331	86
DV 982	73	FJ 2932	8	GC 2052	79	TA 1814	82	UO 2380	71
DV 1082	18	FJ 2932	11	GH 3281	80	TA 1921	92	UO 3287	94
DV 1082	69	FJ 2932	95	GH 3281	80	TA 1961	85	UO 3396	82
DV 1183	80	FJ 3101	88	GH 3281	88	TA 2018	84	UO 3396	86

UO 5792	86	BJY 703	69	EUO 122	27	HFJ 153	22	KDV 226	84
UO 6306	83	BJY 703	71	EUO 122	92	HFJ 300	26	KFJ 55	23
UO 6681	75	BOD 8	71	EUO 123	27	HFJ 300	89	KFJ 172	23
UO 7044	71	BOD 418	79	EUO 123	92	HFJ 390	26	KFJ 173	23
UO 7095	86	BWV 716	80	EUO 250	79	HFJ 390	89	KFJ 222	23
UO 7110	11	CDV 772	31	EUO 508	80	HFJ 507	22	KFJ 606	29
UO 7110	95	CDV 772	86	EVJ 439	29	HFJ 834	29	KFJ 606	69
UO 7597	83	CFB 190	80	EVJ 439	85	HFJ 834	69	KFJ 606	73
UO 7597	95	CFJ 942	15	EYE 144	86	HFJ 834	73	KFJ 607	24
UO 7609	83	CFJ 943	15	FDV 8	84	HFJ 835	29	KFJ 608	29
UO 8211	10	CFJ 995	15	FFJ 112	89	HFJ 835	69	KFJ 608	73
UP 212	88	CTT 943	71	FFJ 116	18	HFJ 835	73	KFJ 609	24
UU 973	13	DCJ 691	76	FFJ 909	19	HFJ 836	22	KFJ 610	24
UU 3012	14	DCJ 691	85	FFJ 916	19	HHP 755	23	KFJ 611	24
UU 3015	14	DDD 166	86	FFJ 917	19	HOD 471	31	KFJ 612	24
UU 3022	12	DDV 662	75	FFJ 918	19	HOD 471	86	KFJ 613	24
UU 4811	14	DFJ 46	18	FFJ 948	19	HSP 144	32	KFJ 614	24
UU 4813	14	DFJ 46	69	FFJ 953	19	HSP 144	79	KFJ 683	29
UV 4079	89	DFJ 47	18	FFJ 954	19	HTA 472	89	KFJ 683	73
UV 4082	89	DFJ 47	69	FFJ 967	21	HTA 938	80	KFJ 684	24
UX 6621	75	DFJ 113	73	FFJ 968	21	HTX 628	80	KOD 276	31
UY 3367	92	DFJ 114	18	FFJ 968	31	HYB 646	76	KOD 276	86
VF 6229	17	DFJ 114	69	FFJ 968	86	HYB 984	76	KOD 363	31
VF 6229	83	DFJ 935	89	FFJ 969	21	HYB 984	76	KOD 363	86
VV 10	19	DFJ 936	89	FFJ 970	21	HYN 420	76	KOD 364	31
VV 10	80	DJF 937	89	FFJ 971	21	IJI 5367	49	KOD 364	86
WW 1661	90	DLX 916	89	FFJ 971	31	JAU 804	76	KOD 983	31
YC 9715	86	DLX 918	89	FFJ 971	86	JAU 808	76	KOD 983	86
YC 9718	83	DRM 36	84	FFJ 972	21	JEH 407	89	KTA 388	69
YD 2142	80	DUJ 253	32	FFJ 996	19	JEP 609	67	KTA 388	71
YD 3193	76	DUJ 253	79	FFJ 997	73	JFJ 14	22	KUX 211	76
YD 4649	75	DUX 586	32	FPT 219	89	JFJ 15	22	KYB 954	80
YF 4170	92	DUX 586	79	FPX 749	79	JFJ 16	22	LDH 712	24
YH 2061	86	DVH 434	27	GCV 806	89	JFJ 178	22	LDH 712	89
YH 3796	12	DVH 434	92	GDM 169	76	JFJ 179	22	LFJ 737	24
YP 9979	89	DVH 531	26	GDV 802	31	JFJ 180	22	LFJ 801	24
YV 1102	13	DVH 531	89	GDV 802	86	JFJ 181	22	LFJ 804	24
YV 1103	12	DVH 837	26	GDV 885	27	JFJ 198	26	LFJ 876	24
YV 1104	12	DVH 837	89	GDV 885	92	JFJ 198	89	LFJ 876	76
YV 1105	12	EBU 13	26	GFJ 40	20	JFJ 259	29	LFJ 877	24
YV 1111	14	EBU 13	89	GFJ 41	20	JFJ 259	73	LFJ 877	76
YV 1112	14	EBU 223	26	GFJ 101	20	JFJ 260	22	LFJ 931	26
YV 3656	80	EBU 223	89	GFJ 102	20	JFJ 261	22	LFJ 931	89
YV 8565	13	EBU 771	27	GFJ 632	21	JFJ 346	26	LIL 7077	67
YV 8567	13	EBU 771	92	GFJ 867	29	JFJ 346	89	LOD 266	30
YV 8568	13	ECX 412	27	GFJ 867	85	JFJ 822	23	LOD 266	69
ACN 682	27	ECX 412	92	GHU 105	86	JFJ 867	29	LOD 266	71
ACN 682	92	ECX 413	27	GRL 70	89	JFJ 867	73	LPC 187	26
AFJ 738	12	ECX 413	92	GTD 460	26	JFJ 938	23	LPC 187	89
AFJ 782	12	ECX 566	26	GTD 460	89	JFJ 939	23	LTA 185	30
AFJ 782	69	ECX 566	89	GUO 114	79	JFJ 949	23	LTA 185	69
AFJ 783	69	EDV 433	31	HDV 357	27	JNC 214	27	LTA 185	71
AGH 212	79	EDV 433	86	HDV 357	92	JNC 214	92	LTA 623	34
AOD 103	92	EDV 975	86	HDV 415	69	JNP 888	80	LTA 623	76
AOD 358	75	EFJ 76	16	HDV 415	71	JOD 354	27	LTA 624	34
AOD 773	92	EFJ 77	16	HDV 754	80	JOD 354	92	LTA 624	76
ATA 507	86	EFJ 78	16	HFJ 117	26	JTA 936	79	LTA 625	34
AUO 334	69	EFJ 79	16	HFJ 117	89	JUO 324	31	LTA 626	34
AUO 334	71	EFJ 90	89	HFJ 147	22	JUO 324	86	LTA 627	34
AUO 454	18	EFJ 91	89	HFJ 148	22	JUO 605	28	LTA 627	76
AUO 454	69	EFJ 92	89	HFJ 149	22	JUO 606	28	LTA 628	34
AUO 454	73	EFJ 548	16	HFJ 150	73	JUO 608	28	LTA 629	34
BFJ 938	20	EFR 226	29	HFJ 151	73	JYA 630	76	LTA 630	34
BFJ 938	83	EFR 226	85	HFJ 152	22	JYA 839	76	LTA 631	34

LTA 632	34		OFJ 792	25		XFJ 591	35		964 HTT	50		CHA 106C	64
LTA 633	34		OFJ 793	25		XFJ 592	35		965 HTT	50		CHA 116C	64
LTA 634	34		OFJ 794	25		XFJ 593	35		966 HTT	50		CHA 122C	64
LTT 138	84		OFJ 795	25		XFJ 875	35		967 HTT	50		CTA 637C	80
LUO 359	32		PDV 692	39		XXI 4976	59		968 HTT	51		DDG 252C	62
LUO 359	79		PDV 693	39		XYD 700	76		312 KYC	76		DDG 253C	62
LYB 996	76		PDV 694	39		YRC 43	50		500 NYD	76		DDG 254C	62
LYD 134	76		PDV 695	39		YRC 44	50		501 NYD	76		DDG 255C	62
LYD 135	76		PDV 696	39		YRC 46	50		1 RDV	51		DDG 256C	62
MFJ 551	25		PDV 697	39		YSV 598	59		2 RDV	51		DDG 257C	66
MFJ 552	25		PYB 240	76		240 MT	49		3 RDV	51		DDG 258C	66
MFJ 552	29		RFJ 12	29		1291 WE	45		4 RDV	51		DDG 259C	66
MFJ 552	73		RFJ 380	29		1292 WE	45		5 RDV	51		DDG 260C	66
MFJ 553	25		RFJ 381	29		1293 WE	45		6 RDV	51		DDG 261C	66
MFJ 608	25		RFJ 395	29		1294 WE	45		7 RDV	51		EOD 24D	51
MFJ 609	25		ROD 749	41		1295 WE	45		8 RDV	51		EOD 25D	51
MFJ 609	69		ROD 750	41		1296 WE	45		649 TAE	59		EOD 26D	51
MFJ 900	25		RTK 808	64		889 ADV	43		627 UYB	59		EOD 27D	51
MFJ 900	69		SDR 249	80		890 ADV	43		697 UYD	59		EOD 28D	51
MFJ 901	25		SFJ 902	30		891 ADV	43		837 XHW	66		EOD 29D	51
MFJ 901	69		SFJ 903	30		892 ADV	43		671 YXA	57		EOD 30D	51
MLF 341	76		SFJ 904	30		554 AFJ	35		AJU 264A	34		EOD 31D	51
MLF 342	76		SFJ 905	30		555 AFJ	35		ARU 80A	49		FFJ 10D	42
MLF 346	76		SFJ 906	30		556 AFJ	35		ARU 99A	60		FFJ 11D	42
MMP 809	84		SFJ 907	30		557 AFJ	35		ARU 500A	49		FFJ 12D	42
MMT 879	27		SFJ 908	30		558 AFJ	35		AAD 247B	57		FFJ 13D	42
MMT 879	92		SFJ 909	30		559 AFJ	35		AAD 248B	57		FFJ 14D	42
MMT 880	26		SFJ 910	30		540 CFJ	36		AAD 249B	57		FFJ 15D	42
MMT 880	89		SJY 61	80		541 CFJ	36		AAD 250B	57		GTA 688D	80
MOD 533	27		SMU 447	80		542 CFJ	36		AAD 251B	57		HFJ 416E	44
MOD 533	92		SNJ 611	49		543 CFJ	36		ABO 144B	55		HFJ 417E	44
MOD 737	33		TFJ 436	30		544 CFJ	36		ABO 145B	55		HFJ 418E	44
MOD 737	84		TFJ 437	30		545 CFJ	36		ABO 146B	55		HOD 32E	51
MPI 624	37		TFJ 438	30		546 CFJ	36		ABO 147B	55		HOD 33E	51
MTA 173	30		TFJ 439	31		670 COD	47		ABO 147B	55		HOD 34E	51
MTA 173	69		TFJ 440	31		140 DBO	62		ABO 147B	55		HOD 35E	51
MTA 173	71		TFJ 440	80		142 DBO	62		AFJ 77B	40		HOD 36E	51
MYD 985	76		TSV 850	53		567 EFJ	38		AFJ 78B	40		HOD 37E	51
NDV 263	30		UFJ 300	33		568 EFJ	38		AFJ 79B	40		HOD 38E	51
NDV 263	69		UFJ 301	33		569 EFJ	38		AFJ 80B	40		HOD 39E	51
NDV 263	71		UFJ 303	33		570 EFJ	38		AFJ 81B	40		JTA 763E	51
NIJ 6060	67		UFJ 303	80		571 EFJ	38		AFJ 82B	40		JTA 764E	51
NTT 578	33		UGR 225	80		572 EFJ	38		AFJ 83B	40		JTA 765E	51
NTT 578	84		UJT 384	31		573 EFJ	38		AFJ 84B	40		NTA 855F	80
NUO 651	31		UMN 137	22		919 EYA	76		AFJ 85B	40		CXF 256G	51
NUO 651	86		UTT 985	33		974 FFJ	39		AFJ 86B	40		CXF 257G	51
NUO 680	37		UTT 985	84		175 GFJ	39		BDV 175B	54		NFJ 619G	45
NUO 681	37		VFJ 991	34		176 GFJ	39		YCV 365B	54		NFJ 620G	45
NUO 682	37		VFJ 992	34		76 GIO	64		CDV 778C	80		NFJ 621G	45
NUO 683	37		VFJ 993	34		934 GTA	46		CFJ 894C	41		NFJ 622G	45
NUO 684	37		VFJ 994	34		935 GTA	46		CFJ 895C	41		NFJ 623G	45
NUO 684	76		VOD 549	33		937 GTA	48		CFJ 896C	41		KCK 381H	66
NUO 685	37		VOD 549	84		938 GTA	48		CFJ 897C	41		KCK 990H	66
NUO 686	37		XDV 850	43		939 GTA	48		CFJ 898C	41		KCK 991H	66
NUO 686	76		XDV 851	43		940 GTA	48		CFJ 899C	41		KCK 994H	66
NUO 687	37		XDV 852	43		941 GTA	47		CHA 83C	64		RCY 55H	68
NUO 688	37		XDV 853	43		942 GTA	47		CHA 94C	64		RFJ 824H	46
NUO 689	39		XDV 854	43		107 GYC	76		CHA 95C	64		RFJ 825H	46
NUO 690	39		XDV 855	44		108 GYC	76		CHA 96C	64		RFJ 826H	46
NUO 690	76		XDV 856	44		109 GYC	76		CHA 98C	64		RFJ 827H	46
NUO 691	39		XDV 857	43		960 HTT	47		CHA 99C	64		RFJ 828H	51
NVM 134	76		XDV 858	43		961 HTT	47		CHA 100C	64		VHT 912H	66
OFJ 790	25		XDV 859	43		962 HTT	47		CHA 104C	64		YTX 322H	56
OFJ 791	25		XFJ 590	35		963 HTT	48		CHA 105C	64		YTX 323H	56

AAX 259J	59	OJN 470P	64	**Alderney**	
ELU 599J	67	STA 378R	67		
ELU 600J	67	STA 379R	67	AY 58	40
HGC 233J	49	STA 380R	67	AY 91	41
UFJ 229J	48	STA 381R	67	AY 305	41
UFJ 230J	48	STA 382R	67	AY 750	41
UFJ 231J	48	VGD 363R	42		
UFJ 232J	48	BNF 151T	66		
UFJ 233J	48	CPM 520T	55		
UUO 450J	48	DEF 822T	66		
UUO 451J	48	JRE 63T	31		
UUO 452J	48	WHT 825T	66		
UUO 453J	48	FTC 2W	65		
UUO 454J	48	STT 295X	41		
ADG 330K	59	WDV 505X	56		
ADG 331K	60	Q364 FVT	68		
ADG 332K	60				
JYT 606K	63	**Guernsey**			
JYT 607K	63				
JYT 608K	63	3989	59		
JYT 609K	63	6768	40		
JYT 610K	63	6769	53		
JYT 611K	63	8228	41		
NRX 149K	60	8229	40		
BFJ 310L	57	8230	41		
BFJ 311L	57	12723	62		
BFJ 312L	57	12727	62		
BFJ 313L	57	16706	41		
BFJ 314L	57	31906	61		
GHH 31L	57	31907	61		
CNB 354M	59	31908	61		
NTT 315M	57	31909	61		
OOD 360M	58	31910	61		
OOD 361M	58	31911	61		
OOD 362M	58	31912	62		
OOD 363M	58	31913	62		
OOD 364M	58	31914	62		
OOD 365M	58	31915	62		
OOD 366M	58	31916	61		
OOD 367M	58	31917	61		
PFJ 351M	58	31918	61		
PFJ 352M	58	31918	61		
JFJ 497N	60	31919	61		
JFJ 498N	60	31919	61		
JFJ 499N	60				
JFJ 500N	60	**Jersey**			
JFJ 501N	60				
JFJ 502N	61	J 2239	31		
JFJ 503N	61	J 6419	31		
JFJ 504N	61	J 9040	31		
JFJ 505N	61	J 9050	31		
JFJ 506N	61	J 16590	41		
JFJ 507N	61	J 16601	41		
JFJ 508N	61	J 16654	40		
NFJ 368P	63	J 16828	41		
NFJ 369P	63	J 16841	41		
NFJ 370P	63	J 16845	40		
NFJ 371P	63	J 22898	31		
NFJ 372P	63	J 29255	55		
NFJ 373P	63	J 51937	55		
NFJ 374P	63				
NFJ 375P	63				
NFJ 376P	63				
NFJ 377P	63				

HISTORICAL COUNTY CODES

Code	County	Code	County
GOV	Government Department		
AD	Aberdeenshire	KK	Kirkcudbrightshire
AH	Armagh	KN	Kesteven division of Lincolnshire
AL	Argyllshire	KS	Kinross-shire
AM	Antrim	KT	Kent
AR	Ayrshire	LA	Lancashire
AS	Angus	LC	Lincoln (City)
AY	Isle of Anglesey	LE	Leicestershire
BC	Brecknockshire	LI	Lindsey division of Lincolnshire
BD	Bedfordshire	LK	Lanarkshire
BE	Berkshire	LN	London Postal area
BF	Banffshire	LY	Londonderry
BK	Buckinghamshire	ME	Merionethshire
BU	Buteshire	MH	Monmouthshire
BW	Berwickshire	MN	Midlothian
CG	Cardiganshire	MO	Montgomeryshire
CH	Cheshire	MR	Morayshire
CI	Channel Islands	MX	Middlesex
CK	Clackmannanshire	ND	Northumberland
CM	Cambridgeshire	NG	Nottinghamshire
CN	Caernarvonshire	NK	Norfolk
CO	Cornwall	NN	Nairnshire
CR	Carmarthenshire	NO	Northamptonshire
CS	Caithness	NR	North Riding of Yorkshire
CU	Cumberland	OK	Orkney Islands
DB	Dunbartonshire	OX	Oxfordshire
DE	Derbyshire	PB	Peebles-shire
DF	Dumfries-shire	PE	Pembrokeshire
DH	Denbighshire	PH	Perthshire
DM	County Durham	RD	Rutland
DN	Devon	RH	Roxburghshire
DO	Down	RR	Radnorshire
DT	Dorset	RW	Renfrewshire
EI	Eire	RY	Ross-shire & Cromarty
EK	East Suffolk	SD	Shetland Islands
EL	East Lothian	SH	Shropshire
ER	East Riding of Yorkshire	SI	Selkirkshire
ES	East Sussex	SN	Stirlingshire
EX	Essex	SO	Somerset
EY	Isle of Ely	SP	Soke of Peterborough
FE	Fife	SR	Surrey
FH	Fermanagh	ST	Staffordshire
FT	Flintshire	SU	Sutherland
GG	Glamorgan	TY	Tyrone
GL	Gloucestershire	WF	West Suffolk
HA	Hampshire	WI	Wiltshire
HD	Holland division of Lincolnshire	WK	Warwickshire
HN	Huntingdonshire	WL	West Lothian
HR	Herefordshire	WN	Wigtownshire
HT	Hertfordshire	WO	Worcestershire
IM	Isle of Man	WR	West Riding of Yorkshire
IV	Inverness	WS	West Sussex
IW	Isle of Wight	WT	Westmorland
KE	Kincardineshire	YK	York (City)

<u>Note</u>: A 'G' prefix (eg GAD) indicates the operator was a Goods operator (in this case in Aberdeenshire).